A SENSE-OF-
WONDERFUL CENTURY

Borgo Press Books by GARY WESTFAHL

*Islands in the Sky: The Space Station Theme in Science Fiction
    Literature, Second Edition*
*The Other Side of the Sky: An Annotated Bibliography of Space
    Stations in Science Fiction, 1869-1993*
*A Sense-of-Wonderful Century: Explorations of Science Fiction
    and Fantasy Films*

A SENSE-OF-WONDERFUL CENTURY

EXPLORATIONS OF SCIENCE FICTION AND FANTASY FILMS

GARY WESTFAHL

THE BORGO PRESS

MMXII

MALCOLM HULKE STUDIES
IN CINEMA AND TELEVISION
ISSN 0884-6944

Number Three

A SENSE-OF-WONDERFUL CENTURY

FIRST EDITION

Published by Wildside Press LLC

www.wildsidebooks.com

DEDICATION

To Steven Kong—

a wonderful son-in-law,
longtime fan of Godzilla movies,
and current resident at a hospital
that is far better than St. Elegius

CONTENTS

INTRODUCTION

With essays to come that will offer both general thoughts on science fiction and fantasy films and focused analyses of specific films and television programs, I will primarily restrict this introduction to a businesslike discussion of how this book came to be assembled. In a sense, its contents are the result of moonlighting; for although I have enthusiastically watched science fiction and fantasy films all of my life, a decision to obtain a Ph.D. in English and American literature, with a dissertation on science fiction, first seemed to qualify me solely for a career of writing about science fiction and fantasy literature, not films, and that is where I long focused my attention. However, in this day and age, no one can be faulted for wanting to both watch and write about films, since these are, as I argued in a column for *Interzone* entitled "Big Dumb Opticals," contemporary society's equivalent to ancient Egypt's pyramids—vast, impressive constructs that many people combine to create so that even more people can gather to gaze in admiration at them. And so it was that two early articles on *Project Moonbase* and *Star Trek* led to more and more work in this area; and now, with my ever-expanding online reference, the Biographical Encyclopedia of Science Fiction Film, and regular work as a film reviewer for the website Locus Online, I have found myself increasingly regarded primarily as an expert in science fiction film, not science fiction literature, emboldening me to begin publishing books about science fiction and fantasy films to accompany my other books on science fiction and fantasy literature. Hence, this volume gathers together most of my writings on film, with exceptions to be noted, while another new book, *The Spacesuit Film: A History, 1918-1969*, will present a detailed survey of over 100 films and television programs involving space travel. And to be sure, I am far from the only literary critic whose focus has gradually shifted from literature to films, mirroring our society's increasing obsession with the form.

(This is not entirely my book, of course, since it includes revised versions of two essays originally credited to my wife, who publishes as Lynne Lundquist, and one essay originally credited to both of us—representing her own form of moon-lighting, since she is otherwise employed as a Lecturer in the Theatre and Dance Department of California State University, Fullerton. However, she has requested that she not receive credit as this book's co-author—though her contributions are still acknowledged in the chapter headings—preferring that I receive all the credit, or blame, for the book's contents.)

The original intent was to include all of my previous writings on science fiction and fantasy film, except for the entries in the aforementioned Biographical Encyclopedia of Science Fiction Film, my Locus Online film reviews, and a few columns involving films written for *Interzone* (since all of these columns will soon be collected in another book from Borgo/Wildside Press). But a few other exceptions were made: including essays already incorporated into books I have authored seemed like inappropriate recycling; a few entries on films published in *The Encyclopedia of Fantasy* (1997) and *The Greenwood Encyclopedia of Science Fiction and Fantasy* (2005) were not available; and a brief review of a book on French documentary filmmaker Jean Painlevé, and entries on *Field of Dreams* (1989) and Ronald McDonald written for, but not included in, *The Encyclopedia of Fantasy*, were deemed too inconsequential to merit inclusion. (These items, however, are all listed in the concluding bibliography of my various writings on film, for anyone who might be interested.)

Most of the essays here were published in officially sanctioned venues—books, journals, websites, and a newspaper—as noted in the bibliography, but three items have more irregular origins: a passage on space films before 1950 written for, but ultimately excluded from, *The Spacesuit Film*, on the grounds that this lengthy book did not require such an extensive discussion of films that did not feature spacesuits; some extended musings on how one might define an animated movie, generated while engaged in discussions with colleagues about a proposed reference book to be entitled *The Encyclopedia of Animated Movies*; and some comments on the television series *St. Elsewhere*, which were spontaneous contributions to a listserv. All were polished up and posted on the World of Westfahl website as interesting curiosities, but they have here been further revised (particularly the piece on *St. Elsewhere*, now expanded into a short essay). Other essays are significantly different from their original published versions: the piece on the novel and film *This Island Earth* (1952, 1955) combines an entry written for a forthcoming reference book with a deleted passage from Gary's book on spacesuit films; "Where No Market Has Gone Before" is a revised and updated version of the original journal article, prepared for a critical anthology that never appeared; the essay on the sequels to *2001: A Space Odyssey* (1968) is the original longer version, not the severely shortened version that was originally published; and "Three Questions and Answers about Science Fiction Films" brings together my three responses to date for the website SF Signal's ongoing series of "Mild-Melds," without the comments of the other contributors. In addition, all essays have been lightly reedited and sporadically revised; scattered errors and omissions have been addressed; all quotations are now properly cited; and a concluding bibliography provides complete data on all of the films, television programs, and printed materials discussed or mentioned in the book.

In terms of the structure of the book, I have tried to arrange the essays to follow the chronological order of when the films and television programs being discussed first appeared, with pieces providing more general overviews clustered near the beginning and end, to provide the overall aura of a historical survey. (However, this book obviously does not pretend to provide a comprehensive history of science fiction and fantasy films.) It will also be noticed that, just as the essays intermingle analyses of films and television programs, they also contains some discussions of related plays, novels, stories, and comic books, particularly in the essays on *This Island Earth* and *2001: A Space Odyssey* and its sequels. For these apparent digressions I make no apologies, having never been respectful toward arbitrary boundaries and fully believing that films are sometimes best illuminated when considered in the context of related works in other media.

I might finally comment briefly on the book's concluding essay, which was not originally going to be included, inasmuch as it was written primarily as my meditation on my marriage to Lynne; however, reading it over, I saw that it was also functioning as a commentary on the reasons why I enjoy science fiction films, and worth featuring for that reason, even if Lynne still feels the piece does not quite do justice to her. She has, however, declined to add her own comments on her marriage, and her contrasting tastes in films, preferring as always to suffer her husband's idiosyncrasies in silence.

1. FLIGHTS OF FANCY: SPACE FILMS BEFORE 1950

It must first be acknowledged that the science fiction films of the silent era, and even of the early sound era, remain a significantly unexplored area. Every new investigation along a different research vector may bring to light a few more obscure items to consider; every year, a film previously believed to be lost may be rediscovered, carefully restored, and released for viewing. (Now that a complete version of *Himmelskibet* [1906] has been located, attention is being devoted to finding the lost 1919 film adaptation of H. G. Wells's *The First Men in the Moon* [1901], which might prove interesting indeed.) Having almost abandoned work in this area before stumbling upon other significant films to discuss, I cannot be confident that I am now dealing with all relevant works, and while I have strived to be reasonably thorough, it is likely that future researchers on this topic will lambaste me for my shameful omissions.

To be sure, it is also likely that the space films before 1950 that I have not seen or considered will prove to be insignificant, from the perspective of the spacesuit film; because virtually all films involving space travel prior to 1950 tended to follow certain conventions. While they might seem moderately plausible in depicting the building of spacecraft and the preparations for launching, in light of then-current technology, they tend to become less and less realistic the further they get away from Earth. In particular, space travelers are rarely concerned about the possible dangers of outer space: during their flights, they wear either street clothes or outfits modeled on the clothing of early aviators, like leather jackets and goggles, which would hardly be useful in the environment of space; they never experience zero gravity or worry about meteors; and when they land on another planet, they step out of their spaceships completely unprotected, confident that they will encounter a breathable atmosphere, suitable temperature, and beings that usually look and act exactly like humans.

The first of these films, George Méliès's *Le Voyage dans la Lune* (*A Trip to the Moon*) (1902), is generally characterized as completely farcical, but this is not entirely true, since this short film does begin with a somewhat serious discussion amongst learned astronomers regarding how a flight to the Moon might be accomplished, and subsequent scenes depicting the construction of the space gun and the cylindrical vehicle for the space travelers seem reasonably well grounded in the available technology of the time as it might have been applied to the challenge of space flight. However, having a chorus line of beautiful girls push the vehicle into position to be launched signals a weakening impulse to project any aura of authenticity, and once the capsule is shot into space, a decisive shift to pure fantasy is announced by a scene in which the capsule buries itself in the eye of an animated Man in the Moon, followed by equally unrealistic scenes involving the travelers moving about on the Moon in street clothes and encountering fantastic apelike creatures. Still, one can recognize this brief film as a precursor to two later film traditions involving spacesuits: its generally comic tone anticipates the humorous spacesuit films, while its menacing Selenites (eventually defeated when it is discovered that they disintegrate when struck by a man's umbrella) are arguably the first of the space monsters that will later epitomize the horrific spacesuit films.

To consider three later films of a similar nature, Méliès soon made another film featuring space travel, *Le Voyage à Travers l'Impossible* (*The Impossible Voyage*) (1904), which is more fanciful in all respects, in that it involves a group of travelers who voyage to the Sun inside a runaway train. However, it might be noted that the way the train is sent flying through space, by speeding it up a high mountain, is not unlike the ramps employed to launch a spacecraft in *When Worlds Collide* (1951) and other later films, and the film has one evocative scene of the train speeding through the blackness of space, passing by the planets, before the train is swallowed by the mouth of the Sun's face and the travelers land upon a hot but absurdly habitable Sun.

There is also a little-known curiosity, Spanish filmmaker Segundo de Chomón's *Excursion dans la Lune* (*Excursion to the Moon*) (1908), which is for the most part a blatant copy of Méliès's *Le Voyage dans la Lune* with a few interesting variations. The projectile here is loaded into the space cannon not by scantily-clad women, but more realistically by uniformed soldiers; the capsule does not hit the Man in the Moon (portrayed by an actual human face) in the eye, but is rather swallowed by him; and while the residents of the Moon again include costumed acrobats who vanish at a touch, the visitors are also entertained in the court of the lunar king by a group of lovely female dancers, anticipating later films like *Cat-Women of the Moon* (1953) that would similarly inhabit the Moon with beautiful women with a predilection for modern dance. As a final departure from Méliès, one of the women is abducted by the visitors and taken back to Earth with them.

A better-known film inspired by Méliès was British director Walter Booth's *The ? Motorist* (1906), in which a motorist drives his automobile up a building, through the sky, on top of a cloud, around the Moon, and around the rings of Saturn before he falls to the Earth in the middle of a courtroom. In these and other short films providing fanciful sequences of space travel, including Méliès's *Le Dirigeable Fantastique* (1906), Chomón's *Voyage sur Jupiter* (1909), and Enrico Novelli's *Un Matrimonio Interplanetario* (1910), however, there was never any effort to portray space travel plausibly.

A later silent film, the Russian Yakov Protazanov's *Aelita:*

Queen of Mars (1924), was reasonably realistic in envisioning a spaceship to Mars being constructed by an engineer named Los (Nikolai Tsereteli), based on plans he had carefully prepared. However, while the spacecraft's exterior looks plausible enough, the interior appears identical to a spacious room in a house, despite pieces of equipment in the background, and the conclusion of the flight seems as fanciful as *A Trip to the Moon*: the ship crash-lands on Mars, but the three crew members emerge unharmed into a completely Earthlike environment and immediately encounter Martians who seem exactly like human beings. (A few Martians do wear costumes and helmets that resemble spacesuits, but they cannot be protective in nature, since other Martians survive perfectly well while wearing normal, or very little, clothing.) After Los has a romantic encounter with the Martian queen Aelita (Yuliya Solntseva), who had been longingly observing him from Mars, and after his crewmate Gusev (Nikolai Batalov) leads a Communist revolution of the oppressed Martian workers, the entire flight and the landing on Mars are revealed to be nothing more than Los's dreams, which completely invalidates any idea that the film was arguing in favor of the practicality of space travel. The significance of *Aelita* is that, along with *Himmelskibet*, it anticipates a third tradition of spacesuit films, the melodramatic spacesuit films, in which space travelers encounter aliens who are identical to human beings and become embroiled in situations that are exactly like conventional conflicts on Earth.

What may be the first talking film to depict space travel, *Just Imagine* (1930), is generally described as the first science fiction musical, though by modern standards it would only be considered a romantic comedy with a few musical numbers. Its central story involves a man of the year 1980, J-21 (John Garrick), who is being forbidden by law to marry the girl he loves, LN-18 (Maureen O'Sullivan), because he is deemed insufficiently accomplished. To win his appeal of the decision, he agrees to become the first person to fly to Mars in an experimental spacecraft built by renowned inventor Z-4 (Hobart

Bosworth); accompanying him are his best friend RT-42 (Frank Albertson) and a man from the past, Single O (El Brendel), who has recently been brought back to life after he was struck by a lightning bolt in 1930. While the film's focus is usually on the mildly amusing antics of vaudeville comedian Brendel (who discovers, among other things, pills that have replaced alcohol), the film is momentarily serious when Z-4 tells J-21 why it is important for someone to undertake this mission:

> [Z-4] Thousands of years ago, man wondered what was across the river. Then he went over and found out. Later, Columbus wondered what was across the ocean, and he went over and found out. Since then, men have sought for and learned every secret of the Earth—on the land, in the water, in the air. But there is one secret, the greatest of all, that remains a mystery.
> [J-21] And that is...?
> [Z-4] The planet Mars![1]

This qualifies as an interesting early argument in favor of space travel, contextualizing such endeavors as a natural continuation of humanity's ancient quest to learn about new and distant realms.

As for the spaceship itself, while it is powered by an otherwise-unexplained "gravity neutralizer," it looks very much like a standard rocketship, although it blasts off horizontally like the spaceships of later serials. Furthermore, the travelers do not wear spacesuits or experience zero gravity, but there is one touch of realism during their journey, an image of distant Earth against a black sky filled with stars. Once they reach Mars, though, a spirit of absurdity returns, since they find the planet inhabited by a mixture of friendly and hostile humans wearing odd, skimpy costumes (all Martians, they deduce, are twins, one good and one bad); but the Martians at least do not speak

---

1. *Just Imagine* (Fox, 1930).

English, and there is a rare acknowledgement that conditions there are different than Earth when the travelers effortlessly move their large spaceship around into position for liftoff, an ability explicitly attributed to Mars's lower gravity. That lower gravity would necessarily mean a thinner atmosphere, naturally, is never acknowledged.

Another film, *Things to Come* (1936), is more serious and realistic than these predecessors, which is natural enough given that its screenplay was based on a novel by, and written by, renowned science fiction writer H. G. Wells. Yet this extended chronicle of humanity's future only involves space travel in its concluding scenes, wherein an advanced future civilization has constructed an immense "space gun" to launch a manned rocket, resembling a cross between a spaceship and a bullet, which is designed to circumnavigate the Moon. Interestingly, the drama of these scenes involves a mob of people who are determined to prevent the flight, which makes this one of the first science fiction stories to envision opposition to space travel and foreshadows the efforts to prevent a pioneering space flight which will be observed in *Destination Moon* (1950). However, the film entirely avoids the question of what might actually happen to its passengers during the flight by ending the story with the rocket's departure being observed by two speechifying spectators, Oswald Cabal (Raymond Massey) and Raymond Passworthy (Edward Chapman).

Still, despite the fact that its two space travelers do not wear spacesuits, this classic film merits some attention in this survey because Cabal's final speech offers a singularly eloquent vision of a human destiny to conquer the universe which, in a sense, makes it the first film to present the full potential range of possibilities in the spacesuit film:

> [Passworthy:] Oh, God, is there ever to be any age of happiness? Is there never to be any rest?
> [Cabal:] Rest enough for the individual man—too much, and too soon—and we call it death. But for

Man, no rest and no ending. He must go on, conquest beyond conquest. First this little planet with its winds and ways, and then all the laws of mind and matter that restrain him. Then the planets about him and at last out across immensity to the stars. And when he has conquered all the deeps of space and all the mysteries of time, still he will be beginning.

[Passworthy:] But...we're such little creatures. Poor humanity's so fragile, so weak. Little...little animals.

[Cabal:] Little animals. If we're no more than animals, we must snatch each little scrap of happiness and live and suffer and pass, mattering no more than all the other animals do or have done. It is this, or that. All the universe, or nothingness. Which shall it be, Passworthy? Which shall it be?[2]

Strangely enough, at the precise moment when the British Wells was articulating this glorious vision of humanity's future in space, American filmmakers were in the process of presenting space travel solely as a novel pathway to the sorts of juvenile adventures that had long appealed to young audiences. Taking their inspiration from two popular comic strips of the day featuring space adventurers, they produced four Saturday-morning serials, three starring Flash Gordon (*Flash Gordon* [1936], *Flash Gordon's Trip to Mars* [1938], and *Flash Gordon Conquers the Universe* [1940]) and one featuring another hero, *Buck Rogers* (1939), which all were later reedited as feature films for television and videocassette release. (There was also a recently rediscovered 1934 short, *Buck Rogers in the 25th Century*, produced for presentation during the 1933-1934 Century of Progress International Exposition, informally known as the Chicago World's Fair.) The serials deal with space flight entirely by means of brief transitional scenes displaying squat rocketships, with sparks emerging from their rear ends, that

---

2. *Things to Come* (London, 1936).

take off and fly horizontally through the sky more like airplanes than spaceships; these are always viewed in flight only against the backdrop of an atmosphere, and never the blackness of outer space. Furthermore, the alien worlds visited in these serials may be inhabited by exotic but humanoid creatures like the Hawk Men and Rock Men encountered by Flash Gordon or the Zuggs that Buck Rogers meets on Saturn, but the planets' environments are otherwise identical to Earth; we may be told that Saturn's atmospheric pressure is ten times greater than Earth's, but visiting humans breath normally while on the planet, and while the evil Ming's minions may at times wear metal masks over their faces, these are clearly not airtight and are in no way related to actual spacesuits.

Evaluated as portrayals of space travel, the Flash Gordon serials are the silliest: Flash Gordon (Buster Crabbe) and his colleagues Dale Arden (Jean Rogers [1936, 1938], Carol Hughes [1940]) and Dr. Zarkov (Frank Shannon) never wear any special clothing when they fly into space; their spaceship features an incongruous periscope borrowed from the design of a submarine; and their adventures tend to involve a single space flight to another planet, either Mongo or Mars, where they stay to struggle against the schemes of the villainous emperor Ming the Merciless (Charles Middleton) until they finally triumph with the help of human-like allies and return to Earth. During these sojourns, they may occasionally get into their spaceship or battle against Ming's spaceships, but these vehicles always stay within the atmosphere.

The Buck Rogers serial was marginally more realistic; if they are not wearing spacesuits, Buck Rogers (Buster Crabbe) and his crew at least are dressed like aviators of the day, a modest acknowledgment that space travel might demand special garments, and their efforts to defeat the future Earth's dictator, Killer Kane (Anthony Warde), with the help of virtuous but easily deluded Saturnians, involve several trips from Earth to Saturn and back, with the story's shifting locales signaled by establishing shots of either Earth or Saturn, observed against a black background with stars, which fleetingly provided an authentic image of outer space. Finally, amidst a crisis during Buck's first flight into space, there is a brief mention of the ship's "oxygen tanks," though these appear to be there as part of the propulsion system and not to help the space travelers breathe during their journey.

It is easy to laugh at these serials when they are viewed today, but their lasting impact cannot be denied: they served as the model for a number of melodramatic spacesuit films and television programs of the early 1950s, including series featuring Buck Rogers and Flash Gordon, and their influence can also be strongly felt in what became the major space franchises of recent decades, *Star Trek* and *Star Wars*. (Indeed, after the success of his *American Graffiti* [1973], George Lucas had initially planned to film a new version of *Flash Gordon*, and it was only when he proved unable to obtain the rights to the character that he decided to instead develop the original space adventure he would call *Star Wars* [1977].)

However, for whatever reasons one might have for celebrating these serials and the other early space films, there were only three films before 1950 that were truly breaking new ground in offering plausible predictions of human space travel: Danish director Holger-Madsen's *Himmelskibet*, which acknowledges the potential dangers of outer space by having its space travelers briefly don crude spacesuits; the German Fritz Lang and Thea von Harbou's *Frau im Mond* (1929), accurately described by David Wingrove as "the first realistic space film about a journey to the Moon,"[3] made with the assistance of German rocket scientist Hermann Oberth; and a less renowned Russian successor, Vasili Zhuravlev's *Kosmicheskiy Reys* (1935), which drew upon the expertise of the pioneering visionary Konstantin Tsiolkovsky. It is with these films, which demand more detailed attention, that the saga of the spacesuit film truly begins.

---

3. David Wingrove, *The Science Fiction Film Source Book* (London: Longman, 1985), 47.

2. WHAT IS AN ANIMATED MOVIE?

In order to compile an encyclopedia of animated movies, one needs a working definition of an *animated movie*, as opposed to a mere *cartoon*, to authoritatively determine which works merit entries. In previous conversations with a few experts, two ways to craft such a definition have been suggested.

First would be the criterion of length: an animated film could be defined as any animated narrative over thirty minutes long, perhaps allowing for some aesthetically pleasing exceptions; one might go a bit further and stipulate a narrative that is over sixty minutes long.

A second possible criterion would be the context of original presentation: an animated film could be defined as an animated narrative first presented in theatres as a feature film or as an advertised short subject, or as a film first presented as a television special or a separate DVD or videocassette. In contrast, one supposes, cartoons are those animated narratives which are shown as unannounced introductory adornments to features, as episodes of weekly television series, or as segments of longer films or television programs.

Criteria like these are certainly reasonable, and they may be functional enough to help one decide whether to give a work an entry in an encyclopedia of animated movies, but they also seem rather arbitrary, and perhaps too specific to the cultural contexts of contemporary America and Europe. After all, different eras and different places might have quite different expectations about the proper length of a film, and/or the method of presentation which characterizes a film. A proper definition of an animated movie, I would argue, must involve qualities which are more intrinsic to the films under consideration.

To develop such a definition, I suggest that we turn to the most ancient work of literary criticism, Aristotle's *Poetics*, and employ his famous list of the six elements of tragedy, more frequently described as his six elements of drama (since a posited accompanying discussion of the elements of comedy has never been found). These are usually given as:

1. Plot
2. Character
3. Thought
4. Diction
5. Song
6. Spectacle[4]

Aristotle's elements can be profitably adapted to serve as the six defining elements of the true animated movie.

That is: an animated movie has a true *plot*—a narrative with a beginning, middle, and end as Aristotle specified; a narrative with dynamics like rising action leading to a climax; and a narrative that may have subplots, double plots, or other complications. In contrast, a cartoon may be little more than the initial definition of a situation (cat wishes to eat bird, bird wishes to escape cat, etc.) followed by a series of repetitive incidents that continue until the piece reaches the proper length and stops—as best illustrated, perhaps, by the Warner Brothers Road Runner cartoons, which typically abandon even the pretense of a unified narrative.

Second, an animated movie has true *characters*—creatures or people that audiences can relate to as genuine personalities, often with some degree of depth or complexity. In contrast, the

4. See Aristotle, *Poetics*, translated by S. H. Butcher, introduction by Frank Fergusson (New York: Hill and Wang, 1961), *passim*.

characters in a cartoon may be only ciphers or stereotypes: dogs intent upon chasing cats, cats intent upon chasing mice, hunters intent upon shooting rabbits, and so on.

Third, an animated movie has *thought*, which in modern terms might be termed a message, a theme, a thesis, or a point. An animated movie, unlike a cartoon, always tries to do more than merely entertain viewers or make them laugh; its story is designed to communicate some potentially important statement about the human (or the sentient) condition, even if it is something as puerile as the admonitions in the *Care Bears* movies that people must "share their feelings." A cartoon, however, may simply be a series of amusing vignettes that offer no real message of any significance (beyond, say, that it is undesirable to have a big homely cat eat a cute little bird).

Fourth, an animated movie has *diction*, or words, as a key element. A mere cartoon may function quite well as a series of speechless events, an essentially silent movie with a musical soundtrack (with the Road Runner cartoons again serving as a good example, since the only words typically found therein are on occasional road signs or labels on boxes from the Acme Company). However, to communicate its genuine plot, genuine characters, and genuine theme, the animated movie must communicate through words—narration, dialogue, or titles.

The fifth criterion seems more debatable, since one might reasonably ask: must an animated movie always have *songs*? Well, it is undeniable that a vast majority of them do; and even those that do not are invariably accompanied and driven by a prominent and compelling soundtrack, closely tied to plot developments, making music at least seem like an essential element of the animated film. In contrast, cartoons generally have no songs, and the music they include may consist simply of repeated passages of stock music that have no particular relationship to the incidents on the screen.

Finally, a true animated movie does strive for an element of *spectacle*. Its animation is not the mind-numbing "limited animation" of the United Artists cartoons of the 1950s, or of the innumerable cartoon series where characters keep moving in exactly the same way in front of the same backgrounds. Instead, the animated movie consistently strives to be visually impressive; in particular, whether it's "Pink Elephants on Parade" in *Dumbo* (1941), "Under the Sea" in *The Little Mermaid* (1989), or Moses parting the Red Sea in *The Prince of Egypt* (1998), an animated movie almost always, I believe, has at least one sequence that is designed to be a "show-stopper," a visually stunning setpiece.

Thus, a proposed definition of an animated movie might be as follows:

> An animated movie, as opposed to a cartoon, is an animated narrative that includes (or at least aspires to include) all six of Aristotle's elements of drama: a true plot, fully developed characters, a theme or message, language, songs and music, and visual spectacle.

What are the advantages of such a definition?

First, there is the appeal to authority. Any formula that springs out the mind of an editor can readily be attacked as *ad hoc* or specious; but who can sneer at a definition based on Aristotle? This is also a definition which accords with general perceptions of the animated movie, since it would offer support for the widely accepted belief that Walt Disney's *Snow White and the Seven Dwarfs* (1937) represents the first animated film, and it would include almost all of the films that most would wish to consider animated movies. (The exceptions might be Disney's musical anthology films—*Fantasia* [1940] *Make Mine Music* [1946], *Melody Time* [1948], and *Fantasia 2000* [1999], since these lack a unified plot, but one could argue that even these films have a unifying theme—increasing audience exposure to and appreciation for various forms of music—and they do have fully developed narratives embedded within them, like "The Sorcerer's Apprentice" from *Fantasia* and "The Whale Who Wanted to Sing at the Met" from *Make Mine Music*.)

More broadly, a definition like this would be very useful in terms of the larger argument that a reference book on animated movies would need to make. The essential point would be that an animated movie is *not* simply an overlong cartoon, but is rather a distinct genre. Further, with Aristotle's support, the book might even maintain that the animated movie, far from being a spurious modern development, actually represents a return to the original and most ancient forms of drama, which were characterized by eclecticism and variety. Thus, in ancient Greece, an evening at the theatre would probably involve a trilogy of tragedies, presenting a familiar mythological story with complex characters, a profound message, a singing chorus, and spectacular effects like the *deux ex machina* descending from above on an elaborate crane; and everything would conclude with a satirical satyr play filled with jokes. And the approach of including something for everybody has remained central to the animated movies of today. In contrast, one might continue, other contemporary movie genres are more limited, lacking one or more of the Aristotelian elements: Merchant-Ivory costume dramas offer no spectacle, slam-bang action movies have no well-developed characters, serious dramas exclude songs, teen comedies lack any thought or message, and so on.

To make the point most boldly, one could posit that if the ancient Greeks returned to Earth today, they would find something like *Beauty and the Beast* (1991) or *The Prince of Egypt* far more like their ancient evenings at the theatre than the other films at the multiplexes. Thus, far from being something to belittle, the animated movie could be valorized as something archetypal, a return to ancient principles of drama, a visual narrative that is more complete and more satisfying than any of the others now available to modern filmgoers.

Now, would such an argument be taking matters a bit too far? Perhaps; but this could also have useful effects. As Kingsley Amis notes while discussing devotees of science fiction in *New Maps of Hell* (1960), "to feel that what one is doing is the most important thing in the world is not necessarily undignified, and indeed is perhaps more rather than less likely to lead to good work being done."[5] One danger to editors of an encyclopedia of animated movies would be a nascent inferiority complex, the feeling that one is analyzing movies which have never been taken seriously and may not deserve to be taken seriously; and such thoughts might subconsciously weaken one's determination to do one's very best work. But grand reference books require editors with grand ambitions who fervently wish to present grand claims about their subject matter. Therefore, to be a truly superior reference work, an encyclopedia of animated movies might fruitfully and energetically maintain that it is a book devoted to the best, and to the most significant, movies of them all.

---

5. Kingsley Amis, *New Maps of Hell* (New York: Ballantine Books, 1960), 52.

3. COMING OF AGE IN FANTASYLAND: THE SELF-PARENTING CHILD IN WALT DISNEY ANIMATED FILMS

(WITH LYNNE LUNDQUIST)

In recent studies of children's literature, it has become commonplace to assert that a work is "subversive" in one way or another, so this once-alarming claim may have lost all capacity to shock or surprise—unless, perhaps, the charge is aimed at a body of works which are universally regarded as extremely conservative and conventional in every way: the traditional Walt Disney animated films, which dominated family entertainment from the 1930s to the early twenty-first century.

Indeed, if one wants entertainment that affirms "traditional family values," there would seem to be no better place to look than Disney, since no other company has so vigorously promoted itself as a purveyor of wholesome, family-oriented movies. Yet if we examine the most well-known and popular of its films—the full-length animated features—we discover one curious feature: in these films purportedly about family values, *there are no families*—at least in the way that they are typically defined: a mother and father, often accompanied by siblings, grandparents, or other relatives, who both nurture and control their children. Instead, in these films, we find children who are separated or estranged from their families, or children living in various types of shattered or dysfunctional families. And this in itself suggests that these apparently innocuous and unthreatening films may conceal a troubling and subversive subtext.[6]

Examining first the major human characters in these animated films, we notice numerous orphans, or children who lack parents: *Pinocchio* (1939), magically brought to life by the Blue Fairy without genuine parents; *Peter Pan* (1953), of course; Arthur in *The Sword in the Stone* (1963); Mowgli in *The Jungle Book* (1966); Penny in *The Rescuers* (1976); Taran in *The Black Cauldron* (1984); Prince Eric in *The Little Mermaid* (1989); *Aladdin* (1992); and *Tarzan* (1999).

Next, there are children with single parents. Strangely—a point to study later—there is only one child with a single mother, Cody in *The Rescuers Down Under* (1990), though two adaptations of famous fairy tales, *Snow White and the Seven Dwarfs* (1937) and *Cinderella* (1950), feature daughters with single stepmothers. And there are boys or young men with single fathers—Prince Charming in *Cinderella* and Prince Phillip in *Sleeping Beauty* (1958); boys with single foster fathers—such as *Pinocchio* and Quasimodo in *The Hunchback of Notre Dame* (1996); and daughters with single fathers—such as Ariel in *The Little Mermaid*, Belle in *Beauty and the Beast* (1991), Princess Jasmine in *Aladdin*, *Pocahontas* (1995), and *Mulan* (1998).

Finally, there are children with parents who appear distant or uninvolved. The parents of Wendy, John, and Michael of *Peter Pan* seem loving and devoted, but they do regularly leave their children in the care of a dog, and they leave the children unprotected and go out on an evening when a visit from a myste-

6. In revisiting this essay, originally written in 1993 and updated in 1999, we have elected to avoid discussion of the Disney animated films of the last decade, which have increasingly featured computer-generated animation and often project a more sophisticated ambiance than the more traditional films that are considered here. However, we can note briefly that some of these more recent animated films, particularly *The Princess and the Frog* (2009) and *Tangled* (2010), do have definite resonances with their earlier counterparts discussed here.

rious stranger seems imminent. *Alice in Wonderland* (1951) has a normal set of parents, we assume, but they are not observed; instead, we only see Alice being supervised by an older sister. The parents of Princess Aurora, the *Sleeping Beauty*, agree to let three fairies take their infant daughter and raise her until the age of sixteen, so they are voluntarily not part of her young life. And the parents of the girl in *Oliver and Company* (1988) have gone on an extended trip—something they do habitually—leaving her in the care of servants.[7]

Confronted with this pattern of absent or broken families, one could respond with two ameliorative explanations. First would be that Disney writers and animators are simply controlled by their source materials, which often stipulate unusual situations, so the reason for these odd families must be sought in the original texts, not the film adaptations. In some cases, this is surely true, and it is hard to imagine, for example, how one might adapt *Cinderella*, *Peter Pan*, or *Tarzan* so as to provide the title characters with a normal set of parents. But in other cases the explanation will not hold: a few films, like *Oliver and Company* and *The Rescuers Down Under*, are basically original creations,[8] while in other films, the source materials do not demand an unusual family structure. The story of "Sleeping Beauty" does

---

7. Because we are interested in how the movies affect young viewers, we consider only human characters; animals, no matter how anthropomorphic, are unlikely to be influential role models. Yet animal characters do display irregular family structures: *Dumbo* (1941) has no father and is separated from his mother; *Bambi* (1942) loses his mother and sees his father only sporadically; *The Aristocats* (1970) are a single mother cat and her kittens; *The Great Mouse Detective* (1986) helps a little girl mouse find her single father; the cat in *Oliver and Company* is an orphan; and the eagle in *The Rescuers Down Under* is a single mother. These movies differ, though, in that the animal frequently not only marry—a typical conclusion in many Disney films—but also go on to have children and establish their own normal families, as in *Lady and the Tramp* (1955), *101 Dalmatians* (1961), and *The Lion King* (1994).

8. Although *Oliver and Company* is derived, very loosely, from Charles Dickens's *Oliver Twist* (1838).

not state that the princess grew up away from her parents, and neither Hans Christian Andersen's "The Little Mermaid" nor the histories of Pocahantas stipulate that the heroine lacks a mother. Most strikingly, while all other versions of the Aladdin story include Aladdin's mother as an active character, the Disney version removes her from the scene; far from being forced to rely on a story about an orphan, here the animators contradicted their source material and deliberately made their protagonist an orphan. Also, there are any number of familiar fairy tales with more conventional families—including "Rumpelstiltskin," "The Elves and the Shoemaker," "The Princess and the Pea," and "King Thrushbeard"—that the Disney company has scrupulously avoided, as if there were some desire to avoid depicting normal families.

A second explanation would be that these absent or shattered families are presented to evoke a sense of pathos, so young characters quickly earn the audience's sympathy because they lack normal parents. Again, there is some truth in this response; but again, it is not wholly satisfactory, for there are other devices for separating children from parents—misunderstandings, accidents, or criminal activities—involving no permanent disruption of the family unit. But the characteristic strategy of Disney animated films is final or injurious separation. How funny would *Home Alone* (1990) have been if Kevin's parents had died, or if his parents had deliberately left him alone? However, such permanent or willful parental absence is exactly the sort of situation that often confronts a child at the start of a Disney film.

We are driven, then, to this hypothesis: that the preferred premise for writers and animators who create these films is the destroyed or shattered family, and the characteristic problem confronting their young characters is the need to compensate for their irremediable lack of one or both of their parents.

Children and young people in Disney animated films employ two strategies to replace their absent or inadequate families. The first could be described as a reconciliation with nature:

without nurturing support from parents, the young person turns to the natural world, to sympathetic and often anthropomorphic animals who can provide that support. Thus, after fleeing through a stormy forest, Snow White is surrounded by forest animals who comfort her. When the Blue Fairy brings *Pinocchio* to life, she appoints an insect named Jiminy Cricket to serve as his mentor and companion. Arthur of *The Sword in the Stone*, when he travels to London, is supervised by a talking owl. Mowgli of *The Jungle Book* is raised by wolves and later guided by a bear and a panther, just as *Tarzan* is raised by apes. Penny of *The Rescuers* is helped by two mice, Bernard and Miss Bianca, from the Rescue Aid Society. King Triton of *The Little Mermaid* at one time appoints the crab Sebastian to serve as his daughter's guardian. Cody of *The Rescuers Down Under* bonds with a mighty mother eagle, and is later rescued by Bernard and Miss Bianca.[9] (Other animals in Disney films also provide support, though they are admittedly more like friends than parents: Princess Aurora of *Sleeping Beauty* frolics with some forest animals; the girl in *Oliver and Company* turns to the kitten Oliver for companionship; Ariel, *The Little Mermaid*, has a flounder and seagull as her friends; *Aladdin* has a pet monkey, Abu, while Princess Jasmine has a protective pet tiger named Rajah; *Pocahantas* has a rambunctious pet raccoon; and *Mulan* is assisted by a small dragon.)

The other strategy is to seek out or find a surrogate parent— a friendly adult, typically a magical being who can provide the support and guidance of a parent. Snow White finds the Seven Dwarfs to protect her from the Queen, *Pinocchio* is adopted by the woodcutter Geppetto, and *Cinderella* finds a Fairy Godmother. *Peter Pan* enjoys the help of the adult Tinker Bell,

---

9. A variation in this pattern occurs in two films featuring artificial structures: *Beauty and the Beast*, largely set in the Beast's mansion, and *The Hunchback of Notre Dame*, largely set in a cathedral. Here the protagonist establishes rapport not with creatures from the natural world but man-made objects from the civilized world—a talking candlestick, clock, teapot, cup, and wardrobe for Belle, and three statues of gargoyles for Quasimodo.

who saves him from the scheme of Captain Hook. Aurora of *Sleeping Beauty* is raised by motherly fairies. Arthur of *The Sword in the Stone* is taken in by Merlin the Magician; Taran in *The Black Cauldron* finds a sorcerer to serve as a father figure; *Aladdin* stumbles upon a friendly genie to help him woo Princess Jasmine; and *Pocahontas* obtains advice and guidance from an ancient talking tree, Mother Willow.

All of these developments might serve as a transitional stage, a way to temporarily help children deal with an unpleasant situation until their normal family can be restored, or until a new normal family can be created. And the films where human characters are subordinate to animal characters—like *The Rescuers*, *Oliver and Company*, and *The Rescuers Down Under*—may move to this kind of conclusion: after being helped by Bernard and Miss Bianca, Penny is adopted by two loving parents; after the crisis provoked by her pet cat, the girl in *Oliver and Company* is reunited with her parents; and although Cody in *The Rescuers Down Under* is last seen as the triumphant master of his natural realm, riding the mighty eagle to America, we assume he will soon be reunited with his mother.

However, in other Disney animated films, something different happens: the children's mentors do not give way to true parents and do not retain the role of surrogate parents. Instead there occurs a role reversal: while animals and magical adults first appear in parental roles, the children later assume parental roles, with the animals and adults recast as their children. In effect, children manage to construct their own families, with themselves as parents.

The pattern is twice enacted in the first Disney animated film, *Snow White and the Seven Dwarfs*. When they first appear, the forest animals comfort Snow White when she is sadly crying in the forest; but after she wakes up and becomes a little more cheerful, she takes charge of the animals and issues commands as they clean up the dwarfs' cottage. Similarly, Snow White initially appeals to the dwarfs for protection against the Queen; then she begins to act like their mother—cooking their meals, scolding them to wash their hands before eating, and kissing them goodbye as they go off to work.

The ostensible child who functions as a parent is also seen in the second Disney animated film, *Pinocchio*. Although Jiminy is assigned to be Pinocchio's conscience, the puppet-boy completely ignores him, never asks for advice, and goes where he pleases, leaving the cricket to literally and figuratively play the role of Pinocchio's follower throughout the film. Pinocchio twice disobeys Geppetto by not going to school and instead joining Stromboli's puppet show and visiting Pleasure Island. Even at the end of the film, when Pinocchio has apparently reformed, he is still willful and disobedient: without asking permission or explaining himself, he sets fire to Geppetto's boat so as to provoke the whale Monstro to sneeze; and later, when the drowning Geppetto tells Pinocchio to leave him and save himself, the boy disobeys him and rescues the woodcutter. From the beginning to the end of the film, Pinocchio is completely in control of his own actions, and Jiminy Cricket and Geppetto are little more than his puppets.

Similar role reversals occur in other animated films. Despite their careful parenting, the fairies in *Sleeping Beauty* cannot prevent Aurora from falling in love with a handsome stranger. Baloo the bear and Bagheera the panther of *The Jungle Book* are powerless to keep Mowgli from doing what he wants; Ariel does what she pleases, despite the advice of her aquatic friends; Aladdin soon learns how to manipulate and control his genie; and Pocahantas becomes an assertive voice for peace in her tribe. The most extreme case is *The Sword in the Stone*: when young Arthur announces that he is going to London against Merlin's wishes, the magician angrily vanishes, abandoning his parental role and leaving Arthur completely in control of his own actions; the owl Archimedes tries to replace Merlin as tutor and guide but remains subordinate to Arthur; and Arthur then pulls the sword from the stone and becomes King of England— making himself the ultimate parental figure.

A variation of the pattern is seen in *Cinderella* and *Peter*

Pan. Here, the child is first seen already in a position of dominance; that is, while Cinderella may have initially turned to the household animals to console her in her times of unhappiness, like Snow White, by the time the movie begins she has established herself as their parent, feeding, dressing, and fussing over them. Similarly, Peter Pan was no doubt a rather helpless figure when he first came to Neverland, but at the start of the film, he is the leader of the Lost Boys and master of Tinker Bell. In these films, the crucial action is a crisis which temporarily returns the child-parent to the status of a child, so that animals and magical beings must temporarily resume the role of parents: so when Cinderella is reduced to despair because she has no dress for the ball, the mice and birds come to her rescue by crafting a beautiful dress for her; and when Peter Pan naïvely opens the deadly present from Captain Hook, Tinker Bell rushes to save him, like a good mother. However, when the crisis passes, Cinderella and Peter Pan return to their parental roles; indeed, it is interesting that in the one major change from J. M. Barrie's original story, the Disney version of *Peter Pan* has the Lost Boys stay behind with Peter in Neverland, so that he can remain a dominant parental figure.

Far from affirming "traditional family values," then, these animated films directly argue against those values. Their message is that parents are not in fact an important element in childhood: children can prosper without true parents or effective parents; and when they encounter parent-like figures, they can learn how to dominate and control those potential surrogate parents. In effect, children in Disney animated films create their own families and make themselves the parents of those families.

Some may not accept that these classic and beloved films are a functional assault on American family values; but the true test of a model is how well it explains otherwise puzzling aspects of its subject. And we can employ this model to propose solutions to a few problems raised by the Disney animated films.

The first problem has been alluded to: the peculiar and conspicuous absence of mothers in these films. This is crucial, for while fathers were once traditionally allowed to periodically leave the home or be absent for extended periods, the established role of the mother was to always be at home, nurturing the children and keeping the family functioning as a unit. Thus, removing the mother rather than the father—the usual preference in the films—is the strongest device for attacking the family. Yet these films rarely lack a strong female figure. However, a key transformation occurs: the mother figure is recast as a powerful villainess.

The transformation is transparent in *Snow White and the Seven Dwarfs* and *Cinderella*, where the evil woman is a *step-*mother, not a true mother, but other films have domineering, malevolent women who are less obviously mothers in disguise—the Red Queen of *Alice in Wonderland*, the fairy Maleficent in *Sleeping Beauty*, Madame Mim in *The Sword in the Stone*, Madame Medusa in *The Rescuers*, and Ursula in *The Little Mermaid*. Watching boys and girls without mothers struggling to free themselves from the evil machinations of powerful older women, we witness an enactment of children struggling to free themselves from their families, as personified by the figures who most strongly hold those families together, the mothers. In contrast, early Disney films featured relatively few male villains, with the prominent exceptions of Stromboli and the Coachman in *Pinocchio* and Captain Hook in *Peter Pan*, who in that film, as in the play, is a version of the children's father, Mr. Darling (on stage, the same actor plays both roles, and in the Disney film, Hans Conreid provided the voice for both roles).

Yet an odd shift has occurred in recent Disney animated films, which also poses a problem: except for *The Little Mermaid*, these films focus on powerful male villains, warped transformations of the father figure: the Horned King in *The Black Cauldron*, Bill Sykes in *Oliver and Company*, McHeath in *The Rescuers Down Under*, Gaston in *Beauty and the Beast*, the Grand Vizier of *Aladdin*, the English colonialist of *Pocahantas*, Frollo of *The*

Hunchback of Notre Dame, Hades in *Hercules* (1997),[10] and the Hun Shan Yu in *Mulan*. Having relied on villainous women in previous films, why has the Walt Disney company suddenly shifted, in the last ten years, to an emphasis on villainous men?

Our answer is this: in recent times, the idealized image of the family has radically changed. Modern fathers are not supposed to be distant or absent, leaving mothers to care for and unite the family; instead, fathers are supposed to be intimately involved in all aspects of family life, participating as an equal in nurturing children and maintaining the family. So, at the very moment when the father has assumed a new prominence as an avatar of practicing family values, Disney animated films give new prominence to the evil, domineering male villain. This cannot be coincidental; rather, it must represent a recognition that a modern attack on family values must focus on the father as well as on the mother.

Our model may also offer some insight regarding what must be regarded as the strangest and most problematic of the Disney animated films, *Alice in Wonderland*. Based on a popular children's classic, the film featured, as most critics would agree, many colorful and entertaining characters, some brilliantly creative animation, and a soundtrack filled with memorable songs. Thus, *Alice in Wonderland* should have been highly successful. However, it is widely viewed as Disney's most spectacular failure: it was one of the few animated features that lost money on its initial release, the first such film to be shown on television (as early as 1954), and one of the few films that was never re-released to theaters. The question we must ask is:

---

10. Though this film does violate the pattern noted here in one key respect: the goddess Hera, formerly portrayed as Hercules's vengeful, antagonistic stepmother, is recast as a loving mother, making this one case where Disney animators altered source material to strengthen a maternal relationship. Perhaps this was done to differentiate the film from the television series then on the air, *Hercules: The Legendary Journeys* (1995-1999), wherein an offstage Hera is a recurring villainess, or perhaps someone else complained about the absence of sympathetic mothers in Disney films, engendering this response.

what's wrong with this movie?

While other explanations have been offered, our model provides an answer: overly constrained by very familiar source material, Disney writers and animators could not make *Alice in Wonderland* fit the pattern of the family-creating, self-parenting child, so the film lacked appeal both to its creators and to its audiences.

At the start of the film, we see Alice as a young girl who wishes to follow in the footsteps of other Disney children. The first song she sings, "In a World of My Own," may be the purest expression of the impulse that drives these independent youths:

> Cats and rabbits
> Would reside in fancy little houses
> And be dressed in shoes and fancy trousers
> In a world of my own.
> All the flowers
> Would have very extra-special powers;
> I would sit and talk to them for hours
> When I'm lonely in a world of my own....
> I would listen to a babbling brook
> And hear a song that I could understand.
> I keep hoping it could be that way,
> because my world would be a Wonderland.[11]

Like other Disney children, Alice is ready to abandon her family, at least temporarily, to establish rapport with anthropomorphic animals (and even plants) and to make herself a parent in her own world.

Unfortunately, Alice cannot accomplish these goals. She tries to establish sympathetic contact with the natural world, but the animals she encounters—the White Rabbit, the talking flowers, the caterpillar, and the Cheshire Cat—are either hostile or enigmatic. She encounters adults who might serve as surro-

---

11. Bob Hilliard, lyrics, Sammy Fain, music, "In a World of My Own" [song], *Alice in Wonderland* (Disney, 1950).

gate parents—Tweedledum and Tweedledee, the Mad Hatter, and the Red Queen—but these people are also unhelpful and sometimes maddening. Unable to dominate these animals or magical adults, or even to connect with them, Alice cannot begin to construct her own family with herself as a parent; and, late in the film, at a time when other Disney children have established themselves as the centers of their own families, we see Alice sitting alone in the forest, crying her heart out, in a scene not found in Carroll's books which is an exact analogue to the forest scene in *Snow White and the Seven Dwarfs*. As she cries, various baffling creatures surround her and cry sympathetic tears. But, as was not the case with Snow White, the creatures do not approach her, and Alice cannot parent them. Instead, they vanish, and she must travel by herself to another unsettling adventure. Unable to commune with or control her Wonderland, Alice must ultimately retreat, returning to her old life under the guidance of her older sister and finding, reassuringly, that her Wonderland was only a dream.

The odd thing is that *Alice in Wonderland* is also the one Disney film that offers a traditional message: "there's no place like home." To stay happy, Alice must remain at home, in what we presume is a normal family; if she goes away from home, she will only get in trouble, find no worthwhile friends, and feel lost and confused. This is, presumably, the messages that parents would want their children to hear; and it is surprising to find it only in a Disney movie that most critics and viewers despise.

Throughout the twentieth century, children have become more independent and more rebellious in dealing with their parents, and one posited explanation has always been the baleful influence of disreputable literature. There have been vigorous crusades to keep children away from pulp magazines, comic books, violent cartoons, and video games, all seen as causes of undesirable childhood or adolescent behavior. And during all these periods of alarm, Disney animated films were cast as wholesome, desirable alternatives to these despised examples of children's subliterature. We suggest here that these films have in fact conveyed a subversive message of their own; and parents who insist upon blaming outside influences for their children's bad conduct now have a new, and surprising, candidate for their concern and condemnation.[12]

---

12. Some may argue these films are not truly "subversive": all children like pretending to be parents, so films appeal to that desire by depicting children who pretend to be parents, and what's subversive about that? However, just as children playing house must eventually return to their roles as children, films with youths acting as adults usually end with the characters returned to their previous status. In the Disney live-action film *Pollyanna* (1960), for example, young Hayley Mills first lords it over grumpy and confused adults, cheering them up and dispensing exactly the right advice to help them solve their problems. But at the end of the film, her aunt forbids her to attend a local fair, reminding everyone of her subordinate position; and when she attempts to defy her aunt by climbing out a window, she experiences a near-fatal fall. Again a vulnerable child, she recovers to learn that her aunt will now marry a suitor, providing her with a normal set of parents. As noted, animated films like *The Rescuers* and *Oliver and Company* also unite children with parents as the conclusion, and other live-action Disney films with animation—*Song of the South* (1946), *Mary Poppins* (1964), and *Pete's Dragon* (1977)—similarly end with once-rambunctious children again supervised by parents. Only the animated films lack such humbling or restorative endings; the child becomes not a temporary parent, but a permanent parent. (Eric S. Rabkin suggested in conversation that audiences may find it easier to observe drastic role reversals involving animated characters, while they prefer more traditional resolutions in films that, while still fantastic, do feature live actors portraying children.)

4. THE TRUE FRONTIER: CONFRONTING AND AVOIDING THE REALITIES OF SPACE IN AMERICAN SCIENCE FICTION FILMS

Though narratives of space travel characteristically resonate with historical and generic references—to pioneering and settling the American West (the Old Frontier), voyaging across vast oceans, diving deep underwater, or trekking into unknown polar regions—the fact remains that outer space is an environment radically different from all those that humans have previously explored. It is a realm without air, without water, and without material resources; a realm of zero gravity, extreme temperatures, and no protection from harmful radiation. A film about space travel, even if designed only to entertain, should in some way acknowledge these harsh realities; in the science fiction films of the last fifty years, I maintain, this has increasingly not occurred.

To distinguish films that confront the facts about space from films that avoid those facts, one can search for a simple but clear visual icon: the spacesuit. In both cinematic and actual space flights, these bulky, cumbersome costumes unmistakably signal that their wearers are in a dangerous and potentially lethal environment which demands an unprecedented degree of protection. Just as millennia of sea travel have not eliminated the need for lifeboats and life preservers, and just as a century of air travel has not eliminated the need for parachutes and emergency oxygen, anyone traveling through space will always need to have a spacesuit readily available, because all forms of defense one can imagine—force fields, tractor beams, photon torpedoes, strengthened hulls—will inevitably be susceptible to failure, and will inevitably fail someday, bringing travelers into contact with the deadly vacuum of space. A space film featuring spacesuits, whatever its other flaws, is realistic in at least one crucial respect; a space film that never displays or alludes to spacesuits, whatever its other virtues, is unrealistic in at least one crucial respect.

With space at a premium (in another sense), I cannot undertake a complete history of spacesuit films in relation to the larger set of space films, but a few important works can be named and discussed. Although there were space films before 1950, including *A Trip to the Moon* (1902), *Woman in the Moon* (1929), and the serials featuring Flash Gordon (1936, 1938, 1940) and Buck Rogers (1939), the first completely authentic spacesuit film was probably *Destination Moon* (1950), produced by George Pal and directed by Irving Pichel. While other critics have noted the film's painstaking efforts to portray outer space accurately, employing black curtains and innovative lighting techniques to achieve a memorable effect, the film was equally attentive to the authenticity of its spacesuits; even Woody Woodpecker, in the film's incongruous cartoon sequence explaining the principles of space flight, wears a realistic spacesuit during his flight to the Moon.

As it happens, the film's co-author and technical advisor, science fiction writer Robert A. Heinlein, was uniquely qualified to provide expert guidance in devising plausible spacesuits, since he had worked during World War II on the construction of "high-altitude pressure suits";[13] and he later wrote a novel, *Have Space Suit—Will Travel* (1958), which incorporated a detailed

13. H. Bruce Franklin, *Robert A. Heinlein: America as Science Fiction* (New York: Oxford University Press, 1980), 14.

and loving description of a functional spacesuit. In his essay "Shooting *Destination Moon*," Heinlein described some of the film's efforts to achieve realistic-looking spacesuits:

> Low gravity and tremendous leaps [require] piano wire, of course—but did you ever try to wire a man who is wearing a spacesuit? The wires have to get inside that suit at several points, producing the effect a nail has on a tire, i.e., a man wearing a pressurized suit cannot be suspended on wires. So inflation of suits must be replaced by padding, at least during wired shots. But a padded suit doesn't wrinkle the same way a pressurized suit does and the difference shows. Furthermore, the zippered openings for the wires can be seen. Still worse, if inflation is to be faked with padding, how are we to show them putting on their suits?... To get around the shortcomings of padded suits we worked in an "establishing scene" in which the suits were shown to be of two parts, an outer chafing suit and an inner pressure suit. This makes sense; deep-sea divers often use chafing suits over their pressure suits, particularly when working around coral.... It is good engineering and we present this new wrinkle in spacesuits without apology.[14]

Now, reading about an "establishing scene" (albeit a very brief one) to explain the design of the film's spacesuits, some will discern misguided priorities, agreeing with Phil Hardy that "the script is colourless and wooden; the dominant concern of those involved was to make the journey to the Moon realistic rather than dramatic."[15] Yet it is infelicitous to describe the

14. Robert A. Heinlein, "Shooting Destination Moon," 1950, *Requiem: New Collected Works by Robert A. Heinlein and Tributes to the Grand Master*, edited by Yoji Kondo (New York: Tor Books, 1992), 120.

15. Phil Hardy, *The Encyclopedia of Science Fiction Movies, 1984* (Minneapolis, Minnesota: Woodbury Press, 1986), 125. Later quotations in

difference between *Destination Moon* and other space films in terms of "realism" versus "drama," since we are actually dealing with two different types of drama: the brilliantly predicted drama of actual space travel versus the conventional drama of popular film.

That is, applying normal standards, one could easily claim that there is no "drama" in *Destination Moon*: there are no villains to overcome, no tensions between protagonists, no thwarted romances or comic misunderstandings. Yet there is a strong and definite conflict in this story—the conflict between frail human beings and the merciless hostility of outer space— and the critical weapon that people need to oppose this enemy is a spacesuit. With space cast as the opponent, a scene describing the spacesuits that the heroes will wear might be regarded as both interesting and necessary, a scene precisely equivalent to the well-loved introductory scenes in the James Bond films in which Q displays and explains the ingenious devices that Bond will use to battle his next foe. Attentiveness to the correct appearance of the spacesuit is also essential, for the same reason that a cowboy in a western film cannot be seen brandishing a toy gun: a hero's weapons must look credible.

In a film that devoted so much energy to its spacesuits, it is only appropriate that its final crisis involves a spacesuit: seeking to reduce the weight of the rocketship so it can return to Earth, the astronauts craft an ingenious scheme to jettison the last spacesuit without endangering the life of Sweeney (Dick Wesson), the crewman wearing it. They tell him to drill a hole in the airlock, attach the suit to a line through the hole attached to an oxygen tank, quickly remove the suit while the air slowly leaks out, return to the ship, and have the suit fall out of the ship once the airlock door is reopened. Even removing a spacesuit, then, in certain circumstances, proves beneficial to human survival in space.

If *Destination Moon* remains an underappreciated film, that

---

the text are to this edition.

might stem from the fact that, as Hardy notes, "for the most part its predictions were remarkably accurate" (125). Its depictions of slow-moving astronauts outside the ship resemble films of actual space walks; its scenes of men walking on the Moon, as others have pointed out, eerily anticipate television coverage of the Apollo missions; and even the improvisational, spit-and-chewing-gum inventiveness of their solution to the weight problem mirrors the actual way that astronauts and engineers on the ground devised answers to problems like those of the *Apollo 13* mission. People rarely watch *Destination Moon* today not because it is undramatic, but because they have regularly watched real-life video footage which conveys the same sense of authentic drama.

For the next eighteen years, no other space film quite matched the stark intensity of *Destination Moon*'s confrontation with space, though some spacesuit films of that era had moments of evocative power. *Project Moonbase* (1953), the lesser film that Heinlein made without George Pal, offered innovative scenes of weightlessness in a space station and an accident on the Moon, while *Conquest of Space* (1955), the lesser film that Pal made without Heinlein, presented an unusually austere portrait of astronauts on Mars. Other reasonably realistic and dignified spacesuit films of that era include Ivan Tors' *Riders to the Stars* (1954), the almost unknown *12 to the Moon* (1960), and the television series *Men into Space* (1959-1960). Displaying some—but not enough—concern for safety, *The Angry Red Planet* (1960) places spacesuited Martian explorers in what look like motorcycle helmets with faceplates, protecting their skulls from dangerous collisions but offering unpersuasive protection from the harsh Martian environment. In the 1960s, there emerged films purportedly about the actual space program; these tended to be farcical at first, like *Moon Pilot* (1962) and *The Reluctant Astronaut* (1967), but later a few such films aspired to gritty realism, like *Countdown* (1968) and *Marooned* (1969).

However, the greatest spacesuit film of this period—and, perhaps uncoincidentally, the greatest science fiction film of all time—was Stanley Kubrick's *2001: A Space Odyssey* (1968). The film took its subtitle seriously; *2001* is very much an odyssey within and through outer space, with co-creator Arthur C. Clarke, famed for his realistic science fiction, constantly on hand to ensure scientific accuracy. Our first glimpse of a person in the future, following the celebrated jump cut from bone to spaceship, is the sleeping Dr. Heywood R. Floyd (William Sylvester), wearing a spacesuit without a helmet, well prepared for any emergency during his flight to near-orbital space. Although Floyd's stopover at the space station, with its comfortable chairs and Howard Johnson's restaurant, may briefly give the impression that future space travel will be a safe and familiar experience, much like today's air travel, subsequent events in the film decisively indicate that will not be the case, for Floyd is back in a full spacesuit for his spartan journey across the lunar surface to the unearthed monolith. A brief scene that usually provokes laughter—members of Floyd's party form a group and pose for the camera in front of the monolith—conveys a serious message: space is an environment unlike that of Earth, and longstanding rituals and activities may no longer be appropriate or logical in this new environment. Here, it makes no sense to take a souvenir photograph to record someone's visit to a noteworthy site when the person in the resulting photograph will appear entirely anonymous, virtually identical to all the other people wearing spacesuits. (The point was also made in *Destination Moon* when Sweeney, just photographed apparently holding up the Earth, complains, "Nobody will know it's me in this diving suit."[16])

The film's most significant spacesuit scene, of course, is the suspenseful episode when astronaut Dave Bowman (Keir Dullea), leaving his spaceship in an unsuccessful effort to rescue fellow astronaut Frank Poole (Gary Lockwood) drifting in space, is locked out by the rebellious computer HAL 9000 and forced to figure out how to get back into the spaceship before his

---

16. *Destination Moon* (George Pal, 1950).

power and oxygen run out. His plight stems from a critical lack of preparedness: hurrying to save his friend, Bowman neglected to put on his space helmet before piloting his tiny craft or "pod." Drawing upon a vignette in his earlier story "The Other Side of the Sky" (1959), Clarke had Bowman come up with a startling solution: first, he opens a manual airlock; next, after positioning the pod by the airlock door, he opens the pod and exposes his body to the vacuum of space; then, since the rush of escaping air from the pod drives him into the airlock, he has a few seconds to reach and operate the manual control, closing the airlock and restoring oxygen to the chamber, before the exposure to space kills him. Thanks to his careful preparation, he manages to do exactly that; then, after finding and putting on a space helmet to guard against further threats, he proceeds to HAL's memory chamber and methodically turns the machine off. While Sweeney briefly faced the same potential danger in the airlock of *Destination Moon*, Bowman's chaotic moments in the airlock of *2001* represent the pinnacle of the spacesuit film, the only time on film when a human being comes into *direct* contact with outer space—and lives to tell the tale.

Considering this episode, and episodes in previous space-suit films, we see that the environment of space radically alters several conventions of filmed narrative. A scene in space *looks* different: with an enveloping background of dark black space filled with sprinkles of white light, and foregrounded figures in white spacesuits (the usual color choice, despite the idiosyncratic bright colors of *Destination Moon*, since white best reflects heat), viewers essentially see a starkly black-and-white environment, even if the film is shot in color. A scene in space *sounds* different, since sound does not travel in space. Some films, like *Project Moonbase*, convey this by having no background noise whatsoever, a brief return to the silent film; in his space scenes, Kubrick provided only the sound of Bowman's breathing—reminding viewers that, when you are deep in space, the only sound you will hear is the sound of your own breathing; and the scenes of Floyd on the moon, and Bowman flying near the final monolith, are backed by the ethereal, discordant vocal music of György Ligeti, suggesting an unfamiliar and alienating realm. A scene in space *moves* differently: for long periods of time, everything may proceed slowly and incrementally, as people in bulky spacesuits gingerly maneuver in an unforgiving environment; then there may be sudden dramatic movements lasting only a few seconds. Finally, for all these reasons, a scene in space often must be *explained* differently: either it must be preceded by expository scenes, so that viewers will understand later events, or it must be accompanied by narration, conversation, or interior monologues providing on-the-spot information. Here, Kubrick boldly assumed that the audience could figure out Bowman's problem, and his risky solution, without any prefatory or concurrent explanation; in fact (though some hasty last-minute editing of the lengthy sequence may have been a factor too), many viewers to this day have trouble understanding this episode, which may be why it usually receives little critical attention.

After the success of *2001*, one might have predicted a new wave of grim, meticulous spacesuit films; but Kubrick and Clarke were a hard act to follow. In fact, the most influential science fiction film of 1968 was *Planet of the Apes*, whose astronauts are never observed in spacesuits and quickly emerge from their spaceship onto the surface of an alien planet resembling southern California, eliminating all impediments to routine adventure. As for stories that focused more on space travel, it was not *2001* but another, different sort of celluloid space adventure that became Hollywood's template of choice.

At the time when *2001* was released, a television series named *Star Trek* (1966-1969) was finishing its second year; and during two seasons of weekly journeys through interstellar space, a spacesuit of any kind had never been mentioned or presented. The crew of the starship *Enterprise* wore only normal clothing, and the women's clothing was positively skimpy. Most of the time, they were comfortable inside their spacious craft, thanks to life support systems and artificial gravity; when they needed to leave, they entered a transporter room to instantly "beam down" to an earthlike planetary surface or into another spaceship. In rare circumstances when the transporter could not be used, crew members traveled through space in a small "shuttle craft"; however, even when they were looking through windows at space only a few feet away, it apparently never occurred to anyone to bring along some protective gear.

For the most part, then, the crew of the *Enterprise* experienced outer space only by watching it on television. To modern viewers, the ship's bridge resembles a futuristic home entertainment center, with all chairs positioned to watch a huge television screen. Unaccountably lacking a remote control device, father-figure Captain James Kirk (William Shatner) must bark out orders to subordinates whenever he wants to change channels. The screen usually shows the space in front of the *Enterprise*, tiny stars moving from the center of the screen to its borders, a pattern now observed in a popular "screen saver" for computer monitors called "Starfield Simulator." When necessary, Kirk can order the camera to zoom in for a close-up or recede for a long-range view. If he wants to speak with someone on another ship or a planet, he says "Screen on," and space vanishes, to be replaced by a picture of a talking alien. In some situations, the screen can also display diagrams or video images from the computer library. For the people on board the *Enterprise*, quite literally, outer space is what you watch on television when nothing else is on.

When *Star Trek* eliminated space as a significant factor in its stories, there were several advantageous results. Certainly, life was simpler for the special effects people, since they did not have to worry about simulating zero gravity or filming actors in spacesuits; only models of spacecraft and planets had to be filmed against the background of space. More importantly, the peculiar and problematic aspects of space drama observed in previous spacesuit films were no longer present; scenes in *Star Trek* episodes could be filled with bright colors and evocative sounds, could be paced in conventional ways, and could be understood without annotation. In one key respect, the series famously ignored the facts of space, as Gene Roddenberry once explained:

> A spaceship traveling through space, where there is no atmosphere, does not make a sound as it passes. When we did the original titles for the pilot, where we have the ship zoom past the camera at seemingly great speeds, we had no sound...just the visual movement of the ship. As a result, that sequence was literally dead. It had no feeling of speed or excitement about it at all. So we added a "swish" sound as the ship passed by, and suddenly it came alive. We are earthbound creatures, and we are used to some thing going that fast making a sound as it goes by. We had to put it in even though we know that scientifically it wouldn't happen.[17]

With this concession to "earthbound" sensibilities, the producer was frankly falsifying the nature of space, making it seem more like Earth with those familiar "swish" sounds (which also accompany all spaceships in subsequent *Star Trek* series and films). It is a small matter, but it suggests a larger pattern of making space seem familiar and comfortable by ignoring its true features.

In one episode during the third season of *Star Trek*, however, spacesuits finally made a telling appearance. In "The Tholian Web" (1968), Captain Kirk and other crew members investigating a devastated spaceship must wear large, clumsy spacesuits when they are beamed aboard. Due to strange energy disturbances in the vicinity, Kirk is stranded on board the ship, which soon vanishes; as the crew gradually recognizes that there is no possibility of rescue, Kirk is officially pronounced

---

17. Gene Roddenberry, cited in Stephen Whitfield and Roddenberry, *The Making of Star Trek* (New York: Ballantine Books, 1968), 116, ellipsis Roddenberry. The book was actually written by Whitfield, with occasional inserted comments from Roddenberry.

dead, and Mr. Spock (Leonard Nimoy) takes over as captain. To those who have only seen this episode as part of an endlessly rerun syndication package, it is hard to convey the impact of this episode when I watched its first airing on November 15, 1968. Even as a teenager, I knew that regular characters were sometimes written out of series for various reasons; and, watching an episode in which Kirk is declared dead and Spock is competently settling into a new role as captain, I and all the others watching that night could not be *sure*, like later viewers, that it was all a trick. The emotional power of the episode was further heightened by a scene in which a quarreling Spock and Dr. McCoy (DeForest Kelley) watch a prerecorded video message from Kirk, who gently tells them that they must stop fighting and work together now that he is gone.

In the end, we do learn that it was all a trick; crew members start seeing fleeting images of Kirk in his spacesuit, flailing about, and after Spock deduces that Kirk is still alive, trapped in another dimension, he figures how to locate him and transport him back to the *Enterprise*—since the spacesuit kept him alive while he drifted through dimensional space. Still, I would argue that it is in this episode that death as a reality—as something that happens to people we know and like, not just villains, guest stars, and extras—first entered the universe of *Star Trek*, long before the more celebrated deaths of Spock (in *Star Trek II: The Wrath of Khan* [1982]), Tasha Yar (Denise Crosby) (in "Skin of Evil" [1988], episode of *Star Trek: The Next Generation*), and Kirk (in *Star Trek: Generations* [1994]). And the apparent death of Kirk occurred at the one time in the first series when someone was wearing a spacesuit—suggesting that the presence of spacesuits in space films can both signal and enforce attentiveness to the true dangers of space.

It is a sign of some fundamental blindness in the *Star Trek* family that the script's co-author Judy Burns, recalling "The Tholian Web," regarded the presence of spacesuits in the episode as a significant *flaw*; announcing that her original plan was to produce "a ghost story based on fact," she explained:

Some of the things I was a little disappointed in were caused by technical problems. Originally there were no space suits when Kirk and the others beamed over to the other ship. There were force field belts which kept them encapsulated in a kind of mini-force field.... Therefore, Kirk would have wandered around the ship looking like he looks, except for a little force field belt. I think it would have made a better ghost story. He looks silly constantly appearing in that space suit. I really had a lot of qualms about that. Not from poor designing or anything, but from a story point-of-view, it would have been better.[18]

Stating a desire for "a better ghost story," though, is also expressing a preference for a more *conventional* story. And does Kirk look "silly" in a spacesuit? At times, yes, just like any other real or fictional astronaut wearing one of those cumbersome suits to stay alive, clumsily trying to maneuver through zero gravity. People who really travel into space must be prepared to look silly, even if it offends Burns'a sense of decorum.

In any event, spacesuits have remained relatively rare in the universe of *Star Trek*; the only one that immediately comes to mind is the suit that Spock wears for a perilous rendezvous with the immense V'Ger ship in *Star Trek: The Motion Picture* (1979). It is one of the most visually impressive scenes in that flawed film, as the tiny human figure reminds us again of the smallness and vulnerability of humans travelling through space—precisely the message that *Star Trek* otherwise endeavors to suppress.

The pattern set by *Star Trek* was generally followed by the other major science fiction franchise of our time—the *Star Wars* films—though these thankfully minimized the role of television screens and returned to the notion of spaceships with windows.

18. Judy Burns, cited in Edward Gross and Mark A. Altman, *Captains' Logs: The Unauthorized Complete Trek Voyages* (Boston and New York: Little, Brown, and Company, 1995), 72.

Still, even within a few feet of space, no *Star Wars* character ever dons a spacesuit. As for the later *Star Trek* series, the only visible concessions to the environment of space are the large picture windows with scenes of space that are often observed in the background of crew quarters and meeting rooms; once a television channel, outer space now also functions as exotic wallpaper.

In the unlikely milieu of the film *Superman II* (1980), there occurs one striking moment of interaction between different styles of space films that in a way dramatizes the death of the realistic spacesuit film and the triumph of the unrealistic space film. Super-villains from the planet Krypton, flying through the vacuum of space without spacesuits in defiance of all scientific logic, encounter American astronauts on the Moon; the female villain casually rips one astronaut's suit, causing his realistically-depicted death from exposure to vacuum. This provides a jarring touch of grim authenticity in a generally ridiculous film, an incongruous juxtaposition that illustrates the generic gap between space film and spacesuit film; and, as the villains abandon the dead astronauts to fly on to Earth to engage in epic battles with Superman, one gets the sense that this era of *Star Wars*, *Superman* (1978), and the revived *Star Trek* signaled the end of the true spacesuit film. Spacesuits would still figure in some serious movies, like the first *Alien* film (1979), and in some light-hearted ones, like the James Bond romp *Moonraker* (1979), but the spacesuit would no longer function as a generic marker that could impose an atmosphere of grim reality on space adventure films.

Now, given the other virtues of *Star Trek*, *Star Wars*, and similar films and television programs, it might seem petty and irrelevant to criticize them because they are insufficiently focused on the dangers and novelties of space travel; and to be sure, some scientific inaccuracy in science fiction film is far from unprecedented. But it is worth noting that films like these have prospered not only because they are aesthetically superior to the spacesuit films—though they usually are—but also because they are more conventional in all respects: films like *Star Wars* (1977) fit comfortably into any number of well-established literary patterns, though the same cannot be said of *Destination Moon* or *2001: A Space Odyssey*. Further, a lack of realism in fiction does become an issue when the fiction begins to influence real-life decisions—which arguably happened in the case of *Star Trek*.

That is, during the 1970s, when support for the space program started to fade, the National Aeronautics and Space Administration visibly sought new popularity by riding on the coattails of *Star Trek*. In response to a letter-writing campaign, the prototypical space shuttle was named the *Enterprise*; members of the *Star Trek* cast attended several NASA functions, including a well-photographed visit to NASA's *Enterprise*; and *Star Trek*'s Nichelle Nichols was recruited to make a promotional film designed to attract women and minority astronauts. All this was harmless enough, but it soon seemed that NASA was also embracing the *Star Trek* philosophy that space was a safe and comfortable environment, suitable not only for trained astronauts but for "ordinary citizens" as well—the idea that led directly to Christa McAuliffe and the 1986 *Challenger* disaster. To be sure, the causal chain from Roddenberry's mini-skirted spacefarers in starships that go "swish" to *Challenger* exploding in the upper atmosphere is tenuous at best; still, it is at least an unsettling coincidence that the final flight of the *Challenger* had a seven-person crew whose visible and politically attractive diversity—including two women, an African-American, and an Asian-American—mirrored the diversity of the original seven-person cast of *Star Trek*. The universe of *Star Trek* might well provide attractive role models for an embryonic space program, but one should never forget that the actual universe is more strange and deadly than Roddenberry and his successors ever acknowledged.

Today, although America continues to maintain a doggedly conservative pace in human exploration of space, and although *Star Trek*, *Star Wars*, *Babylon 5* (1994-1998), and all their cousins are still going strong, there nevertheless are signs of a possible revival of the spacesuit film. Some might be heartened by two major 1998 films, *Deep Impact* and *Armageddon*, which featured heroic astronauts in spacesuits engaged in desperately improvised missions to stop a large object from colliding with the Earth; but despite their scenes of implausible space heroics, these films retain an earthbound sensibility, terrified of space and entering that realm only to prevent a major disruption in our daily routines.

More noteworthy are the recent spacesuit films associated with the genre's unlikely new hero, actor Tom Hanks. A lifetime devotee of the space program, Hanks was happy to appear as astronaut James Lovell in the big-budget film *Apollo 13* (1995), which offered an authentic account of the most spectacular near-disaster during America's lunar missions. Interestingly enough, one of the film's most emotional moments, and one of its rare fictional touches, featured a spacesuit: swinging around the Moon in his dangerously crippled spacecraft, Lovell looks at the Moon and imagines himself standing on its surface, wearing a spacesuit, looking up at the Earth. Though space-suits could not help the *Apollo 13* astronauts, in life or on film, we again see a visual linkage between spacesuits and the grave dangers of space travel.

Immediately after *Apollo 13*, Hanks persuaded HBO to finance a major mini-series, co-written and co-directed by Hanks, recounting the entire saga of the first American space program, *From the Earth to the Moon*, which appeared to great acclaim in early 1998. Once again, as in 1950 and 1968, audiences eagerly watched films about men in bulky spacesuits awkwardly attempting to survive in a bizarre and harsh new environment. When asked by *The Los Angeles Times* why he launched this project, Hanks said he wanted to "show people what an amazing and cool thing it is to go up in space." This was necessary, he continued, "Because in all honesty, that's been lost.... We're all awash in Capt. Kirk and *Babylon 5* and *Star Wars*, in which the whole idea is reduced to essentially cowboys and Indians."[19] The contrast between what Hanks was doing, and what others had been doing, was recognized by the interviewer, who then explained: "In other words, Hanks didn't want to do a thriller or a creepy sci-fi epic; rather, he wanted to film space history, and in so doing bolster a genre that has one benchmark work (Stanley Kubrick's *2001: A Space Odyssey*) and a host of other films that played fast and loose with the facts of space travel" (92). On the day that I first drafted this essay, it was eerily appropriate to stumble upon such overt support for my developing argument.

One more issue must be addressed: in mentioning *Apollo 13* and *From the Earth to the Moon*, I have in a sense gone beyond the boundaries of my announced subject, "science fiction films." After all, how can films about events that really happened, accurately related, qualify as science fiction films? Yet in placing them in this context, I am hardly alone: *Apollo 13* was nominated for the science fiction Hugo Award as "Best Dramatic Presentation," and television coverage of the *Apollo 11* Moon landing actually *won* the Hugo Award in 1969. And other fact-based space films like *Return to Earth* (1976), based on Buzz Aldrin's autobiography, and *The Right Stuff* (1983), based on Tom Wolfe's book about the Mercury astronauts, are regularly linked to science fiction film. While this might be only an atavistic response, a lingering feeling that all films about space must be "science fiction," I suggest that other factors are at work here.

That is, since space is such an unprecedented and outlandish environment, it may continue to seem like science fiction, even when over a hundred people have traveled into space and recorded their exploits in words and on film. The problem is that many people may resist believing, at some level of their consciousness, that this strange realm is actually what travelers report it to be, preferring to believe that it is really similar to

19. Tom Hanks, cited in Paul Brownfield, "Fly Him to the Moon" [interview with Tom Hanks], *The Los Angeles Times*, Sunday Calendar Section, April 5, 1998, 92. Later page references in the text are to this edition.

Earth, that it will serve as a colorful new playground for stories about cowboy and Indians, or cops and robbers. The films that cater to this illusion, the space films, may be better regarded as fantasies; the films that seek to counter this illusion by depicting space as it truly is, the spacesuit films, are science fiction precisely because the truths they present are still not widely accepted.

Before World War II, science fiction predicted the atomic bomb, but after two of them were detonated with catastrophic results, stories about atomic bombs were no longer viewed as science fiction; everybody now believed in the atomic bomb. Science fiction also predicted space travel, which has been regularly occurring for nearly forty years, yet stories about space travel continue to be regarded as science fiction because people still do not really believe what space is truly like. And so, as long as people can listen to the dramatic "swish" of the *Enterprise* without protesting, as long as they imagine that *Star Trek* and similar programs represent a plausible future for humanity, there will remain a need for true science fiction stories to remind them of the ominous silence, and lethal power, of outer space.

5. THE DARK SIDE OF THE MOON: ROBERT A. HEINLEIN'S *PROJECT MOONBASE*

Whenever I teach one of my infrequent science fiction classes, I begin by showing my students two short films: *Project Moonbase* (1953) and *La Jetée* (1962). These films, I explain, exemplify the two extreme points of the spectrum of science fiction: the juvenile melodrama and plodding didacticism of *Project Moonbase*, and the *avant-garde* lyricism and haunting imagery of *La Jetée*. And those works prepare my students rather nicely for the final movie I show, *2001: A Space Odyssey* (1968)—a film, after all, that is not unlike two reels of *Project Moonbase* spliced on to one reel of *La Jetée*.

However, the announced reasons I offer my students for showing *Project Moonbase* are disingenuous; for if my only objective was to display the cinematic equivalent of the original Gernsbackian paradigm—adventure stories with scientific explanations and logical predictions—there are any number of movies that could serve that purpose, including *Destination Moon* (1950), *Riders to the Stars* (1954), and *Conquest of Space* (1955). But while those films have their momens, only *Project Moonbase* fascinates me—because it is the only piece of celluloid I know of that even partially reflects the writing style and idiosyncratic philosophy of its noted co-author, Robert A. Heinlein.

Of course, this movie has generally not been valued—or even noticed—by filmgoers, Heinlein scholars, or film critics. After being thrown together from an unsold television pilot entitled *Ring Around the Moon*, written by Heinlein and producer Jack Seaman, the film was only briefly released, and has been rarely seen since; the only time it has been shown on television, I believe, was as part of the *Canned Film Festival* series of avowedly awful movies hosted by comedienne Laraine Newman. One scholar who prepared a definitive Heinlein bibliography, Marie Guthrie, reported that she had never been able to see the film.

Also, unlike Heinlein's earlier film *Destination Moon*, *Project Moonbase* did not become a Heinlein short story or the subject of a Heinlein article; indeed, by all accounts, Heinlein was dissatisfied with the film and to my knowledge never mentioned it in print. Most critical studies of Heinlein—including Alexei Panshin's *Heinlein in Dimension* (1968), George Slusser's *Robert A. Heinlein: Stranger in His Own Land* (1976), and *The Classic Years of Robert A. Heinlein* (1977), and Joseph D. Olander and Martin H. Greenberg's anthology *Robert A. Heinlein* (1978)—do not even mention the movie, while H. Bruce Franklin's usually thorough *Robert A. Heinlein: America as Science Fiction* (1980) dismisses it in less than a page.

In reference books and studies of science fiction films, *Project Moonbase* is similarly neglected, either omitted altogether—as in books ranging from John Baxter's pioneering *Science Fiction in the Cinema* (1970) to James Gunn's *The New Encyclopedia of Science Fiction* (1988)—or subjected to brief criticism: in *Future Tense: The Cinema of Science Fiction* (1978), John Brosnan summarizes the plot and comments that "it's not a very good film,"[20] and in his entry on the movie for *The Encyclopedia of Science Fiction* (1993) Brosnan says that its "ambitious idea... is undermined by melodramatics, poor performances, and

---

20. John Brosnan, *Future Tense: The Cinema of Science Fiction* (New York: St. Martin's Press, 1978), 77. Later page references in the text are to this edition.

sets designed for tv."[21] John Stanley's *Revenge of the Creature Features Movie Guide* (1988) finds the film "uninteresting" and "pseudo-scientific,"[22] and Phil Hardy's *The Encyclopedia of Science Fiction Movies* (1984) complains of its "melodramatic plot" that "contains everything that the makers of *Destination Moon* tried to avoid."[23] Just about the only positive comment on *Project Moonbase* comes in Bruce Lanier Wright's *Yesterday's Tomorrows: The Golden Age of Science Fiction Movie Posters, 1950-1964* (1993), where, after repeating some familiar criticisms, he says that the film "deserves points for a more adult approach."[24]

A recurring theme in these curt commentaries is that *Project Moonbase* does not display any of the influence of Robert A. Heinlein: Stanley asserts that Heinlein's "style and themes are not to be found" in the movie (271); David Wingrove's entry on the film for his *Science Fiction Film Source Book* (1985) says the film "has little of the zest of Heinlein's written work of the period";[25] Brosnan in *Future Tense* suspects that "not much remained of Heinlein's original" in the shooting script (77); Wright says that "The movie's overall tone bears little resemblance to Heinlein's literary work" (28); and Hardy concludes that "the film lacks the sense of confidence that even Heinlein's

---

21. John Brosnan, *"Project Moonbase,"* *The Encyclopedia of Science Fiction* edited by John Clute and Peter Nicholls (New York: St. Martin's Press, 1993), 964.

22. John Stanley, *"Project Moonbase,"* *Revenge of the Creature Features Movie Guide*, Third Revised Edition (Pacifica, California: Creatures at Large Press, 1988), 271. Later page references in the text are to this edition.

23. Phil Hardy, *"Project Moonbase,"* *The Encyclopedia of Science Fiction Movies*, 1984 (Minneapolis, Minnesota: Woodbury Press, 1986), 141. Later page references in the text are to this edition.

24. Bruce Lainer Wright, *Yesterday's Tomorrows: The Golden Age of Science Fiction Movie Posters, 1950-1964* (Dallas, Texas: Taylor Publishing Company, 1993), 3. Later page references in the text are to this edition.

25. David Wingrove, *"Project Moonbase,"* *Science Fiction Film Source Book*, edited by Wingrove (London: Longman, 1985), 185.

worst novels have in abundance" (141).

Still, Hardy does concede that the film is "only of interest for a few of the odd quirks that Heinlein introduced" (141); and while I would agree that *Project Moonbase* is a terrible movie by conventional aesthetic standards, my own argument, based on repeated viewings of the film, would be that this film is far odder and more distinctive than Hardy's comment would indicate. Furthermore, in contrast to the bland and rather anonymous *Destination Moon*, I would maintain, despite the opinions cited above, that the oddities of *Project Moonbase* can be directly related to themes and concerns expressed in Heinlein's written science fiction; and for that reason, if only for that reason, the film merits closer consideration than it has previously received.

The movie must first be understood in the overall context of Heinlein's career at the time. Between 1945 and 1958, Heinlein primarily wanted, as he later reported in *Expanded Universe*, "to break out from the limitations and low rates of pulp science-fiction magazines into anything and everything: slicks, books, motion pictures, general fiction, specialized fiction not intended for SF magazines, and nonfiction."[26] Whenever Heinlein first entered a new market, he made himself appear very eager to please, and his early efforts in each field seem to conform completely to its usual conventions. However, as soon as Heinlein achieved some success in a given market, he began to push at the boundaries of those conventions, gradually moving toward an approach that combined a conventional surface with unconventional undercurrents. Thus, as is frequently discussed, Heinlein's juvenile novels gradually moved from the simplistic melodrama of *Rocket Ship Galileo* (1947) and *Space Cadet* (1948) to the complex tensions of *The Star Beast* (1954) and *Have Space Suit—Will Travel* (1958); and two of his later stories for the mass-market magazines, which both appeared in December, 1949, had unexpected features: "Delilah and the

---

26. Robert A. Heinlein, "Foreword" to "The Last Days of the United States," *Expanded Universe: The New Worlds of Robert A. Heinlein*, by Heinlein (New York: Ace Books, 1980), 145.

Space Rigger," as H. Bruce Franklin notes, "shows a relatively high level of consciousness about one form of the oppression of women";[27] and "The Long Watch," though originally published in *The American Legion Magazine*, surprisingly criticizes the military, since the menace in the story is a planned military takeover of the government.

This pattern of initial acquiescence to generic conventions, and later efforts to bend and stretch those conventions, can be seen in Heinlein's two screenplays. *Destination Moon* is primarily a straightforward and unchallenging depiction of a first flight to the Moon, with few disturbing elements or unexpected touches; *Project Moonbase*, apparently a retelling of the same story with some added juvenile adventure, repeatedly offers some surprising features and dark undercurrents.

To describe what is conventional, and what is unconventional, about *Project Moonbase*, one could speak of a series of tensions between the apparent messages, and the actual messages, in the movie. Four of these are most prominent.

* * * * * * *

First, there is the conflict of *The ordinariness of space versus The strangeness of space*. In most scenes of the movie, there is no particular effort to make the environment of space seem disorienting: as in other films of the period, the spaceship itself is a typically roomy two-story chamber, an obvious set with no discomfiting features. Once they are on the Moon, the space travelers often do not move in any peculiar way in the lower gravity, and the final scene of their marriage ceremony is thoroughly conventional.

However, other scenes reveal the influence of an author who understands just how strange life in space can be. Some of them recall scenes in *Destination Moon*: the facial contortions of

---

27. H. Bruce Franklin, *Robert A. Heinlein: America as Science Fiction* (New York: Oxford University Press, 1980), 70. Later page references in the text are to this edition.

the space travelers during the launch, the effortless lifting of massive weights in the low lunar gravity, and the soundless fall of the saboteur down a lunar mountain. Others are more innovative: when the discovery that one crew member is an enemy imposter triggers both sudden acceleration of the spaceship and a hand-to-hand battle, the fight is carried out in eerie slow motion, as heroic Major Bill Moore (Ross Ford) and the fake Dr. Wernher (Larry Johns) struggle against the force of acceleration to gain the upper hand.

The most striking scenes in the movie, however, take place during the brief visit to the space station. As soon as they disembark, Colonel Briteis (Donna Martell), Moore, and "Wernher" walk down a corridor, to be greeted by a station resident walking in the opposite direction—upside down on the ceiling—which resembles a space scene in Stanley Kubrick's *2001: A Space Odyssey*. They next walk past a sign, "Please Do Not Walk on the Walls," an example of Heinlein humor.[28] Finally, they enter a room for a discussion with the station commanders—who are seated on the opposite wall at a ninety-degree angle to them. While there is nothing impressive about the special effects involved—crudely spliced split-screen footage—these scenes do establish how disorienting it would be to live in a zero-gravity environment, and they do so far more effectively than the later and more expensive film *Conquest of Space*, which included extended scenes on a large space station with little attention to the effects of zero gravity.[29] Wright also singled out this portion of the film for praise, saying that the "sequences set on the zero-gravity space station are rather nice....anticipating

---

28. *Project Moonbase* (Galaxy, 1953).

29. A similar lack of imagination can be seen in other space station films, including the *Outer Limits* episode "Specimen: Unknown" (1964), *The Green Slime* (1968), the television movie *Earth II* (1971), and the television series *Star Trek: Deep Space Nine* (1993-1999). Arguably, out of all the filmed depictions of space stations, only *Project Moonbase, 2001: A Space Odyssey*, and *Solaris* (1971) display any sensitivity to the unusual characteristics of a space station environment.

similar scenes in *2001*" (28).[30]

More so than many other writers of the postwar period, Heinlein recognized the importance of space stations in the coming exploration of space, and his stories during this time regularly featured space stations (although often in a very minor role).[31] It is appropriate, then, that *Project Moonbase* is, to my knowledge, the first of many films to depict a space station. And the fact that it remains, surprisingly, one of the most imaginative of those films must be credited primarily to Heinlein's insight.

* * * * * * *

The second conflict is *Glorification of the American military versus Criticism of the American military.* In many ways, to be sure, *Project Moonbase* presents itself as a glowing endorsement of the work of American military forces. The written prologue that scrolls down the screen proudly describes how the United States military has established a space station "as a military guardian in the sky...to consolidate the safety of the world," and the film displays America's triumph over evil foreign saboteurs trying to destroy the station—implicitly arguing that the participation of other nations in the space program would only cause problems. The two space travelers of the film are military officers, under the command of a general. The one civilian added to the mission, a scientist named Wernher taken along to photograph the back side of the Moon, is included, the commander tells his astronauts, exclusively as a gimmick—playing the "science angle"—in order to get the flight approved; and, since

30. For the record, when she hosted the film for the Canned Film Festival, as I recall, Laraine Newman also noted—facetiously, of course—that the "parallels" between *Project Moonbase* and *2001: A Space Odyssey* were "amazing."

31. My bibliography of science fiction works involving space stations, *The Other Side of the Sky* (2009), lists in addition to *Project Moonbase* twelve Heinlein stories and novels published before 1955—more entries involving space stations than any other writer in that period can claim.

enemy agents succeed in replacing him with an imposter who almost destroys the space station, the civilian element is clearly projected as the weak link in the program. When the spaceship crashes on the Moon, orders from the Pentagon establish the site as an American military base. Thus, while other movies at the time at least gesture toward a civilian and international presence in the space program—a character in the original screenplay of Heinlein's other film *Destination Moon* announces that "the only Government to control the Moon must be a sovereign government of the whole of man" (cited in Franklin 97)—*Project Moonbase* appears to celebrate an entirely American, and entirely military, space program as most desirable.

However, scenes in the later part of the movie seem designed to ridicule the military mind. When the stranded space travelers finally establish contact with their commanding officer, General "Pappy" Greene (Hayden Rorke), and inform him that they have unexpectedly crash-landed on the Moon, his surprise and confusion are almost comically exaggerated; he must check with his superiors, he tells them, before he can say anything at all. When he calls them back, his first announcement is that their mission has been officially reclassified as "Project Moonbase"—so their accidental landing is now cast, after the fact, as a deliberate effort to establish a base on the Moon. Only after issuing these incongruous orders does the general tell the space travelers that, by the way, vital supplies will soon be rocketed to them. Surely, the scene is designed to function as a scathing critique of the bureaucratic mind—an overt attempt to disguise a major failure by an after-the-fact renaming which makes it seem a success— and surely any space travelers in this position would be baffled and irritated by the priority given this message. (Imagine, for example, two early aviators on a pioneering military flight across the Pacific who crash on a deserted island; after desperate efforts to make contact with their superiors, the first news they receive from home is that their mission has been reclassified as

"Project Pacific Island Base.")[32]

This bifurcated attitude towards the military is consistent with Heinlein's developing philosophy. On one hand, as a former Navy officer, Heinlein had obvious respect and admiration for the military life and attitudes; on the other hand, he evidenced a growing dislike for large government bureaucracies, which he saw as stultifying and repressive.[33] It is only logical, then, that Heinlein would show admiration for his astronaut protagonists while seeming to ridicule their seen and unseen superior officers.[34]

* * * * * * *

The third set of tensions involves *The continued subjugation of women versus The new domination of women.* In this area, *Project Moonbase* plays a more complex game, offering three

---

32. In one respect, though, the feeling that the film burlesques the military mind may be the accidental result of later events: the actor playing the General, Hayden Rorke, went on to play the befuddled commander in the television comedy *I Dream of Jeannie* (1965-1970), so it is particularly easy, I suppose, to see him as a buffoon in this movie. Still, I would argue that the comical aspects of his portrayal are to a large extent intrinsic to the film, and do not emerge simply because of the impression left by his later television role.

33. Indeed, elements of this philosophy can also be detected in *Destination Moon*: early scenes criticize the shortsightedness of the American government and military in failing to mount a space program, and the privately-sponsored flight to the Moon is almost halted by bureaucratic interference. However, these aspects of that film could be interpreted simply as efforts to interject a sense of drama into a narrative that otherwise has very little conflict; in *Project Moonbase*, a story about enemy agents trying to sabotage the American space program, there was no compelling reason to introduce criticisms of military thinking.

34. Also, while the all-American character of this space mission cannot be overlooked, the two rockets that are launched from Earth to the space station are interestingly named "Canada" and "Mexico." At least on a metaphoric level, then, there is some international participation in the conquest of space.

distinct levels of argument: an overt, nominal commitment to feminine superiority; a poorly concealed, residual belief in masculine superiority; and a deeper, ameliorative message affirming feminine superiority within certain restraints.

First, a summary of the plot suggests the movie presents a strongly feminist viewpoint. *Project Moonbase* may qualify as the first—and certainly, it is one of the few—science fiction stories that depicts a woman, Colonel Briteis, as the first human in space; the same woman then becomes the commander of the first circumlunar mission, and when her ship crashes, she becomes by default the first commander of Project Moonbase. Also, the President of the United States is ultimately revealed to be a woman. Apparently, then, this is a future society when women routinely assume dominant roles.

However, three aspects of the movie undermine this proto-feminist theme and instead suggest a more traditional stance. Carefully written dialogue in the film's early scenes withholds the information that Colonel Briteis is a woman, so it is not until she walks into the room that viewers learn her sex. That the President is a woman is also not revealed until the final scene, when she appears on television to congratulate the newlyweds. Thus, despite these revelations, the film functionally depicts a male-dominated world, with knowledge of the sex of certain major figures deliberately concealed while on-screen men act as the decision makers.

In addition, there is clearly nothing impressive about the way the women characters are depicted in *Project Moonbase*. Colonel Briteis consistently acts like a spoiled child, given to emotional outbursts; she is belittled by the nickname used by her male comrades, "Bright Eyes"; a comment by Major Moore indicates that she was chosen for the first manned flight solely because she only weighed ninety pounds, not because of her superior qualifications; despite her position, she is rarely observed making command decisions; in the crucial battle with the saboteur, she is merely a bystander while Moore and the imposter fight it out; and the Presidential decision to make her, and not

Major Moore, the commander of the first lunar flight is revealed by the final scene to be little more than a woman's favoritism toward a member of her own sex. Another woman character, a journalist friend of the President named Polly Prattles (Barbara Morrison) who interviews the General, provides comic relief in one scene by displaying her almost complete ignorance of space travel. As for the President herself, she is pictured as a sweet, grandmotherly sort of woman, with no particular aura of authority about her.

Most notably, the conclusion of *Project Moonbase* seems to overthrow previous pictures of feminine superiority, as Colonel Briteis's new husband, Major Moore, is immediately promoted to General so that he, not she, can become the commander of Project Moonbase. It is this scene that inspires an arch comment by Franklin about the limited extent of Heinlein's feminism: "Heinlein has no problem projecting a female pilot or even President, but when a woman relates to a man she has to know who is the boss" (98).

Despite these features of the film, however, it can still be seen as a curious affirmation of female dominance. After all, the General in charge of the space program is under the direct command of the President; she allows him to maintain apparent control over its affairs, while intervening only occasionally with direct orders, like the one which made Colonel Briteis the commander of the first lunar mission. And, it must be noted, Major Moore is promoted to be the commander of Project Moonbase *only because Colonel Briteis specifically requests that promotion.*

A complex and ameliorative recommendation thus emerges: women should have ultimate control over situations, both in title and in fact; but they should also stay in the background and allow men to have apparent control. In a way, then, the movie appears to affirm old clichés about "the hand that rocks the cradle, rules the world," and "behind every successful man, there is a woman"; the difference is that Heinlein grants women both official and covert power, while enjoining them from overly obvious exercise of that power. It is, then, a solution to the problem of male-versus-female dominance that grants women genuine and supreme authority, while preserving the male ego by granting men the appearance of superiority.

In keeping with the spirit of the film, then, one can anticipate that the marriage of Briteis and Moore, despite Franklin's remark, will not produce a traditional husband-controlled family; rather, Briteis will continue to make all the decisions, even as she allows Moore to believe that he is making the decisions. And this stance arguably represents one aspect of Heinlein's later expressed attitudes towards women, inasmuch as two later novels, *I Will Fear No Evil* (1970) and *To Sail beyond the Sunset* (1987), both feature assertive female protagonists, totally in control of their own lives, who are nevertheless willing to act subservient in the presence of men.

* * * * * * *

The fourth and final conflict is *The endorsement of traditional values versus A challenge to traditional values.* The President's final suggestion—virtually a command—that Major Moore marry Colonel Briteis seems to be not only a reaffirmation of male dominance but also a commitment to conventional morality: while an unmarried man and woman on a brief space mission might be tolerable, having such a pair serving indefinitely as sole residents of a lunar base would be an overt invitation to adultery, and therefore unacceptable in the American society of 1953. Their arranged marriage eliminates the possibility of illicit sex, and since Moore and Briteis are revealed to be secretly in love with each other, it is also an appropriate decision in a society that insists that marriage should be a matter of personal choice, not the result of someone's directives.

Despite its apparent acceptability, however, there are provocative undercurrents in this denouément. In their earlier encounters, Moore and Briteis are constantly squabbling, in a manner that suggests an ongoing competition for the affections of their superior officer, the General. They act, then, not as would-be lovers, but as an older brother engaged in sibling rivalry with a younger sister. Such a characterization of their relationship is strongly reinforced by the fact that both Moore and Briteis regularly address the General as "Pappy," labeling him as their father, not simply their commanding officer; and the General assumes an especially parental role in the final scenes of the film, when he has separate conversations with Moore and Briteis and gives them each his personal advice as their "Pappy."

On a symbolic level, then, *Project Moonbase* is the story of an older brother and younger sister who are secretly in love with each other; and with the approval—indeed, at the urging—of their father, they finally get married and thus establish a sexual relationship. What the movie affirms, then, is not the importance of traditional marriage, but the appropriateness of incest. In particular, the film argues for a sexual relationship between an older man and a younger female relative, a theme that is also apparent in later Heinlein works. Thinly disguised incest of this sort figures in *The Door into Summer* (1957), where Daniel Boone Davis arranges through suspended animation to marry his twelve-year-old "niece," Ricky; the story "—All You Zombies—'" (1959), wherein a time traveller sleeps with an earlier, female version of himself; and *Time Enough for Love* (1973), where Lazarus Long has sex with his young female clones. And in Heinlein's final novel, *To Sail beyond the Sunset*, such incestuous love is explicitly endorsed when Maureen Smith's husband sleeps with his daughter, with her mother's knowledge and approval.

* * * * * * *

It is therefore fitting that the mission of the space travelers in *Project Moonbase* is to photograph the dark side of the Moon, and that they ultimately crash on the dark side of the Moon, so they must walk some distance to set up a transmitter that can reach the Earth. For, by the conventional standards of its day, the film does indeed have a dark side. Apparently a straightforward affirmation of the routine of space exploration, the American military, male superiority, and conventional morality, *Project Moonbase* covertly argues for the strangeness of life in space, the absurdity of American military thinking, concealed female control of the government, and socially approved incest. We may never know exactly why *Ring around the Moon* was rejected as a television series, but it may well be that television executives could dimly perceive in the pilot that there was something disturbing about Heinlein's vision, something that would not be appropriate in a medium whose involvement with science fiction at the time was otherwise a matter of routine juvenile fare like *Captain Video* (1949-1955), *Tom Corbett: Space Cadet* (1950-1955), and *Space Patrol* (1950-1955).

In sum, instead of dismissing *Project Moonbase* as a standard Hollywood product that suppressed all signs of Heinlein's influence, critics should instead embrace the film as an integral part of the Heinlein canon, a film which despite its many flaws significantly prefigures attitudes about bureaucracy, women, and sex that are made explicit in later Heinlein novels. Perhaps, for those who wish to view films solely for their aesthetic appreciation, *Project Moonbase* will always be a film that must be endured rather than enjoyed; certainly, that is the typical response of my students who are obliged to watch it. Yet there are clearly other reasons why the film should be interesting, especially for Heinlein scholars. Worthwhile projects would include a search through the Heinlein archives for scripts that would reveal exactly how much Jack Seaman contributed to the final film, and for evidence of any further work on story or script development Heinlein might have done for the television series that was supposed to grow out of *Project Moonbase*. Also, although the initially released film was sixty-three-minutes long, all versions now available were cut to fifty-one minutes. Perhaps, if some enterprising scholar can track down and examine those missing twelve minutes, there will be more surprises in store for Heinlein critics.

6. GODZILLA'S TRAVELS: THE EVOLUTION OF A GLOBALIZED GARGANTUAN

If the topic under consideration is the role played by science fiction in an ongoing process of globalization, there is one iconic figure who literally and figuratively towers above them all. The Japanese monster Gojira, better known by his Americanized monicker Godzilla, burst into international cinema with a series of well-received films of the 1950s and 1960s that played to packed houses in the United States and inspired many imitators there and in other nations. After several films of declining quality drove Godzilla into temporary retirement in the 1970s, he stormed back during the 1980s with a new series of high-profile Japanese films, and in the 1990s he was recruited to star in one of the most expensive and heavily publicized Hollywood films ever made. Still observed in countless films, cartoons, novels, comic books, video games, toys, and merchandise, and the only non-human recipient of an MTV Movie Lifetime Achievement Award, Godzilla has earned a place alongside Tarzan and Superman as one of the most famous literary creations of the twentieth century.

Chronicling the entire history of Godzilla in his various incarnations would demand an entire book, more likely several of them; all I can attempt in one essay is to examine eight key films—including three that ostensibly have nothing to do with Godzilla—that will help to explain how the character has changed and evolved as he has been adapted to different situations and subjected to more and more diverse influences, finally becoming the overdetermined symbol who collapses under his own weight in the colossal fiasco of the made-in-America *Godzilla* (1998). Glances at numerous other films along the way will indicate that the roots and branches of the Godzilla family tree are vast and variegated.

While earlier literary and cinematic influences—prominently including Arthur Conan Doyle's novel *The Lost World* (1912) and the film *King Kong* (1933)—cannot be entirely overlooked, the modern saga of Godzilla truly begins, I would argue, with two prose narratives by noted American science fiction writers published around the middle of the twentieth century. Robert A. Heinlein's *Rocket Ship Galileo* (1947) describes a visionary engineer who builds a moon rocket with the aid of three teenagers who fly to the Moon and encounter renegade German Nazis working to establish a Fourth Reich. Ray Bradbury's "The Fog Horn" (1951) is an atmospheric vignette about a dinosaur who somehow survived for millions of years under the sea and was drawn to shore by a lighthouse's fog horn that resembled the call of his own kind. Both works were purchased by Hollywood producers and transformed into films that had little to do with their source materials—*Destination Moon* (1950) and *The Beast from 20,000 Fathoms* (1953), respectively—and together these films laid the foundation for the Godzilla mythos.

Destination Moon, at first glance, seems out of place in any discussion of Godzilla, for it endeavors to provide a realistic portrayal of how a moon voyage might actually be accomplished, with nothing resembling a dinosaur involved. Yet it is a film that will later make its mark on the Godzilla series, and it further signals a noteworthy shift in science fiction films that had direct effects on the genre of giant monster movies. In earlier science fiction films, the scientific menaces or challenges tended to be on a small scale—a mad scientist conducting secret experiments, a horribly transformed human on a rampage—and the typical agents who dealt with the situation were police officers or detectives. If a troublesome creature was eluding their grasp, said officials might recruit a posse of torch-wielding citizens to assist in tracking it down, but that would represent the full extent of any broader civic involvement; even King Kong, it may be recalled, was defeated by a modest number of single-pilot aircraft. Perhaps this recurring pattern of localized scientific disruptions handled by local officials reflected a widespread belief that scientific progress was, all in all, a relatively minor issue with little broad impact on society. However, after the appearance of the atomic bomb in 1945—the event that reverberates through virtually all science fiction films in the coming decade—the overarching importance of science could hardly be denied, and the scientific menaces or challenges depicted in films would radically expand in their visibility and consequences. In the face of such problems, mere police officers would be impotent, a point dramatically conveyed by the scene in *The Beast from 20,000 Fathoms* when New York City's finest are conspicuously ineffectual in their efforts to fend off the invading dinosaur with their handguns and rifles. Instead, these bigger, and worse, scientific crises would demand the formation of broad coalitions of university-based scientists, government officials, and military forces.

Destination Moon was the first major film to depict precisely such a coalition in action, as the script eliminated Heinlein's isolated scientist and instead had its moon rocket constructed by a small army of scientists and industrialists working in cooperation. Their success in this endeavor might make the movie seem, in the words of H. Bruce Franklin, "a hymn of praise to the industrial-military complex."[35] However, the film is also highly critical of some members of that complex: the retired General Barnes, rebuffed by a short-sighted American government after his official efforts to launch an Earth-orbiting satellite are thwarted by apparent sabotage, must employ patriotic

35. H. Bruce Franklin, *Robert A. Heinlein: America as Science Fiction* (Oxford: Oxford University Press, 1980), 76.

fervor to forge a team of scientists, engineers, and leaders of private industry to construct an atomic-powered rocket to the Moon; later, the flight is almost thwarted by legal actions undertaken by officials in response to public pressure. Most science fiction films of the 1950s would similarly display both respect for intelligent figures of authority and contempt for obtuse figures of authority, leading to subplots involving conflicts between different factions in "the industrial-military complex" regarding the best course of action to take in response to the problem at hand.

Further, despite the absence of a monster, a few recurring conventions of later monster movies first figured prominently in *Destination Moon*: the introductory gathering of officials to be informed about the problem, usually involving visual aids such as maps, photographs, and films—here, incongruously, an educational cartoon starring Woody Woodpecker explaining how a Moon rocket would work; scenes of workers making their own small but vital contributions to the larger effort, sometimes including stock footage; and conferences of worried team leaders discussing terrible setbacks and possible responses to them. These devices undoubtedly created a certain sense of drama, but the problem in *Destination Moon* was that the focus of their energies—constructing a rocket that would travel to the Moon undistracted by enemy agents, aliens, or monsters—was inherently less than thrilling, leading to the standard complaints that the film suffered from "severe shortcomings" and was "colourless and wooden."[36] To sustain a film genre, these leagues of scientists, officials, and soldiers would require more exciting and spectacular challenges—aliens invading the Earth, as in *Invaders from Mars* (1953) and *Earth vs. the Flying Saucers* (1956), or the topic under discussion here, gigantic monsters on the rampage.

The film that first presented the blueprint for giant monster

---

36. John Baxter, *Science Fiction in the Cinema* (New York: Paperback Library, 1950), 102; Phil Hardy, *The Encyclopedia of Science Fiction Movies* (1984; Minneapolis, Minnesota: Woodbury Press, 1986), 125.

movies was *The Beast from 20,000 Fathoms*. Abandoning Bradbury's efforts to sympathetically characterize the dinosaur as a lonely relic of a forgotten era, filmmakers depict the monster as implacably evil, the only remnant of the original story being a brief sequence in which the dinosaur, like the dinosaur of "The Fog Horn," indifferently smashes a lighthouse. (Consequently, the film's credits can honestly say only that the movie was "suggested by" Bradbury's story.[37]) The film's radically different scenario introduces virtually all the elements that would be replicated in scores of monster movies of the 1950s and 1960s. The monster appears in a faraway, unpopulated area—such as the Arctic (this film), the deserts of the American west (*Them!* [1954], *Tarantula* [1955]), or the middle of the ocean (*Godzilla, King of the Monsters* [1954, 1956])—usually created or reawakened by the explosion of an atomic bomb. The creature steadily makes its way into more and more populated areas before ending up in a major metropolis, such as New York City (this film), Tokyo (*Godzilla, King of the Monsters* and its sequels), London (*Gorgo* [1961]), Chicago (*The Beginning of the End* [1957]), San Francisco (*It Came from Beneath the Sea* [1955]), or Copenhagen (*Reptilicus* [1961]). Initially, scattered sightings of the monster are met with incredulity and ridicule, but one scientist, or a few scientists, recognize what is happening and urge generals and government officials to take action. The usual triumvirate is an older scientist, his beautiful daughter, and a young scientist romantically involved with the daughter, although the daughter figure in *The Beast from 20,000 Fathoms* is atypically the older scientist's unrelated assistant. When the monster's increasing visibility and destructiveness make the threat undeniable, scientists join forces with politicians and military leaders to craft an organized, institutional response to the monster. The monster enters the big city, causing crowds of panicking people to run away screaming while it smashes buildings and steps on cars. After conventional defenses fail,

---

37. *The Beast from 20,000 Fathoms* (Warner Brothers, 1953).

and all hope seems lost, members of the inner circle agree to go along with one scientist's desperate suggestion, and as a result of the innovative idea, the monster is finally destroyed.

Even though the film may now be overlooked by viewers who anachronistically interpret it as a routine rendering of the formula it actually invented, there are some aspects of *The Beast from 20,000 Fathoms* that were not precisely replicated in its successors and thus command attention. The special effects of Ray Harryhausen employed stop-motion animation to create a dinosaur that was considerably more impressive than those created by what would become the era's standard techniques: rear-projected insects and lizards (as in *The Beginning of the End* and the 1960 *The Lost World*) or men in rubber suits trampling on miniature sets (as in *Godzilla, King of the Monsters* and its sequels). Eventually, computer animation would engender a renaissance of quality in depictions of giant monsters. Second, in a rarely noticed subplot, the dinosaur, in addition to its nasty habit of destroying everything in its path, is said to be spreading a virulent disease incapacitating scores of soldiers and citizens. This aura of virulence, of a medical menace associated with the monster, will later be reintroduced into the genre. Finally, the film interestingly reaches its climax with the monster in Coney Island Amusement Park, smashing around its famous roller coaster and inexorably suggesting that, despite the film's unrelentingly serious tone, a dinosaur in contemporary times might also be an object of entertainment and amusement, a theme that came to the forefront in the novel and film *Jurassic Park* (1993). (One might also term the film prophetic, in that dinosaurs now figure in actual amusement park rides, such as Universal Studio's Jurassic Park: The Ride and Knott's Berry Farm's Kingdom of the Dinosaurs.)

Despite legions of American imitators (*Them!*, *It Came from Beneath the Sea*, *Tarantula*, *The Land Unknown* [1957], *The Beginning of the End*, *The Giant Claw* [1957], *The Deadly Mantis* [1957], *The Black Scorpion* [1957], etc.), the most significant offspring of *The Beast from 20,000 Fathoms* was unquestionably Toho Studio's 1954 film *Gojira*, released in America in 1956 as *Godzilla, King of the Monsters*. The American version actually qualifies as a Japanese-American co-production, since American producers added numerous scenes with Raymond Burr as American reporter Steve Martin and smothered the entire film with Burr's incessant narration. However, to balance this intrusive American presence, the film, unlike later Godzilla films reedited for American audiences, employed relatively little dubbing into English; most scenes feature actors speaking in Japanese, their words explained to Burr by an observing translator or paraphrased by Burr as the narrator. It oddly seems, then, more of a Japanese film than its successors that include American actors in their original casts and dub all dialogue into English.

Watching *Godzilla, King of the Monsters*, one notices obvious borrowings from *The Beast from 20,000 Fathoms*, such as the first appearances of both monsters as huge heads looming over mountain ridges. Yet the Japanese film also departed from the American template in several ways, some of which have been well documented. Certainly, there is less emphasis on scientific rigor: in comparison to the extensive scientific discussions intended to justify the existence of the monster in *The Beast from 20,000 Fathoms*, little time is devoted to faux paleontology in *Godzilla, King of the Monsters*; instead, Godzilla is briefly and vaguely described as an ancient hybrid of land and sea creature from "two million years ago," though dinosaurs of course actually perished about sixty-five million years ago.[38] And Godzilla's fire breath, as commentators regularly note, connects him more to legends of dragons than to fact-based accounts of dinosaurs. (And how might a purportedly half-aquatic creature develop fire breath in the first place?)

Further, despite its famous scenes of monstrous mayhem, *Godzilla, King of the Monsters* is actually more attentive to

---

38. *Godzilla, King of the Monsters* (Toho Studios, 1954); English-language version with added scenes released in America by Embassy Pictures in 1956.

human drama than its American counterparts. The standard triad of old scientist, daughter, and young scientist, with a perfunctory romance between the latter two figures, is expanded to include a fourth character and a romantic triangle; the scientist's daughter has fallen in love with a handsome sailor, even though she wishes to remain loyal to her fiancé, a brilliant young scientist who wears a distinctive eyepatch. More significantly, the film devotes much more attention to the suffering of Godzilla's victims; whereas *The Beast from 20,000 Fathoms* had only a few brief scenes of injured people in hospitals, *Godzilla, King of the Monsters* lingers on scenes of pain and mutilation. The film begins with Raymond Burr lying underneath the rubble of a smashed building; he is carried to an overcrowded hospital and laid on the floor, since there are no beds available; and later scenes depict him with head bandages and his arm in a sling. Scene after scene shows people getting injured or killed; it is repeatedly emphasized that Godzilla has caused thousands of deaths; and there is an extended scene showing a televised memorial service with two hundred young women solemnly singing a musical tribute to Godzilla's many victims.

Although the factor of atomic energy transforms almost every monster movie of the 1950s into a potential allegory of the devastating effects of nuclear weapons, this film's prolonged preoccupation with the suffering caused by Godzilla makes this linkage impossible to deny. It was a reaction, as noted in J. D. Lees and Marc Cerasini's *The Official Godzilla Compendium*, not only to the bombings of Hiroshima and Nagasaki in 1945, but to a more recent incident in 1954 involving Japanese sailors disastrously contaminated by an American H-bomb test in the Pacific Ocean, described in Japanese newspapers as "the Second Atomic Bombing of Japan."[39] To make the connection even clearer, the older scientist of the film specifically attributes the emergence of Godzilla to the effects of H-bomb tests. *Godzilla, King of the Monsters*, therefore, introduced to the monster

39. J. D. Lees and Marc Cerasini, *The Official Godzilla Compendium* (New York: Random House, 1998), 12.

movie a message about postcolonial guilt, with the monster as both a product of the more powerful developed countries and a symbol of the damage they characteristically inflict upon their less powerful, less developed counterparts. Like other themes so far touched upon, it is a motif that will be echoed in later monster films.

Since their first Godzilla movie was a tremendous success, Toho Studies promptly produced a sequel, sometimes given the American title *Godzilla Raids Again* (1955), which included in its otherwise-familiar story a battle between Godzilla and another giant dinosaur, later to become a standard plot device. Yet the film was originally released in America under the title *Gigantis the Fire Monster*, providing Godzilla with an alias and making no reference to the original film. Clearly, the message received by Toho Studios was that American audiences wanted to see new monsters, not old favorites, and the company accordingly devoted the next several years to films about other giant creatures, including the giant bird *Rodan* (1956); *Varan the Unbelievable* (1962), variously described as a giant squirrel or giant winged lizard; and *Mothra* (1961), a giant moth who gives birth to two giant caterpillars that carry on her struggle. When Willis O'Brien's suggestion for a *King Kong vs. Frankenstein* film was taken by producer John Beck to Japan and refashioned into the film *King Kong vs. Godzilla* (1962), a new cycle of Godzilla films built around monster slugfests began, followed by *Godzilla vs. the Thing* (1964), with Godzilla battling Mothra, and *Ghidrah the Three-Headed Monster* (1965), with Godzilla, Mothra, and Rodan teaming up to defeat the titular menace, a three-headed flying dragon. The latter film marked a key shift in characterizations of Godzilla; previously the villain, the horrible destructive force that must be stopped by human ingenuity or by the intervention of kinder, gentler monsters like King Kong or Mothra, Godzilla would now figure primarily as an heroic figure, defending Japan and the rest of humanity against implacable foes like Ghidrah or alien invaders. *Ghidrah the Three-Headed Monster* also had a strange subplot involving a woman prophet who rediscovers her Martian ancestry, anticipating the next ingredient that would soon be added to the Godzilla stew: adventures in outer space.

The plot of *Godzilla vs. Monster Zero* (1966), to say the least, resists easy summary; it is as if the film's creators went rummaging through the American science fiction films of the 1950s in search of tropes and ideas to borrow, then clumsily combined their gleanings with the battle-of-the-monsters storyline of *Ghidrah the Three-Headed Monster*. The opening sequence, in many respects, surprisingly recapitulates and pays homage to *Destination Moon*: a new Planet X has been discovered behind Jupiter, and a spaceship has been dispatched by the World Space Authority to land on and explore this world. Astronauts Fuji (Akira Takarada) and Glenn (Nick Adams) wear garish orange spacesuits that recall the brightly colored suits of the astronauts in *Destination Moon*, and glimpses of them upside down or sideways in their spaceship fleetingly reference depictions of zero gravity in the earlier film. They turn around their streamlined spaceship to land, like the space travelers in *Destination Moon*, and images of their approach to the barren surface, and the first moments of their arrival on the surface, are strongly reminiscent of similar scenes in *Destination Moon*. However, just as Fuji is about to plant the combined flags of the United Nations, Japan, and the United States on Planet X, presumably to claim the world in the manner of the earlier lunar explorers, the atmosphere of realism dissipates; the spaceship and Glenn vanish, elevators emerge from the surface of the world, and unseen voices command Fuji to enter an elevator and descend into the aliens' underground realm.

At this point, the story abruptly shifts to a pastiche of a considerably less realistic science fiction film of the 1950s, *This Island Earth* (1955); like that film's Metalunans, the scientifically advanced denizens of Planet X have been forced to live underground because of destructive attacks on their world's surface, and they are seeking Earth's assistance in combatting the menace. Here, however, the attacks come from Ghidrah, renamed Monster Zero on Planet X, and the assistance being requested is the right to transport Godzilla and Rodan from Earth to Planet X to drive Ghidrah away. The aliens recall that Godzilla and Rodan were previously efficacious in ridding Earth of Ghidrah in *Ghidrah the Three-Headed Monster*, though they have inexplicably overlooked the equally important contributions of a third Earth monster, Mothra, perhaps omitted from this film as a cost-cutting measure. In exchange for the monsters, the aliens will provide Earth with a "miracle drug that will cure all disease." The astronauts then return to Earth in another sequence that recalls *Destination Moon*, and when senior officials agree to the deal, flying saucers from Planet X appear and take Godzilla and Rodan away to Planet X. Another flying saucer takes Fuji and Glenn back to Planet X, where they watch Godzilla and Rodan take care of Ghidrah with amazing ease and are given a tape with the formula for the miracle cure to return to Earth in a duplicate of their original spaceship.

The overcomplicated story now lurches into a redaction of *Earth vs. the Flying Saucers*, since the tape contains only an ultimatum, demanding that Earth surrender to Planet X or face a devastating invasion. Soon, flying saucers are patrolling Earth's skies, zapping random vehicles with death rays, and Godzilla, Rodan, and Ghidrah, now all mentally controlled by magnetic alien rays, have been returned to Earth and dispatched to destroy various areas and cause masses of horrified people to flee in scenes that briefly harken back to *The Beast from 20,000 Fathoms* and *Godzilla, King of the Monsters*. This time, however, there are no scenes of wounded victims or over-crowded hospitals; far too much is going on for anyone to worry about such trivialities.

Alongside its distinguished older scientist Dr. Sakurai (Jun Tazaki) and beautiful young woman, Miss Namikawa (Kumi Mizuno), *Godzilla vs. Monster Zero* has provided not one or two but three male heroes, whose disparate activities now converge: astronaut Fuji, the brother of Namikawa, has somehow reemerged as the brilliant young scientist in charge of efforts to find some way to block the magnetic mind-controlling rays and get Godzilla and Rodan back on Earth's side; astronaut Glenn has romanced a beautiful agent from Planet X, who despite being under computerized mental control (like all residents of Planet X) has fallen in love with Glenn and provides him with a vital clue before being disintegrated by her disappointed masters; and an eccentric young inventor, Tetsuo Teri (Akira Kubo), in love with Namikawa, has been imprisoned by agents from Planet X after selling them the rights to his latest invention, a device that produces a loud, unpleasant sound. Learning from a note left by the dead alien seductress that residents of Planet X are vulnerable to loud noises (another borrowing from *Earth vs. the Flying Saucers*), Glenn and the inventor use his noisemaker to escape from the agents of Planet X; they obtain Fuji's assistance in broadcasting the noise all over Earth to disable the aliens; and Godzilla and Rodan are simultaneously freed from alien mental control so they can combine forces to defeat Ghidrah and bring this increasingly incoherent story to a welcome end. There is one final bombshell: Glenn cannot go on vacation because he has been appointed the new ambassador to Planet X, though what sort of diplomacy he is expected to practice with the computer-controlled scoundrels who just slaughtered his girlfriend and laid waste to planet Earth is left unspecified.

If the failure of *Godzilla vs. Monster Zero* can be attributed to its reliance on too many disparate influences, the multiple and contradictory roles being played by Godzilla are particularly striking. It will be recalled that the story that arguably started it all, "The Fog Horn," invited sympathetic consideration of the reawakened dinosaur as a pathetic lost soul, and *Godzilla vs. Monster Zero* unexpectedly includes one scene that invites such an emotional reaction. When Fuji and Glenn leave Planet X a second time after Ghidrah's first defeat, Godzilla and Rodan look up with seeming frustration and regret at their departing spaceship. The astronauts express a bit of guilt about leaving these loyal monsters on a barren alien world, and viewing the monsters from the high perspective of the rising space-ship unusually makes them look small and helpless, like pets being abandoned by their masters. Another role played by the giant monster—the implacable enemy—will increasingly be assumed by Ghidrah, but Godzilla and Rodan briefly return to that characterization in their destructive rampages. In this film and most future films, Godzilla will primarily figure as Earth's heroic champion, defending humanity against one threat after another and by default representing the benevolent converse of whatever evil he battles—defending individuality and freedom in opposing brainwashed invaders from Planet X in this film, fighting to preserve the environment by battling Hedorah in *Godzilla vs. the Smog Monster* (1971), standing up for the natural world and organic life by overcoming a giant robot in *Godzilla vs. Mechagodzilla* (1974), and so on. Finally, in this film's introduction of the theme of monsters under the mental control of others, Godzilla and other monsters take on a fourth role—the powerful but morally neutral weapon, ready to serve whatever good or evil entity contrives to seize control of it. In sum, *Godzilla vs. Monster Zero* alternately invites audiences to feel sorry for Godzilla, to fear and despise Godzilla, to root for Godzilla, and to have no feelings whatsoever for Godzilla.

The next nine Godzilla movies display similar confusion, and often downright silliness, in various attempts to recombine familiar elements and import new influences. In two films, Godzilla is provided with an adorable little son to underline his burgeoning aura of avuncular benevolence; new aliens launch monster-assisted invasions of Earth to enhance Godzilla's reputation as Earth's defender; a place called Monster Island, a safe haven for all of Earth's monsters in the near future, provides a domesticating context for Godzilla and other monsters and a convenient starting point for adventures; and Godzilla's robot counterpart, Mechagodzilla, provides an enemy that overtly represents not simply the evils of atomic energy but more broadly the evils of modern technology. None of these developments, however, could bring a genuine sense of novelty to a monster-movie formula that seemed increasingly played out and incapable of further creative growth. Accordingly, Toho's decision to end the series in 1975 with *Terror of Mechagodzilla* represented at the time the appropriate mercy killing of an ailing franchise.

However, events in the outside world would soon offer a foundation for a revitalized genre of monster movies. First, scientists in the 1960s and 1970s were becoming aware of a new type of dinosaur, the raptor, that was about the size of a human being but fast-moving and lethally ferocious. The sheer difference in size between gigantic monsters and people had always made efforts to establish personal relationships awkward and implausible; one wondered why Mothra was so fond of those two miniature women, or why the giant turtle Gamera of rival studio Daiei was said to be so fond of tiny human children. The raptor offered the intriguing possibility of a dinosaur that could look a man or a woman in the eye, a formidable but modestly dimensioned opponent. Another portentous development in the 1970s was the rise of feminism. With the exceptions of Mothra and the British *Gorgo*, both mothers accompanied by their offspring, cinematic dinosaurs and giant monsters had implicitly been gendered as male, and the people who led the battles against those monsters were invariably men. How might the dynamics of the monster movie change if the monster were portrayed as a dynamic female, and/or if the struggle against the monster featured an assertive woman? An American film, ostensibly unrelated to the Godzilla saga, would soon begin the process of exploring these new options.

Given the huge amount of scholarship and commentary focused on the film *Alien* (1979) and its sequels, and my lack of familiarity with that literature, I am understandably reluctant to discuss the film at length, for fear of unknowingly replicating what has already been observed. Perhaps, however, there is a modicum of novelty in arguing that *Alien* can be fruitfully considered as an inspired transformation of the Godzilla movie. Other influences on the film certainly cannot be overlooked, most notably A. E. van Vogt's 1939 story "Black Destroyer" (van Vogt sued the filmmakers and garnered a cash settlement), the 1958 film *It! The Terror from Beyond Space*, and John Carpenter's satirical *Dark Star* (1974). Yet resonances with the Godzilla films and their predecessors are present as well.

First, as the robot Ash (Ian Holm) admiringly remarks, the Alien is, like Godzilla, "a survivor," who endured for a long time in inhospitable conditions before its revival.[40] Like *Godzilla vs. Monster Zero*, the film begins with the first human landing on an alien planet, and as in *The Beast from 20,000 Fathoms*, the monster is first discovered in a cold, barren environment. The creature's projected trajectory is the standard one observed in *The Beast from 20,000 Fathoms*, *Godzilla, King of the Monsters*, and countless other monster films; beginning its journey in a remote territory, the creature is steadily traveling toward the big cities of Earth (even if, in the case of the Alien, its trip to Earth is only completed in the series' fourth film). While the adult Alien is humanoid in shape, it also appears reptilian, much like a miniature Godzilla or a raptor, and the octopus-like tentacles of its initial parasitic form suggest that it shares with Godzilla an aquatic origin, as does the large net initially deployed in an effort to capture it. The deadly acid that drips from its parasitic form, and the manner in which it infiltrates and takes over its victim's body, display a linkage with infectious disease that also recalls *The Beast from 20,000 Fathoms*. And, if the Alien serves as a miniaturized giant monster, and the ship of the first film as the miniaturized wilderness in which it destructively wanders on its way to civilization, then the seven-person crew of the *Nostromo* represents the miniaturized bureaucracy assembled to combat the monster, combining initial respect for and reliance on authority with the eventual rejection of one member of the team who is revealed to be complicit in the alien's progress.

Yet *Alien* both replicates and reinvents the giant monster movie. With a creature the size of a raptor, not a tyranno-

---

40. *Alien* (Twentieth-Century Fox, 1979).

saurus rex, *Alien* offers a more intimate aura of menace, and the hostility toward its monster takes on a personal tone; it is hard to imagine, for example, someone condemning Godzilla's destruction of Tokyo by calling him a "son of a bitch." Further, despite the masculine nature of that particular insult, members of the Alien species in this and later films are generally gendered as female; here, we essentially have a creature who lays eggs in human torsos and whose homicidal impulses are driven by its desperate determination to reproduce. And the most effective opposition to the Alien is provided by a female crew member, Ripley (Sigourney Weaver), who is consistently the person who figures out and executes the best course of action, while her male comrades display either inappropriate compassion and docility to the monster (Dallas [Tom Skerritt] and Ash) or inappropriate and ineffectual machismo (Parker [Yaphet Kotto] and Brett [Harry Dean Stanton]). In these respects, Ripley offers a refreshing contrast to the submissive romantic objects of 1950s American science fiction films and the Godzilla movies.

Predictably, *Alien* quickly inspired a flood of imitative films featuring small, virulent monsters, including *Inseminoid* (1980), *Alien Contamination* (1981), *Mindwarp: An Infinity of Terror* (1981), *Forbidden World* (1982), and *Parasite* (1982), but there also appeared a well-received homage to the older model of the rampaging gigantic reptile, *Alligator* (1980), which may have played a more direct role in inspiring Toho Studios to re-release some of their classic monster films in 1982. When these proved profitable, a decision to relaunch the Godzilla series was inevitable. This time, however, not only were there new cinematic and cultural influences to assimilate, but Godzilla would be emerging from a vastly transformed nation: Japan, the global economic superpower, in contrast to the devastated vassal state that originated the monster. There was little novelty in the first film of this new series, *Godzilla 1985* (1984), a straightforward sequel to the first Godzilla film with Raymond Burr reprising his role as reporter Steve Martin. But the next film, *Godzilla vs. Biollante* (1989), would offer filmgoers a striking mixture of the old and the new.

At the heart of this film, one might argue, is the standard Godzilla storyline—Godzilla emerges from the sea, approaches populated areas, and eventually destroys a major metropolis (here, oddly, Osaka instead of Tokyo)—but this familiar drama occupies at most fifteen minutes of the film's two hours. More attention is focused on the strange creation of Biollante: a scientist grieving over the sudden death of his daughter decides to blend her genes with those of a rose bush, then further combines the rose genes with genes from Godzilla cells to create a gigantic monster plant, sporting tentacle-like vines with snapping jaws that recall both the carnivorous plant of *Little Shop of Horrors* (1960) and the baby Alien that spurts out of William Hurt's chest. Yet Biollante is a also a gentle female monster, determined to stop Godzilla's destructive attacks, inasmuch as she is imbued with the benevolent spirit of the scientist's daughter, whose face mysteriously materializes when Biollante drifts into orbit to metamorphose into a huge red rose at the film's conclusion. The battle against Godzilla also requires the assistance of a young woman whose psychic powers enable her to detect the monster's presence when he is hiding beneath the sea. In this film, then, Godzilla is singularly defeated almost entirely by girl power.

The influence of *Alien* is further suggested by the film's theme of infectious disease (perhaps reflecting the fact that the story was written by a dentist who entered and won a contest to determine the plot of the next Godzilla movie): scientists are using Godzilla cells to create "anti-nuclear bacteria" which they hope can infect and destroy Godzilla—and might, incidentally, also make all nuclear weapons obsolete. This attracts the attention of foreign governments and, not incidentally, makes this the first Godzilla movie since *Godzilla, King of the Monsters* to have a mildly anti-American tone, for two of the foreign agents attempting to steal some Godzilla cells are Americans. However, not unmindful of a potential American audience, the agents are presented as likable and ineffectual; the real villain is a ruthless assassin from the Middle Eastern nation of "Saradia"—a transparent renaming of "Saudi Arabia"—which seeks Godzilla cells in order to create a superstrong form of wheat capable of growing in the desert that will provide the country with a new source of income and global clout when its oil reserves eventually diminish. Since even the resurgent Japan of the 1980s depended upon the increasingly influential nations of the Middle East for oil, they can now join the United States in functioning as representatives of postcolonial forces seeking to oppress Japan.

If the geopolitical tensions and violence of the spy thriller seem unduly sophisticated for a Godzilla film, there is the offsetting factor of another subplot openly aimed at children. As part of its plans to deal with the expected return of Godzilla, the Japanese government has constructed an amazing futuristic vehicle called the "Super X-2," closely resembling the space fighters of *Star Wars* (1977) and always accompanied by a musical fanfare highly reminiscent of John Williams's theme for the film *Superman* (1978). The Super X-2 soars through the air and employs various weapons in its visually dramatic but ultimately ineffectual engagements with Godzilla. Since this vehicle could have been eliminated from the film without altering the plot in any way, its presence must be explained in cynical terms. Toho Studios may have figured that putting a bit of *Star Wars* into the film might enhance its popularity, perhaps anticipating that this series of Godzilla films, like the last one, was bound to end up in outer space anyway (as it did). It might also represent a plan to profit from the toy market, with Toho Studios hoping that little Japanese boys would clamor to own their own little Super X-2's to deploy in mock battles with a miniature Godzilla.

However confused and variegated *Godzilla vs. Biollante* might seem, it is a model of coherence and thematic unity when compared to the next Godzilla film, *Godzilla vs. King Ghidorah* (1991). In some respects, this seems a redaction of *Godzilla vs. Monster Zero*: again, technologically advanced visitors to Earth emerge from a flying saucer, seeking to remove Godzilla from Earth for everyone's benefit, and again they prove to be duplicitous and evil. But these visitors are from Earth's future, and their appearance and motives seethe with undeniable political overtones. Two of these Futurians are white men named Wilson and Girencheko; one is clearly American, with a name that recalls Woodrow Wilson, the first American president to play a dominating role in world politics, while the other is clearly Russian, whose name blends the name of the then-current leader of the U.S.S.R., Mikhail Gorbachev, with that of his immediate predecessor, Konstantin Chernenko. The third Futurian is a Japanese woman, Emmy, who is not a party to her comrades' insidious scheme. The visitors announce that Godzilla is soon destined to completely destroy Japan, so they seek to remove him so that Japan can exist in the future. In actuality, however, Japan will thrive and will become the wealthiest, largest, and most powerful nation in the twenty-third century; Wilson and Girencheko's actual intent is to replace Godzilla with the even more dangerous Ghidorah, so that Japan will be devastated and never achieve its dominant status. The provocative storyline, then, has the United States and Russia plotting to repress Japan by removing its monstrous champion.

An anti-American spirit, however, is even more apparent in the way that Godzilla's origins are re-explained. In previous films, Godzilla had somehow shifted from being a representative of other nations oppressing Japan, created by an American H-bomb, to being a representative of Japan, defending the nation against attackers; *Godzilla vs. King Ghidorah* gives Godzilla a new origin story that stresses his empathy with Japan. During World War II, Japanese soldiers on a remote island are improbably saved from an American attack by the appearance of a dinosaur, dubbed the godzillasaurus, who routs the Americans; though the survivors kept this dinosaur a secret, they continued to admire and revere this creature, because the men who survived turned out to be "the very same men who rebuilt our economy."[41] Ten years later, when Americans tested an H-bomb near the island, it was this dinosaur that mutated into the larger and more dangerous Godzilla. In scenes of the smaller Godzilla killing American soldiers, and in the affection the soldiers show to the wounded dinosaur who saved Japan's leaders and benefitted the nation, Godzilla is reconfigured as a champion of Japan, rendered a menace only due to American intervention before it rediscovers and reasserts its kinship with Japan.

The Futurians teleport the godzillasaurus to the bottom of the Pacific Ocean so that it will never be exposed to the H-bomb radiation and never become Godzilla; however, as part of their plot, the Futurians also bring with them three cherubic little flying monsters called Dorats, which they know will mutate into the horrific Ghidorah when they are exposed to that same H-bomb radiation. When a Japan without a Godzilla is subsequently attacked by Ghidorah, a Japanese official suggests that the undersea dinosaur be located and exposed to radiation to make it into Godzilla again, revealing in passing that Japan secretly possesses a nuclear submarine armed with nuclear missiles. Any action on Japan's part turns out to be unnecessary, however, when it is revealed that a sunken Russian atomic submarine has already done the job of recreating Godzilla, now even taller and more savage than before. The political message seems to be: the Americans, who created the original Godzilla, are bad; but the Russians, who created the second and more deadly Godzilla, are even worse.

While the analysis above might suggest a conclusion to the film in which Godzilla sheds his evil influences and reasserts his status as Japan's hero, the Godzilla films at this stage have started to manifest a tendency toward maximal complexity which mitigates against such moral clarity. Instead, after Godzilla defeats Ghidorah, Godzilla looms as a menace to Japan; the good Futurian and her present-day comrades then

_____

41. *Godzilla vs. King Ghidorah* (Toho Studios, 1991).

have the bright idea of reviving Ghidorah to defeat Godzilla. (The circularity of this logic, which might lead to Ghidorah defeating Godzilla and becoming the new menace, creating a need to revive Godzilla to defeat Ghidorah, on to infinity, goes unnoticed.) Ghidorah then becomes this film's unlikely avatar of girl power, as Emmy arranges to turn the moribund Ghidorah into the cyborg Mecha-King Ghidorah, with herself controlling the monster from a cockpit of sorts installed near his three heads. The female psychic from *Godzilla vs. Biollante* is also lurking about, occasionally pitching in to provide some piece of information about Godzilla or Ghidorah, but there is so much going on in the film that it is difficult to pay any attention to her. When Godzilla and Ghidorah fall into the sea while locked in battle, it seems that they have defeated each other, allowing for at least a sense of temporary closure; however, the film ultimately refuses even that, by means of a final scene in which we see Godzilla's undersea eye glowingly open up, laying the groundwork for the next sequel.

Concurrent with these efforts to demonize the previously benevolent monster, *Godzilla vs. King Ghidorah* simultaneously makes an unprecedented effort to arouse sympathy for Godzilla. Harkening back to the spirit of "The Fog Horn," the Japanese soldiers during World War II bond with the injured dinosaur who defended them, protectively surrounding him as he lies wounded and helpless on the ground and apologizing for the necessity of their departure. Later, in one of the most extraordinary scenes in the entire Godzilla series, the Japanese soldier who most admired Godzilla, waiting in an abandoned skyscraper, comes face to face with the giant dinosaur while he is flattening the city. In alternating closeups, man and monster stare intently at each other, and one momentarily wonders if the film will lapse into the implausible bathos of a scene right out of *Androcles and the Lion* in which Godzilla recognizes his old benefactor and ends his attack. Instead, however, Godzilla resumes his rampage, killing the old man with a blast of fire breath and reverting to his sinister persona.

The borrowings and homages permeating this film are so numerous as to defy cataloging. The evil, humanoid robot of *Alien* is borrowed to serve as the Futurian's super-powerful accomplice (performing astounding feats that also seem derived from television's *The Six Million Dollar Man* [1974-1978] and the film *The Terminator* [1984]), though Emmy reprograms him to become the sort of helpful, reliable robot observed in *Aliens* (1986). One American in World War II observing the dinosaur is told by his commander to someday describe it to his son, the punchline being that he is then identified as "Major Spielberg"; however, one isn't sure if filmmakers are acknowledging the influence of Spielberg's *Close Encounters of the Third Kind* (1977) in the design of the Futurians' flying saucer, are linking the cute little Dorats to Spielberg's cute little *E.T.: The Extra-Terrestrial* (1982), or are joking about Spielberg's then-forthcoming dinosaur film *Jurassic Park*. In a more general tribute to Godzilla's predecessors, the hero of the film, who first theorizes that Godzilla is the transformed dinosaur of World War II, is said to be a "science fiction writer"; also, after apparently building a romantic relationship with Emma, the woman from the future finally reveals that she is one of his descendants, recalling the incestuous adventures of Robert A. Heinlein's Lazarus Long in *Time Enough for Love* (1973). The "anti-nuclear bacteria" of *Godzilla vs. Biollante* have not been entirely forgotten—they are said to have kept Godzilla alive after the last film's battle—and when Godzilla is observed foaming at the mouth in one battle scene, there is the momentary suggestion that Godzilla is like a rabid, diseased animal.

Despite this film's undeniable energy and evocative moments, *Godzilla vs. King Ghidorah* conveys the aura of a project that has gotten out of control, a snowball rolling madly down a hillside picking up and absorbing whatever materials happen to lie in the way. Godzilla is simultaneously an implacable enemy and a poor lost soul, the embodiment of overreaching colonial superpowers and the champion of anticolonialism, a symbol of the evils of technology and symbol of the natural world opposing technology, a wily and intelligent adversary and a mindless destructive force. In four more films after this one, Toho Studios carried on the saga in a similarly variegated fashion, finally and officially killing Godzilla in *Godzilla vs. Destroyah* (1995) while also developing his new son, Godzilla Junior, as the potential centerpiece of additional films. In the end, however, the next Godzilla film would surprisingly be an all-American product, a massive epic produced by an American studio and the creative team that gave us *Independence Day* (1996), producer Dean Devlin and director Roland Emmerich.

Godzilla (1998) seemed like a film that could not fail, and two sequels were already in the works before the unexpectedly lukewarm response to the film brought a halt to such plans. Many explanations might be, and have been, advanced for its failure. Perhaps, the film needed a stronger leading man than Matthew Broderick; perhaps the new, more lizard-like design of Godzilla made the creature seem less human, less appealing, and not quite a "true" Godzilla, who always walked upright like a man; perhaps the film was so relentlessly publicized and promoted that it inspired a critical and popular backlash.

To me, however, the central problem is that *Godzilla* is not a movie, but is a mixture of numerous different movies. It is as if the filmmakers watched every single Godzilla movie ever filmed, along with scores of related films, and resolved to include elements from every single one of them while also crafting a film that could appeal to every conceivable audience. Instead of a fresh new start, filmmakers instead carried on with Toho Studio's process of ever-burgeoning borrowing and complication to produce the most multifaceted and muddled Godzilla film of them all.

Consider, for example, how the filmmakers deal with the issues of nuclear energy and postcolonial guilt. In keeping with longstanding tradition, their Godzilla will be created by an H-bomb test in the Pacific Ocean; further underlining the theme of irresponsible use of nuclear energy is the fact that the film's heroic scientist is working on a project to investigate mutated earthworms at the scene of the Soviet Union's Chernobyl disaster. However, in a film aimed primarily at American audiences, even the slightest hint of anti-Americanism must be avoided, so Godzilla would have to be attributed to a *French* H-bomb test, further engendering a subplot involving agents of the French secret service who surreptitiously join the battle against Godzilla to deal with their own "mistake."[42] Now, if Godzilla had gone on to attack Algeria or another country victimized by French imperialism, this theme might have had some evocative power, at least for filmgoers in the impacted nation; yet it had also been decided, for maximum appeal to Americans, to emulate *The Beast from 20,000 Fathoms* in having Godzilla rampage through New York City. Inexorably, then, Godzilla becomes a symbol of the damage inflicted upon America by French colonialism—which is to say, Godzilla becomes a symbol that makes no sense whatsoever, depriving the film of any deeper resonances to underscore its spectacular action scenes.

Further confusion results from an evident desire to have it both ways, to deal with every set of conflicting options by embracing both of them. Should Godzilla be an embodiment of traditional masculine strength or contemporary girl power? Why not do both? Thus, while Godzilla rampages with the usual sort of unrestrained machismo and is consistently referred to as a "he," the monster is also a mother figure, capable of reproducing asexually and laying up to 200 huge eggs that undeniably recall the sinister eggs laid by the Alien.

Should Godzilla resemble the traditional gigantic dinosaur or a more modestly dimensioned raptor? Why not feature both types? Thus, while the film begins and ends with battles against the huge, towering Godzilla, an interlude in the middle of the film pits the heroes against a horde of baby Godzillas who strikingly resemble both the original Alien and the attacking raptors of Spielberg's *Jurassic Park*.

---

42. *Godzilla* (Centropolis Films 1998).

Should members of the military forces opposing Godzilla be depicted as ineffective or effective? Why not both? Thus, for most of the film, military firepower seems helpless against Godzilla, and the general leading the defense of New York seems to blunder again and again; near the end, however, the general starts heeding the advice of Dr. Tatopoulos (Broderick), makes good decisions, and can ultimately kill Godzilla with an aerial attack.

Should Godzilla be unrelentingly menacing, or a somewhat sympathetic figure? Why not have him be both? Thus, for the bulk of the film, Godzilla and his offspring function as little more than malevolent killing machines, but there are moments when we are invited to feel sorry for him—in a scene recalling *Godzilla vs. King Ghidorah* when Tatopoulos stands next to Godzilla and looks him in the eye, when we observe Godzilla saddened and enraged by the corpses of his children, and when we watch Godzilla die at the film's end. There are even efforts to make Godzilla seem comical, in a scene where a fisherman feels a strong tug on his line, thinks he has caught a big one, and then watches in horror as Godzilla emerges from the water, and in another scene where the little Godzillas roaming through Madison Square Garden are eating huge bags of popcorn, even though it has been previously established that Godzilla is a carnivore—a scene perhaps designed to encourage some audience members to hit the concession stands. The two sides of Godzilla are suggested by two fleetingly observed television images: the menacing octopus from *It Came from Beneath the Sea* (1955) and the lovable dinosaur who entertains toddlers, Barney.

In addition, during the film's two hours, any number of other themes or motifs from previous films are briefly introduced but never developed enough to have any impact. The short-sighting interfering governmental officials who figure in *Destination Moon* make an appearance here, though the more immediate influence seems to be the film *Jaws* (1975): not only does Godzilla have one scene when he swims through the ocean like a menacing shark, but there is the recurring character of New York's mayor (Michael Lerner), up for re-election, who is consistently grouchy and unhelpful during Godzilla's attacks. Just as the civic leaders in *Jaws* sought to hastily re-open the beach in order to make money, despite the ongoing threat of the shark, the mayor and others wish to hastily allow citizens back into New York City in order to make money, despite the ongoing threat of Godzilla and his children. As in films like *Godzilla vs. Monster Zero* and *Godzilla vs. King Ghidorah*, people make efforts to manipulate Godzilla into serving their own ends—the mayor seeking political advantage, and Harry Shearer's anchorman trying to win big ratings with coverage of Godzilla's attack. Indeed, while journalists in previous Godzilla films were typically benign but impotent observers, *Godzilla* borrows from films ranging from *The Thing (from Another World)* (1951) to *Broadcast News* (1987) in presenting journalists both as heroes (Broderick's girlfriend Audrey [Maria Pitillo], who devises a way to employ television to alert the city to the menace of Godzilla's nest, and her friend "Animal" [Hank Azaria], the brave cameraman) and villains (Shearer's vain, self-serving anchorman). With Godzilla portrayed as a creature capable of quickly giving birth to 200 counterparts, and Broderick warning that Godzilla represents "a new species" that might replace humanity, we are invited to view Godzilla as a sinister sort of *homo superior*, echoing the paranoia of *Invasion of the Body Snatchers* (1956) and countless depictions of advanced beings poised to take our place as rulers of the planet.

To any reasonably informed viewer of science fiction films, virtually every scene in *Godzilla* seems a borrowing from a previous film. The initial destruction of a Japanese fishing vessel recalls the destroyed ship in the original *Godzilla: King of the Monsters*. Images of tiny aircraft darting through the corridors of streets surrounding by large buildings in pursuit of Godzilla recall scenes of space dogfights in *Star Wars*. The octopus of *It Came from Beneath the Sea* emerges on the Golden Gate Bridge; Godzilla ends up on the Brooklyn Bridge. The soldiers patrolling through the subways of New York in search of Godzilla recall the soldiers searching the Los Angeles subway system for giant ants in *Them!* Some scenes have occurred in so many previous films that they can only elicit groans. To slow down a squadron of baby Godzillas, Broderick upturns some racks of balls and gumball machines so as to make the monsters trip and fall. And incredibly enough, the exciting climax to *Godzilla* is nothing more than an extended car chase, similar to those in innumerable television cop shows, with Godzilla taking the place of the pursuing vehicle as Broderick and company race through the streets of New York endeavoring to lure Godzilla to the Brooklyn Bridge where he can be attacked and killed. Given all of these innumerable borrowings, it is only appropriate that the filmmakers did not commission any new songs for the film; instead, they recruited the Wallflowers and Puff Daddy to offer lame remakes of old songs by David Bowie and Led Zeppelin. It is as if the film's script went through countless rewrites by uncredited writers, each one adding another tried-and-true device.

A film stuffed with too many elements paradoxically becomes empty, meaningless. Godzilla is simultaneously humanity's enemy, victim, successor, and clown. His intrusion into contemporary society brings to mind every conceivable issue; his story is a chaotic patchwork of bits and pieces from a century of filmmaking. The giant dinosaur who could never be killed has been smothered by thematic overkill, sheer cinematic excess that is breathtaking in both its relentless cynicism and its utter incoherence.

Still, just as Godzilla had lived through countless other deaths in previous films, the indefatigable dinosaur proved capable of surviving the debacle of his American debut and was soon starring in another sequel—though not the sequel that Devlin and Emmerich had envisioned. For, in response to the horrible mutilation they had inflicted upon the character, demands arose in both Japan and America that Toho Studios bring back the original Godzilla, and Toho obliged with *Godzilla 2000* (1999), which became the first Japanese Godzilla film since *Godzilla 1985* to receive a theatrical release in America. In launching their third series of Godzilla films, however, it seems that Toho had learned some lessons from past experiences, because these new films were characterized as the "alternate history" Godzilla movies: films in this series, it was announced, would have no relationship to any previous film and would make no effort to lead up to another film; instead, each would tell its own individual story about Godzilla. It was an approach that might help to minimize the influence of Godzilla's past, place limits on his multiple personalities and roles, and keep the narratives from spinning out of control; and this proved to be the case with *Godzilla 2000*.

Here, then, the saga of Godzilla was intermingled only with precisely one new influence, chosen with insidious shrewdness—Devlin and Emmerich's own *Independence Day*. (It is as Toho Studios was saying: you bastardized our film, so we will bastardize yours.) Thus, Earth is again invaded by an immense spaceship that hovers over cities and causes mass destruction; this time, Godzilla is recruited to battle the alien ship, and evidently impressed by what they see, the invading aliens then seize a piece of Godzilla's tissue and employ it to transform their spaceship into a monstrous dinosaur, named Orga, who is finally defeated by Godzilla in a typical battle of the monsters. Unambitious, derivative, and entertaining, *Godzilla 2000* was followed by four additional Godzilla movies along similar lines before the character was retired, yet again, with *Godzilla: Final Wars* in 2004, but this time, the retirement was announced as temporary, for only ten years, and Toho Studios has also sanctioned another American reboot of Godzilla, provisionally scheduled for a 2014 release. More Godzilla films, in both Japan and America, are sure to follow.

Godzilla, it would seem, has finally absorbed a lesson in survival already illustrated by the other iconic figures already mentioned, Tarzan and Superman: to remain viable, the most ubiquitous characters of popular culture must periodically abandon their pasts and reinvent themselves, so as to avoid being crushed by an overaccumulation of attributes and resonances. Thus, over the years, the Tarzan of novels and films has alternately been a cultured gentleman and an inarticulate savage, the head of an extended family and a lonely wanderer, a visitor to contemporary New York and a traveler to other worlds. The saga of the comic-book Superman has been periodically revised to erase large chunks of his past, to eliminate or reinvent redundant characters, and reduce his overdeveloped powers. Similarly, it seems, Godzilla must, like other reptiles, periodically shed his skin, abandon the built-up residues of past adventures, and start afresh. And as long as this continues to occur, then Godzilla may be able to dominate the twenty-first century just as he dominated the latter half of the twentieth century.

7. METALUNAR MISADVENTURES: DIVERGENT VOYAGES FROM *THIS ISLAND EARTH*

The strange saga of *This Island Earth* begins with Raymond F. Jones's 1949 short story "The Alien Machine," which launched a narrative that would extend into two additional stories, a novel which incorporated all three stories and extended the adventure, and a more heralded film adaptation. "The Alien Machine" is also the only part of Jones's story which was replicated almost exactly in the film, and its events are a major reason for the film's enduring appeal. In the story, a radio engineer named Cal Meacham, after receiving an amazingly advanced piece of equipment and a catalog from a mysterious company, orders the parts needed to build a machine with an unknown purpose called an interocitor. After he successfully assembles the device, a man appears on its television screen to tell Meacham that he has passed the test and has shown himself qualified to work for the company. Accepting this unusual job offer, Meacham shows up at the stipulated place and time and is greeted by a pilotless plane, suggesting that his future employers are indeed aliens.

I have previously suggested that if Jones had stopped the story of Cal Meacham with "The Alien Machine," that story might have eventually earned recognition as a science fiction classic—since it conveys with striking clarity two messages which were crucially important to the scientifically precocious but socially inept male adolescents who were once the genre's main audience. Such readers want to be told, first, that there exists, or will someday emerge, a larger and more interesting universe, filled with strange wonders, which most residents of our mundane, everyday world are unable to imagine. Second, within this broader context, certain individuals that society now disrespects and marginalizes—namely, the intelligent young nerds who read science fiction—will be valued and celebrated as the true heroes of this advanced realm. Thus, the unseen aliens of "The Alien Machine" do not seek out Earth's movie stars, top athletes, or political leaders—all professions that geeky science fiction readers could not realistically aspire to—but rather choose to recruit a working scientist, a likely career for those readers, who the aliens manifestly regard as one of the most important people on the planet.

However, Jones soon set out to write a sequel to "The Alien Machine," and so he had to devise an answer to the first story's obvious question: *why* are these aliens interested in the services of a skilled radio engineer? Jones's answer is prosaic but logical: when Meacham's plane lands in Arizona in "The Shroud of Secrecy" (1949) and he meets with several other people who have been recruited by the aliens, one of them tells Meacham that he is going to be asked to oversee a factory to manufacture interocitors—which explains why he was given the task of assembling an interocitor as his initiation test. He then speaks with the head of the organization he will be working for, a man named Jorgasnovara, who explains that his group of Peace Engineers is an ancient society dedicated to secretive but benevolent scientific research. During the following months of work, Meacham develops a romantic relationship with another recruit, a psychiatrist named Ruth Adams, and eventually makes two interesting discoveries—that the real function of interocitors is telepathic communications, and that the completed interocitors are being sent into outer space.

In the third story, "The Greater Conflict" (1950), Meacham

attempts to escape from the Peace Engineers after learning that they are embroiled in an interstellar war, but he is instead taken to the Moon, where Jorgasnovara finally admits that he is indeed an alien, a member of a race which is engaged in a vast and prolonged war against other, evil aliens, and that his people are necessarily recruiting less advanced races to assist in their efforts. He likens his race's actions to what the Allies did during World War II in a way which undoubtedly suggested the eventual title of the novel:

> "You have had experience during your own recent World War.... You saw these primitive peoples sometimes employed or pressed into service by one side or the other. On the islands of your seas they built airfields for you; they sometimes cleared jungles and helped lay airstrips. They had no comprehension of the vast purpose to which they were contributing a meager part, but they helped in a conflict which was ultimately resolved in their favor....This greater conflict of which I have spoken has existed for hundreds of generations. Your people were barely out of caves when it began. It will not be ended in your generation or mine....But we need your help."
>
> "To build an airstrip?"
>
> Jorgasnovara smiled. "These interocitors which you find so interesting are a small item of communication equipment which is used in some of our larger vessels....They are simple devices, comparable, say, to your pushbuttons. We need you to make some pushbuttons for us."

After this humbling explanation, Meacham returns to Earth and rededicates himself to the task of making "a lot of—pushbuttons."[43]

---

43. Raymond F. Jones, *This Island Earth* (Chicago: Shasta Publishers, 1952), 127-128.

From one perspective, these sequels have spoiled the impact of Jones's original story: it is now revealed that the aliens sought out Meacham not as a valued colleague, but rather as an inconsequential underling, and instead of the person of authority he initially seemed, he now must spend his time obeying the instructions of other, superior beings. Yet one could also say that Jones is interestingly contradicting what was then the consensus opinion of science fiction—that the rapidly advancing and innovative race of human beings was destined to rule the universe—to argue that humans, upon venturing into the cosmos, might actually learn that they are properly regarded as weak and powerless. This is a theme that will be vigorously returned to in the film, a major reason why it seems so different from other films of its era.

As the story continues in the novel *This Island Earth* (1952), Meacham does recover a bit of his original stature: it emerges that he knows exactly what to do in order to successfully manufacture interocitors on Earth, while his alien overseers (now called the Llanna) do not, as their inept micromanagement leads to disgruntled workers, a strike at the interocitor factory, and sabotage led by a disguised agent of the enemy aliens, recognized as such by Meacham but not the aliens, who has been assigned to prevent the construction of interocitors. Yet Meacham's final act of "heroism" essentially amounts to successfully begging for help: after Jorgasnovara tells Meacham that his people, based on computer projections indicating that they will eventually lose their battle in Earth's region of space, have decided to withdraw from the area and allow their opponents to conquer Earth, Meacham is granted permission to travel into space and meet with the ruling council of aliens, where he vigorously argues that the only way they will ever succeed is if they stop relying on computers and instead start making their own decisions. Impressed by his words, the aliens change their minds and resolve to continue defending the Earth. What emerges from all of this is that the aliens, like Meacham, have also been revealed to be less capable than they originally seemed, as they make one stupid decision after another and eventually must be prodded into doing something intelligent by one of their subordinates.

It would not be unfair to say that the makers of the film *This Island Earth* (1955)—screenwriters Franklin Coen and Edward G. O'Callaghan, principal director Joseph M. Newman, and producer William Alland—essentially decided to throw away everything in Jones's story after the events of "The Alien Machine" and to create an entirely new narrative about what happened after Meacham boarded that pilotless plane. Yet two key aspects of the entire novel are clearly visible in the film: an essentially helpless hero, and equally helpless alien overseers who are in the process of losing an important war.

One significant change, a concession to the era's new fascination with atomic energy, is that the Cal Meacham of the film (Rex Reason) is a renowned nuclear physicist, seeking to figure out how to turn lead into uranium in order to ensure abundant atomic energy in the future. This is why the aliens living on Earth, now called the Metalunans, are interested in his services and are constantly monitoring his activities; early in the film, they disable his aircraft and then employ eerie energy to save him from a fatal crash landing, for reasons never explained. But given these circumstances, the Metalunans' decision to make Meacham assemble an interocitor now seems senseless—since they already know that he has the knowledge they need, why waste precious time by giving him a pointless, time-consuming task? Further, since he will now be working on atomic energy, not building interocitors, they have no reason to be interested in his ability to construct the device.

After Meacham assembles his interocitor and receives his televised summons from the Metalunan leader in Earth, Exeter (Jeff Morrow), the pilotless plane takes him not to Arizona but to an elegant mansion in Georgia. That location, the patrician name Exeter, and the unusual appearance of the Metalunans—prominent brows and huge pompadours of white hair—all suggest that these aliens, unlike the novel's bumblers, are better regarded as members of a decaying aristocracy, destined to be swept away by war and changing times—a saga that might be termed *Gone with the Solar Wind*. With the exception of the benevolent Exeter, the Metalunans are also more malevolent—it transpires that they are turning most of their recruited scientists into mind-slaves, and they are planning to relocate their race to Earth, and take over our world, should they lose their war, here restricted to a defense of their home planet against attacking aliens named Zahgons. Echoing the novel's plot, Meacham meets and befriends fellow scientists Ruth Adams (Faith Domergue), now a nuclear physicist like Meacham, and Steve Carlson (Russell Johnson); eventually, they attempt to flee the premises, but Carlson is killed and Meacham and Adams are taken into outer space by the Metalunans—who have been summoned home to assist in their planet's increasingly difficult struggle to survive.

The journey to Metaluna commands attention as an early example of how science fiction films would increasingly strive to avoid the introduction of awkward spacesuits. Already filled with all sorts of scientific nonsense, the film is unsurprisingly unrealistic in depicting space travel as well: for when Meacham and Adams are forced into the alien flying saucer to be taken to the distant planet Metaluna, we immediately notice that they and their alien hosts are walking around as they did on Earth, showing no effects of zero gravity. However, Exeter explains that "we create our own gravitational field," making this yet another film to refer to a form of "artificial gravity" to account for the natural way that space travelers move around within their spaceships.[44] We then learn that on Metaluna, the "atmospheric pressure is like that of your deepest oceans," meaning that a typical Earthman would "be crushed to death" upon entering "Metaluna's orbit." Since this means that Metaluna must be much larger than the Earth, it would also suggest that its atmosphere has a different composition and could not be breathed by humans. Thus, any human visitor to Metaluna, it seems, would

---

44. *This Island Earth* (Universal, 1955).

have to wear some sort of protective gear, probably a spacesuit with an exoskeleton.

However, it turns out that none of this is necessary, because all Meacham and Adams have to do is to undergo "a little procedure" called "conversion," which will enable them to stay alive on Metaluna; the process involves being placed inside of a large tube, which is sealed and filled with gas, and then being subjected to some form of radiation that briefly reveals their skeletons. All of this is colorful enough, but one would struggle to come up with some sort of reasonable scientific explanation as to how such a treatment would enable an Earthling to survive and move about effortlessly on the surface of a massive alien planet. To add to the silliness, Exeter also asks Meacham and Adams to change into clothing "such as ours, especially conditioned for life on Metaluna," although these silver jumpsuits have no obvious features that would help anyone adjust to a different planetary environment. However, all of this does mean that the filmmakers never need to introduce any spacesuits: the Metalunans could survive on Earth without protective gear because they had been "converted" to live in that environment, just as Meacham and Adams can survive on Metaluna because they were also "converted." (Still, all of this mumbo-jumbo does require a certain amount of screen time to explain and to illustrate, creating an incentive for a simpler way to keep characters out of spacesuits, which would soon be illustrated by *Forbidden Planet* [1956] and other subsequent films.)

Having completely abandoned Jones's story at this point, the film now has Meacham and Adams land on Metaluna, which is being devastated by a steady rain of huge rocks hurled by the Zahgons (fearful that neophyte director Joseph M. Newman was not up to the task, producer Alland asked veteran Jack Arnold to direct this portion of the film). The Metalunans have been protecting their planet with defensive energy shields, but these are now faltering and allowing rocks to land due to inadequate supplies of energy, explaining why the Metalunans are desperately interested in new ways to generate atomic power.

When Exeter sadly points out his planet's once-impressive but now destroyed buildings, such as schools and recreational facilities, he again suggests that his race represents a once-noble but now decadent society. Then, fearful that the Metalunans, unflatteringly represented by their arrogant leader, the Monitor (Douglas Spencer), will again attempt to enslave their human captives, Meacham punches Exeter and runs away with Ruth, but in a bizarre and almost immediate reversal they are soon accepting Exeter's help as he strives to guide them back to his spaceship so the three of them can escape from a planet that is now clearly doomed.

The trio is also menaced by the most controversial aspect of the film—the "Mutant" (pronounced "Mute-Ant" by Jeff Morrow, who evidently was not familiar with the word)—a hideous, insect-like humanoid created by the Metalunans to serve as slave labor, and added to the film at a late date, despite opposition from many people working on the film, in order to provide publicists with a colorfully *outré* image for posters and advertisements. While designed to function solely as a frightening menace, contemporary audiences may instead feel sorry for the Mutant, clearly a cruelly exploited being who in attacking his uppity and contemptuous masters may only be giving these faltering aristocrats exactly what they deserve.

Up to this point in the film, viewers of *This Island Earth* have had to endure more than the era's normal quota of scientific idiocies: the idea of turning lead into uranium (since, as a result of natural radioactive decay, uranium actually turns into lead); the "flame barrier" that the Metalunar spacecraft must pass through in outer space (since no flames could burn in the vacuum of space); Exeter's claim that the planet Zahgon "was once a comet" (since comets are tiny chunks of rock and ice, usually only a few miles in diameter, while planets are at least a thousand times larger); and so on. However, what happens after Exeter, Meacham, and Adams escape from Metaluna is especially spectacular both for its visual splendor and its blatant disregard for basic science. Somehow, as Exeter tells Meacham while they observe the planet from space, the constant Zahgon bombardment is turning the planet Metaluna into a sun, leading to the film's most memorable speech:

> Those flashes of light...they're meteors...hundreds of them! Intense heat is turning Metaluna into a radioactive sun. Temperature must be...thousands of degrees by now. A lifeless planet. And yet...yet still serving a useful purpose, I hope. Yes, a sun. Warming the surface of some other world. Giving light to those who may need it.

Strangely enough, this absurd development probably influenced the conclusion of Arthur C. Clarke's sequel to *2001: A Space Odyssey* (1968), *2010: Odyssey Two* (1982), and its film adaptation *2010: The Year We Make Contact* (1984), when Clarke's unseen aliens send innumerable monoliths raining down on Jupiter, increasing its mass so as to turn it into a star—but Clarke at least is on solider ground in so transforming Jupiter, which by some accounts is nearly massive enough to become a star all by itself, instead of the obviously smaller and more Earthlike Metaluna, which could never become a star no matter how many meteors land on its surface.

A final drama during the flight back to Earth underscores just how ineffectual Meacham has been throughout his adventures: when Adams is menaced by the wounded Mutant, which somehow managed to sneak aboard the spacecraft, Meacham is poised to rescue her in a properly manly fashion—but he never needs to, as the monster collapses of its own accord before he reaches her. (Indeed, it is significant that *This Island Earth* is filled with numerous references to the then-new media of television—the interocitor is among other things an advanced television set, Exeter communicates with his superiors on Metaluna and spies on the recruited scientists by means of television, and all events in outer space are watched on television screens; for television, after all, is the medium not of the active participant but of the passive observer of events, which is precisely the role that Meacham has played throughout the film.) When the travelers finally reach Earth, the injured Exeter declines Meacham's offer to settle on Earth, drops off Meacham and Adams, and promptly dies when his ship crashes into the sea—probably a deliberate act of suicide by the last surviving Metalunan, though it may also have been an accident.

Overall, *This Island Earth* is clearly a film that defies all stereotypical perceptions of 1950s science fiction film: its hero accomplishes absolutely nothing, and both his failures, and those of his apparently superior adversaries, the Metalunans, convey a deeply pessimistic message about humanity's ultimate ability to understand the universe and conquer space. It even offers an argument against paranoia, inasmuch as the menace of the mysterious, manipulative Metalunans ends up collapsing like a house of cards before the humans' eyes. Thus, critics who endeavor to treat the film as a typical product of its era are doomed to failure, as aptly illustrated by Cyndy Hendershot's essay "The Atomic Scientist, Science Fiction Films, and Paranoia," which should be read by all aspiring scholars as an object lesson on the importance of reconsidering one's argument in face of clearly contradictory evidence.[45] Oblivious to all the obvious problems, Hendershot undertakes to bludgeon the square peg of Cal Meacham into the round hole of "heroic atomic scientist," with genuinely embarrassing results. Other scholars of the era have tended to steer clear of *This Island Earth*, perhaps well aware that their own, similar arguments would probably crash upon its shores; only Raymond Durgnat and Gary Westfahl have offered lengthy and sympathetic readings of the film.[46]

---

45. Cyndy Hendershot, "The Atomic Scientist, Science Fiction Films, and Paranoia: *The Day the Earth Stood Still*, *This Island Earth*, and *Killers from Space*," *Journal of American Culture* 20:1 (Spring, 1997), 31-41.

46. Raymond Durgnat, "The Wedding of Poetry and Pulp—Can They Live Happily Ever After and Have Many Beautiful Children?," *Films and Feelings* (Cambridge, Massachusetts: M.I.T. Press, 1967), 251-267; Gary Westfahl, "From the Back of the Head to Beyond the Moon: The Novel

It is finally a strange tribute to this strange film that it was chosen as the centerpiece of *Mystery Science Theater 3000: The Movie* (1996), for as its producers acknowledged, that project required a film that, unlike most of its targets on television, was actually worth paying to watch in a theatre—with or without sardonic wisecracks in the background. However, instead of ridiculing the film's singular oddities, one should more properly celebrate them, since there is literally no other film from the 1950s that is quite like *This Island Earth.*

---

and Film *This Island Earth,*" *Science Fiction, Children's Literature, and Popular Culture* (Westport, Connecticut: Greenwood Press, 2000), 49-68.

8. 1958: SCIENCE FICTION FILM'S SENSE-OF-WONDERFUL YEAR

It would be an interesting question for a panel at a science fiction convention: What was the most important year in the history of science fiction film? One might choose the year that saw the appearance of a single landmark film, such as 1927 (Fritz Lang's *Metropolis*) or 1936 (William Cameron Menzies's *Things to Come*). 1950 would be a good candidate, since that was the year when *Destination Moon* and its cheap imitation *Rocketship X-M* effectively established science fiction as a recognized film genre. I am tempted to argue for 1968, the year that brought us the greatest science fiction film of all time (the intriguingly cryptic *2001: A Space Odyssey*) and the most influential science fiction of all time (the comfortably familiar *Planet of the Apes*, which showed Hollywood executives that they could profit by investing in exotic-looking adventures while still following conventional formulas, making this landmark film the direct ancestor of most modern science fiction films). It would be hard to overlook 1977, with its one-two punch of the classic *Star Wars* and the risible *Close Encounters of the Third Kind*, films that had an unprecedented impact upon popular culture. And of course there is 1982, the year that showed us how high science fiction film could reach (*Blade Runner*) and how low it could sink (*E.T.: The Extra-Terrestrial*).

However, my own personal choice as the most important year

in the history of science fiction film is a year that most people would not even consider: 1958. And while there remains time for a discussion of that year's science fiction films to qualify as a fiftieth-anniversary celebration, I would like to explain why I believe that year represents a uniquely fascinating and significant moment in the genre's history.

The year 1958 commands special attention, I wish to argue, because a convergence of three separate developments combined to make the films of that year unlike any other films that had preceded them, or would follow them.

First, by the time that year began, the major Hollywood studios had effectively given up making science fiction films. In the early 1950s, feeling threatened by the new media of television, they were driven to all sorts of strange innovations in an effort to keep people coming to theatres, and along with Cinemascope, 3-D, extravagant all-star productions, and investigations of the new phenomenon of "juvenile delinquents," they invested in several big-budget science fiction films, prominently including the aforementioned *Destination Moon, The Day the Earth Stood Still* (1951), *The War of the Worlds* (1953), *This Island Earth* (1955), and *Forbidden Planet* (1956). But I don't think film executives of that era ever enjoyed making films so obviously outside of their comfort zones—films about spaceships, aliens, robots, and other things they didn't really understand—and once they felt reassured that even people with television sets were still going to go to the movies, they happily abandoned oddities like 3-D films and science fiction films and retreated to more familiar territory. If they were in the mood for something out of the ordinary, their typical choice in the late 1950s and early 1960s was that subgenre of fantasy films that no one ever dares to label as fantasy films, namely, biblical epics. Otherwise, until the appearance of *Fantastic Voyage* in 1966, their dabblings in science fiction were almost entirely limited to safe, respectable adaptations of the works of Jules Verne (*From the Earth to the Moon* [1958], *Journey to the Center of the Earth* [1959], *Master of the World* [1961], *Mysterious Island* [1961]) and H. G. Wells (*The Time Machine* [1960], *The First Men in the Moon* [1964]). And this meant that the making of science fiction films became almost exclusively the territory of low-budget, independent filmmakers, and while their budgets were miniscule, and their talents on and off the screen often questionable, they had to little to lose in making their cheap, hasty productions, and hence they were open to taking risks that no major studio would consider.

Second, the Soviet launch of the Sputnik satellite on October 4, 1957, soon followed by the American launch of Explorer 1 on February 1, 1958, abruptly and exponentially increased public interest in outer space. Now, it no longer seemed impossible to imagine that human beings might soon travel into space, or that aliens from other planets might soon visit the planet Earth. The major studios were too cautious, or too obtuse, to respond to this sudden new curiosity about space, but minor studios had no such scruples, and they were perfectly willing to cancel plans for another exploitative saga of troubled youth and seek greater profits by improvising a new scenario having something to do with rocketships or aliens. (Thus, in response to Sputnik, Roger Corman literally came up with *War of the Satellites* [1958] in a matter of days and had the film in theatres six months after its launch.)

Third, by the year 1958, science fiction films, even though they had essentially emerged only eight years ago, were in a sense facing their first crisis, a palpable sense that certain basic formulas had now been exhausted. After so many films following similar patterns had appeared, a filmmaker could no longer feel comfortable making yet another film simply involving a giant mutated insect rampaging through the countryside, a scientist transforming a man into an ugly rubber-masked monster, or sinister humanoid aliens intent upon conquering the Earth. These time-honored tropes did not have to be entirely discarded, but filmmakers felt impelled to come up with some novel variation on the theme, some new approach or gimmick, that would make their films seem different from their innumerable predecessors.

Thus, by the year 1958, a small army of innovative film-makers on the fringe of the industry had been given science fiction film as their own private domain; the embryonic Soviet and American space program had made such films more appealing than ever as ways to lure audiences to theatres; and the people creating these films were especially motivated to develop fresh ideas to enliven their old stories. The stage was set, in other words, for the production of films that, despite their palpable flaws, were singularly unique and fascinating.

* * * * * * *

Yet abstract arguments can never establish the special qualities of the science fiction films made in 1958; one must examine the evidence. And, confronting all the extraordinary and bizarre films that were released that year, the only problem is: where, oh where, to begin?

Well. For reasons that will become apparent, one cannot epitomize this year by attempting to compile a list of its Ten Best Films; but I can offer my own personal list of its Ten Most Interesting Films, all films I have seen at least once (though in some cases a long time ago), discussed in alphabetical order, with 1958 release dates confirmed by the Internet Movie Database.

Attack of the 50-Foot Woman. (Director, Nathan Juran as Nathan Hertz; writer, Mark Hanna.) It is at times a bit too farcical for my own tastes, but this film remains fascinating as a treatise on the sexual politics of the 1950s. Was it really the work of a bumbling alien, or is Alison Hayes' explosive growth really a literalization of a burgeoning strength and self-empowerment triggered by her husband's infidelity? Is it a sign of the era's determination to constrain women that its enormous men are permitted to merely be "colossal" (*The Amazing Colossal Man* [1957], *War of the Colossal Beast* [1958]) while the women are always measured? (This film and *The Thirty-Foot Bride of Candy Rock* [1959]) Does the fact that she is so often represented only by her huge hand signify a lingering, stifling commitment to domestic "women's work"? A 1993 television remake with Daryl Hannah attempted to tell this story more seriously, but the results were predictably both less interesting and less entertaining.

The Blob. (Director, Irwin S. Yeaworth, Jr.; writers, Theodore Simonson and Kate Phillips, story Irvine Millgate.) For once, a giant monster is not a dinosaur or a radioactively enlarged animal, but rather a strange pulsating growth run amok, apparently without intelligence or malevolent intent but menacing nonetheless as it expands and oozes through a small Pennsylvania town (an unusual, and evocative, setting for a monster movie). Teenagers Steve McQueen and Aneta Corsaut are the first to understand and respond to the menace, and unlike other science fiction films of the era that drafted teenagers to function as heroes, *The Blob* demonstrates enormous respect for its youthful protagonists. A concluding sequence with the blob menacing the audience at a movie theatre is interesting on several levels, and even a jarringly inappropriate, jazzy score only serves to heighten the film's strange ambience.

The Colossus of New York. (Director, Eugene Lourié; writer, Thelma Schnee, story Willis Goldbeck.) Accompanied by crashing piano chords (making this another film with an unusual, but effective score), idealistic young scientist Ross Martin is saved from death by having his brain transplanted into an enormous metal body, whereupon he predictably begins acting more like a robot than a human being. But ultimately, inspired by his son, he is able to integrate his new mechanical powers with his enduring compassionate nature, although to conform to the sensibilities of its era the film must end with this hybrid creature's death. Overall, this probably qualifies as the most *moving* science fiction film of 1958, and if you are interested in studying "cyborgs in science fiction film and television," this is where you must begin.

The Crawling Eye. (Director, Quentin Lawrence; writer, Jimmy Sangster, story Peter Key.) This is the cuckoo in my nest, as a film made in Great Britain and based upon an earlier television series, but somehow it just seems to fit in. Purists may insist upon using its original British title, *The Trollenberg Terror*, but despite the fact that the American title does spoil the suspense, even purists must admit that it's a much better title. Essentially, this is two films: for much of its length, it is a crisp, atmospheric account of a mountain resort where a strange cloud comes to hover and a woman with psychic powers disquietingly detects an alien presence; then, after we learn that the cloud conceals enormous, one-eyed creatures with tentacles (surely the inspiration for the recurring alien villains in the "Treehouse of Horrors" episodes of *The Simpsons*), it abruptly becomes a very different sort of movie, much more akin to its American counterparts. It is a film that lingers in one's memory when other, apparently more worthwhile films are long forgotten.

The Fly. (Director, Kurt Neumann; writer, James Clavell, story George Langelaan.) Yes, one can appreciate the more nuanced and gradual blending of man and fly exhibited by Jeff Goldblum in David Cronenberg's 1986 remake, but perhaps the sheer horror of becoming half-man, half-fly was better conveyed by the simpler device of placing a huge fly head on David Hedison's shoulders. And while the first sequel *Return of the Fly* (1959) contrives to provide its scientist hero with a happy ending, the original film singularly embraced the inevitably tragic result of his misguided experiment—that the scientist, to end his misery, would be compelled to ask his wife to kill him off by crushing his insect head with a huge vise. And one is awed by the compounded pain of the film's surprise ending: the chance discovery of the other sad product of the scientist's mishap, a fly with a tiny human head crying "Help me" as it struggles to escape from a spider's web. In sum, the remake was an admirable film in many respects, but even a talent like Cronenberg could not quite outdo the impact of its clumsier predecessor.

I Married a Monster from Outer Space. (Director, Gene Fowler, Jr.; writer, Louis Vittes.) Unquestionably it sports one of the best titles ever devised for a science fiction film—testifying to a 1950s paranoia so pervasive as to penetrate even into the bridal suite—and the film also includes one of the genre's most memorable scenes (when a flash of lightning abruptly reveals that a woman's new husband is really a loathsome alien in disguise). Since the alien is portrayed by real-life closeted gay Thomas Tryon, there is the inevitable suggestion of a gay subtext (since many homosexual men in the 1950s, compelled by society to marry women they had no feelings for, undoubtedly felt like aliens, and seemed like aliens to their wives)— especially considering that at the end of the film, in search of "real men" to help her combat the alien menace, the distraught bride goes to the waiting room of a hospital's maternity ward, knowing that fathering a child proves that a man is really human (and is really macho too). Yet, more broadly, the film also speaks to the way that science fiction fans both straight and gay may feel that they are effectively aliens living in a society that conspicuously does not share their values.

It! The Terror from Beyond Space. Director, Edward L. Cahn; writer, Jerome Bixby.) This film is renowned as a precursor to *Alien* (1979), even though its menacing stowaway is more prosaically humanoid in appearance and the weapon of choice to be used against it is an ordinary gun which would, if fired on board an actual spaceship, penetrate the hull and doom its inhabitants to a swift and airless death. But the disturbing message is the same: we can build spaceships to protect ourselves from unknown dangers, but those dangers may be able to overcome our best defenses and menace us within our most secure chambers. And the film projects a subdued but furious energy that makes it hypnotically compelling viewing even for those disinclined to search for deeper meanings.

Queen of Outer Space. (Director, Edward Bernds; writer, Charles Beaumont, story Ben Hecht.) In the late 1950s, as the story goes, veteran Hollywood writer Ben Hecht had shrewdly seen where the industry was going—toward idiotic yarns about male astronauts who travel to planets inhabited only by beautiful, man-hungry women—and when he jokingly described that scenario at a Hollywood party, an eavesdropping producer proved him right by immediately buying the rights to his story and giving him screen credit for the completed film. Proceeding with the polite stiffness of a high school play, the film functions as both an expression or, and a commentary on, the worst tendencies of 1950s science fiction films, its thoroughgoing lack of conviction displaying, I would argue, the lingering influence of Hecht's original satiric intent. Though its response to the protofeminist dilemma is most conventional—namely, that women must liberate themselves by rejecting the guidance of other, bitchy women and falling into the arms of handsome men—it is a film which suggests, like *Attack of the 50-Foot Woman* and *I Married a Monster from Outer Space*, that women's issues were indeed an increasing preoccupation of American society in the 1950s.

Space Master X-7. (Director, Edward Bernds; writers, George Worthing Yates and Daniel Mainwaring.) By ordinary standards, this is undoubtedly the most awful film on my list, its brief story largely conveyed by a voiceover narration suggesting that most of its soundtrack was accidentally lost. Yet this tale of a contaminated woman who engenders lethal alien goo— "bloodrust"—wherever she goes was surely the film that scared me the most as a child, impelling me to start looking under hotel beds to see if any bloodrust had been left behind by the previous guest. In a way, this film cunningly domesticates the menace of *The Blob*, taking the alien amoeba out of the street and hiding it in your closet; and while, as already indicated, a conspicuous lack of artistry on the screen can have its own special power, this is the one film on my list that I wish had been made with a little more care, and the film that would provide the best basis for an updated remake.

Teenage Cave Man. (Director, Roger Corman; writer, R. Wright Campbell.) You've probably been wondering when Roger Corman would appear on this list, since it would indeed be impossible to omit him. And while *War of the Satellites* proved rather dull, *Teenage Caveman* is one of his better films, despite a story line that, even at the time, was a cliché to science fiction readers: a prehistoric caveman disobeys orders and ventures into a forbidden zone where he discovers that he is actually living in a future world devastated by nuclear war that has retreated to savagery. But Corman tells the tale with an appealing, child-like sincerity, and even its awkwardly interpolated footage of dinosaurs from *One Million B.C.* (1940) and *Unknown Island* (1948) only serves to underline the fact that protagonist Robert Vaughn is living in a world disturbingly suggestive of several eras of human history, requiring him to puzzle out how such a world might have emerged. And its final message undoubtedly appealed to his youthful audiences: no matter how much adults have screwed up the world, teenagers will always be able to make things better again.

This list of examples to illustrate the peculiar merits of 1958 science fiction films might be greatly expanded. For example, even though it is not really a science fiction film, I regret not being able to include *The Curse of the Faceless Man*, another soundtrack-less saga exploiting the haunting notion that one of those ash-covered bodies observed in the ruins of Pompeii might come back to life and, in the manner of Hollywood's mummies, seek out a woman resembling his ancient paramour to carry her around in his arms in the vain hope of rekindling a lost romance. Then there are *Attack of the Puppet People* (John Hoyt decides to replay *Dr. Cyclops* [1940] for laughs, though the people he miniaturizes don't seem to appreciate his sense of humor); *Earth vs. the Spider* (an enormous spider emulates King Kong by going on a rampage, being captured to serve as a tourist attraction, and escaping to go on another rampage, with teenagers displaying far less *gravitas* than McQueen and Corsaut coming to the rescue); *Fiend without a Face* (a scientist unwittingly unleashes flying brains that attack hapless victims—a literalization of the power of scientific thought?); *Frankenstein—1970* (Boris Karloff, finally a member of the Frankenstein family, uses atomic energy to create a space-age monster which, after stumbling about menacingly with bandages around his head, turns out to look exactly like—Boris Karloff); *Monster on the Campus* (a professor's experiment goes awry and turns him into a murderous monster, liberated to respond to his students in the manner that most professors would *like* to respond to their students); and *War of the Colossal Beast* (*The Amazing Colossal Man* [1957] returns, much uglier and now portrayed by an actor even worse than John Langan, though a poignant victim nonetheless, finally driven to commit suicide by colliding with electrical wires). And there are other science fiction films from 1958 that I have not yet been able to see, though their outlandish plot descriptions indicate that they might qualify for my honor roll, such as *The Brain Eaters, The Flame Barrier, How to Make a Monster, The Lost Missile, Monster from Green Hell, Terror from the Year 5000*, and *The Thing That Couldn't Die*.

In sum, I argue, there was no other year in the history of science fiction film that produced so many films that, however ineptly, evoked a genuine sense of wonder, so many films that were so undeniably strange in every conceivable fashion...that wonderful year, 1958.

* * * * * * *

In response to this argument, I can anticipate a minor objection, and a major objection.

The minor objection would begin: but why single out the year 1958? Weren't there just as many memorably odd films in 1957, or 1959, or even the years before 1957 or the years after 1959? And I can sympathize with such a viewpoint. Clearly, the forces I described which brought these singular films in being did not start operating precisely on January 1, 1958, and cease functioning precisely on December 31, 1958, and in fact I regret that the technicality of a late-1957 release has prevented me from considering such remarkable films as *The Brain from Planet Arous* and *I Was a Teenage Frankenstein*, just as the technicality of an early-1959 release dictated the omission of *The Cosmic*

Man and *First Man into Space*. I still personally believe that the science fiction films of 1958 collectively outshine the films of nearby years, but an informed observer of the era's films might well feel justified in choosing another year as its high point.

The major objection would be that all of this represents nothing more than self-indulgent nostalgia; I cherish these films only because these were the films that I watched as a child, and I am too blinded by fond memories of my youth to recognize that these films, for the most part, are nothing more than inferior trash, properly neglected in favor of the better science fiction films more recently produced.

The prosaic rebuttal would be that, as it happens, I first saw several of these films, including *The Colossus of New York*, *I Married a Monster from Outer Space*, *It! The Terror from Beyond Space*, and *Teenage Cave Man*, when I was well past adulthood, and hence cannot be appreciating them solely because I was deeply affected by them as a child. I would also note that there are many films I enjoyed as a child, ranging from *Pollyanna* (1960) to the television series *Leave It to Beaver* (1957-1963), which I no longer value in any way; for that matter, I have never regarded my childhood as particularly idyllic and devote little time to thinking back fondly about it. Thus, I'm sure that there is something more to my fondness for the science fiction films of 1958 than a simple desire to recapture or celebrate the lost pleasures of my youth.

I think the issue here is clear enough: as I've been saying in print since 1991, I like my science fiction weird, unsettling, unconventional, unpredictable. We would like to believe that films meeting these criteria can only emerge from a deliberate artistic intent, meticulously realized; but they might also be the serendipitous result of inadequate resources, sheer incompetence, or blinding haste. That is, if you don't have enough money to do what you really want to do, if you don't really know what you're doing, or if you don't have enough time to think about what you're doing, you may well end up going, willy-nilly, where no filmmaker has gone before. And, with the major studios out of the picture, the field of science fiction film in the late 1950s was essentially left open to minor filmmakers who all too often lacked the resources, talent, or time to produce more conventional work, resulting in the singular collection of films that I have been discussing here. Sadly, the circumstances changed in the 1960s, as the B-movie market gradually collapsed and the big players got back into the business of making science fiction films.

Now, when you have millions and millions of dollars to spend on a science fiction movie, and thus need to earn a large profit, you are going to hire the best talents available and take as much time as you need to make your film; and as you become more and more risk-averse and demand more and more rewrites and more and more reshoots, your product will inevitably become more and more unadventurous. And that's why I am so often disappointed with contemporary science fiction films: they are very well made, they function very smoothly as diverting entertainment, but they aren't taking any chances, and they aren't making me think.

So, to fittingly conclude this look into the past by turning to the future, let us consider how it might be possible to recreate the circumstances that led to the memorable science fiction films of 1958. Already, we can observe a vast new array of filmmakers, armed with video cameras and ready to post their work on YouTube or similar websites, who are producing some striking films for viewing on the Internet. If the big producers again drift away from making science fiction films, and if some new event reawakens interest in stories about space travel or new technologies, these talents may focus more and more of their energies on science fiction, perhaps drawing their inspiration from the independent, iconoclastic filmmakers of the late 1950s who would best function as their role models. Then, science fiction film might again become what it was in 1958—cheap, unpolished, and fascinatingly strange.

9. "THE PIT OF MAN'S FEARS": REVISITING *THE TWILIGHT ZONE*

Submitted for your consideration: a television program, a very old television program, one that should be long forgotten by now. Its episodes are all more than forty years old, shot in the now-unpopular format of black-and-white film. It was the type of series that has consistently been the least popular, an anthology series with no regular characters. Even by the low standards of its time, the series was visibly produced cheaply and hastily, with "special effects" that were often on the verge of being ludicrous. As even its creator would admit, many of its stories were little more than over-extended jokes or desperate contrivances.

And yet, the late Rod Serling's *The Twilight Zone* (1959-1964) remains on the air today, decades after its last original episode was aired. Every weeknight, Los Angeles's Channel 56, KDOC, airs one or two episodes of the series, and on most holidays, the Sci-Fi Channel will garner respectable ratings by presenting a *Twilight Zone* marathon featuring twenty or more episodes back to back. Noting its improbable durability, other producers have created a feature film, a television movie, and two additional series based on the original series, all shot in color with big budgets, prominent stars, and state-of-the-art special effects, but none of them have succeeded in recapturing the magic of Rod Serling's unique creation. What, one must ask, is so special about this series? Why does it remain such compelling viewing for millions of people, many who were not even born when the series first aired?

The answer, it occurred to me today, can be summed up in one word: tragedy.

It is a word, of course, that can be defined in at least three ways. To the ancient Greeks, as famously articulated by Aristotle, it is a special sort of drama featuring a noble and generally admirable character who, nonetheless, succumbs to *hubris* and makes one mistake that inexorably drives him to an unhappy fate. In the twentieth century, feeling that this sort of story no longer resonated with modern audiences, Arthur Miller devised a new sort of tragedy, exemplified by his *Death of a Salesman* (1949): here, the doomed protagonist is a very ordinary person who, while lacking the overweening pride of the classic tragic hero, simply seems unable to cope with the demands of the contemporary world, which leads to his downfall. Finally, in general discourse, a "tragedy" is simply any sort of unhappy event; thus, when Vic Morrow and two child actors were accidentally killed during the filming of *Twilight Zone—The Movie* (1983), the event was universally described as a "tragedy," even though the circumstances conspicuously failed to match either Aristotle's or Miller's formula.

During its five seasons on the air, *The Twilight Zone* regularly offered its viewers all three types of tragedy. Consider three episodes that aired on the Sci-Fi Channel on July 4, 2007, also the day I am writing this essay. "Of Late I Think of Cliffordville" (1963) resembles an Aristotelian tragedy: its hero is a successful business tycoon who is unwisely dissatisfied, as he confesses to a janitor that he is bored by his own triumphs. When the Devil offers him the opportunity to go back in time and relive his own climb to the top, he eagerly agrees. But, pridefully, he does not inquire too much about the details of the arrangement (the Devil makes him *look* younger, but he retains the body of an old man), and he relies too much on his faulty memory and makes bad decisions (purchasing property filled with oil which is inaccessible using the technology of 1910 and hence worth-less at the time). When the Devil finally allows him to return to the present, he finds that history has been changed by his visit: he is now the janitor, and the janitor is the successful tycoon.

"A Stop at Willoughby" (1960) is very much in the mold of *Death of a Salesman*. An advertising executive, incredibly stressed out by the constant demands of his job, begins to dream that the train taking him home is stopping at an idyllic nine-teenth-century town named Willoughby, that seems to offer a soothing alternative to his maddening life. One day, when the transformed train of his dreams stops at Willoughby, he decides to get off and is briefly exhilarated by the experience of being in that town. It turns out, however, that he actually jumped off the speeding train and fell to his death; and the funeral home that comes to claim his body is called the "Willoughby Funeral Home."

A third episode, "The Invaders" (1961), fits no tragic patterns: a solitary old woman in a rural home finds herself suddenly afflicted by tiny invaders from another planet, whose spaceship enters her house. After a few skirmishes, she manages to smash the spaceship with an ax, and one of its dying inhabitants sends a final message, identifying himself as an American who has encountered dangerous giants on a distant alien world. Since we never get to know these astronauts, their deaths are simply sad, lacking the emotional impact of the death of a tragic hero, and the old woman, in destroying the beings that were threatening her, has apparently achieved a happy ending. Yet the circum-stances of her lonely life are sordid and unpleasant, and the removal of those annoying invaders will clearly do nothing to improve the miserable routine of her daily existence.

Again and again, and in various ways, episodes of *The Twilight Zone* end unhappily, whether it is the last man on Earth, anxious to spend his time reading, who breaks his glasses ("Time Enough at Last" [1959]), the beautiful woman who cannot be transformed to comfortably match the ugliness of other members of her race ("Eye of the Beholder" [1960]), or the alcoholic ventriloquist who ends up trading places with his malevolent dummy ("The Dummy" [1962]). True, there are also episodes with happy endings, such as the Christmas episode "The Night of the Meek" (1960), or episodes that at least soften the sadness with an overlay of sentimentality, like "In Praise of Pip" (1963), in which the bookie's death also allows his son to live. But these are generally not the episodes that people remember or cherish. Rather, I submit for your consideration, what keeps attracting viewers to Rod Serling's *The Twilight Zone* is its steady diet of tragedy, in all its varied forms, because we now live in an era which, in life and in the media, has strived to banish tragedy at all costs.

Consider: today, if a few cheerleaders are killed in a bus accident, you can be sure that a small army of "grief counselors" will descend upon the high school to comfort the distraught classmates and strive to make their feelings of sadness as brief and as minimal as the situation will allow. We have identified the overriding psychological problem afflicting contemporary civilization as "depression"; quite literally, feeling sad is now defined as a mental disorder which must be attacked and eliminated by means of therapy or medication. Wherever you go in California, you are daily commanded to "Have a nice day," defining the perpetually happy life as the normal, desirable life.

And all of this is horribly, unspeakably wrong. Let's face it: tragedy and sadness are an inescapable part of everyone's life. If your friend and classmate dies in a bus accident, "grief counselors" be damned, you *should* be sad, you should be *very, very sad*, and you should be very, very sad for a *very long time*; responding in any other way is virtually inhuman. The first time I realized that *The Simpsons* was going to be an extraordinary series came when I watched the first-season episode "Moaning Lisa" (1990) wherein Lisa announces that she is feeling sad; Marge, like any well-trained modern parent, insists that she break out of her funk and put on a happy face. But Lisa meets and is schooled by a blues musician in the fine art of being depressed, and the episode ends with a wiser Marge telling Lisa that it is perfectly all right for her to feel sad sometimes. How strange, I thought, that only a cartoon would have the courage to speak such heretical truths.

Instead, contemporary film and television have, in pursuit of profits, relentlessly offered only the upbeat messages that they are sure their audiences crave. Hence, however one breaks down the contemporary formula of the box-office blockbuster, one absolutely essential ingredient is clearly a happy ending. In Frank Wu's delightful short film *Guidolon the Giant Space Chicken*, the monster representing the Hollywood studio is appalled that a main character in the monster's film heroically sacrifices herself while killing the monster and insists that the film must be changed so that she survives. Here, Wu must be recalling the original *Godzilla* film (1954, 1956)—still the best one ever made—which in fact does conclude with a scientist who kills himself in order to destroy Godzilla. Four decades later, imagine suggesting to Roland Emmerich that the proper ending to his American *Godzilla* (1998) would be to have scientist Matthew Broderick die as part of his own effort to kill Godzilla. "No, no, no, are you crazy?," he would have responded; audiences will want to see Broderick live, and hug his girlfriend, and presumably go on to live happily ever after, or at least until Godzilla's inevitable return. With such an ending, and all of the other ingredients for sure-fire success in place, he knew that his *Godzilla* would prove to be overwhelmingly popular and was already planning two sequels before the film opened.

In reality, of course, the film was not a big hit at all—which suggests to me an unacknowledged truth about modern life, and modern movies. Contrary to popular belief, people aren't stupid; they recognize that occasional sorrows have to be part of their lives, and part of everyone's life, and they are starved for entertainment that displays and validates such sorrows. Consider the one film of the last two decades which really was overwhelmingly popular—James Cameron's *Titanic* (1997)– and note that it had an undeniably tragic ending (albeit one lightened a bit, in the manner of Serling's *The Twilight Zone*, with a final uplifting moment). At some point during the filming, some idiot no doubt told Cameron that the ending would never work and insisted that Jack Dawson had to survive, and if he had followed that advice, no one would remember the film today. But one likes to imagine Cameron responding indignantly: look, the sinking of the *Titanic* was a genuine tragedy that resulted in the undeserved deaths of many good people, and any honest film about that disaster has to feature the undeserved death of one good person. Did audiences object? Hardly. Instead, they kept coming back to see the film again and again and again, sensing that it was providing them with something they needed, something that all of the other blockbuster films were desperately striving to avoid—namely, tragedy.

When it was on the air, *The Twilight Zone* seemed very strange because, in the midst of the generally realistic series and films of its day, it was offering stories about aliens, monsters, robots, angels, and devils. Today, such stories are commonplace, and episodes of the original *The Twilight Zone* might seem strange only because their makeup and special effects, in contrast to the computer-generated marvels of today, seem so laughably crude to modern viewers. And that is undoubtedly why the other, similarly crude black-and-white science fiction series of the 1950s and early 1960s, ranging from the juvenile *Rocky Jones, Space Ranger* (1954) to the highly commendable *The Outer Limits* (1963-1965), are so rarely watched today. *The Twilight Zone* continues to command attention because it now seems very strange in another way—that it so frequently defies contemporary expectations by presenting stories with unhappy endings, stories that honestly and truthfully convey the point that a lot of people, a lot of the time, are inevitably destined to have considerably less than a nice day.

And it is a point that, especially today, strikes me with extraordinary force. For, although there are no major tragedies to report, the past year of my life has been extremely difficult and stressful, and there have been many times when I, and the other members of my family, have felt very sad indeed. I could easily relate to the harried executive of "A Stop at Willoughby," feeling trapped in a painfully unpleasant routine and longing for escape, any sort of escape; and there have been many days when I would have been happy to end the day by boarding a train and going to some magical place where I could get away from the unpleasant realities of my life. Watching such a story doesn't make me feel any better, but it does help me realize that my situation is not an aberration, that I am simply experiencing the pain and frustration which many people have experienced and are experiencing, and that, while I can always hope for the best, I must also realize that life never guarantees happy endings. And, I can be sure, there was no other film or television program being shown on July 4, 2007 which was bold enough to present this important message.

In sum, we continue to watch Rod Serling's *The Twilight Zone* because we urgently need to hear what it has to say, and few if any other films and television programs are saying it. Paradoxically, to fully understand the realities of our own lives, we now must keep traveling into another dimension where, in Rod Serling's words, humanity (described as "man") can singularly confront not only "the summit of his knowledge" but also "the pit of man's fears."

10. VICTIMS OF
A GLOBALIZED,
RADICALIZED
TECHNOLOGIZED WORLD;
OR, WHY THE BEATLES
NEEDED *HELP!*

(WITH LYNNE LUNDQUIST)

It is a film that is routinely ignored or derided as an inferior follow-up to a more admired predecessor. Despite several
features that obviously identify the film as science fiction—
including a serum that shrinks a man to the size of an insect and
a "relativity condenser" that slows down time—it has never to
our knowledge been critically examined in the context of science
fiction film and is never rarely included in standard reference
books.[47] And since it appears to be set in the present day, despite
its uses of fictional technology, the film manifests no desire or
intention to predict the future. Still, Richard Lester's Beatles

---

47. Thus, we could find no entry on the film in science fiction film references
that strive to be comprehensive, such as Ed Naha's *The Science Fictionary*
(1980), Phil Hardy's *The Encyclopedia of Science Fiction Movies* (1984),
and David Wingrove's *Science Fiction Film Source Book* (1985). However,
Help! is given a brief entry in John Stanley's *Revenge of the Creature
Features Movie Guide* (1988), which describes it as "A marvelous satire on
genre movies (dig that crazy incredible shrinking man parody)" (Pacifica,
California: Creatures at Large Press, 1988), 139-140.

film *Help!* (1965) arguably commands attention, over forty five years after its release, as its era's most accurate depiction of the twenty-first-century world we now live in.

One lesson to be learned from the film, then, is that genuinely visionary prophecies may result not from careful consideration of scientific realities and logical extrapolation, but rather serendipity; for the elements that made *Help!* so prescient largely resulted from the simple desire of its creators to craft a film that would be "completely unlike the original" Beatles film, *A Hard Day's Night* (1964).[48] That had been a cheap, black-and-white film; this film would have to be a more expensive color film. *A Hard Day's Night* had limited itself to drab English locations; this film would include glamorous international settings. And the first film had strived to provide a sanitized but realistic portrayal of the Beatles' daily life; this film would be an extravagant fantasy, generating conflict with cartoonish adversaries and absurd situations. To a remarkable extent, these mundane considerations engendered a film that today seems to eerily anticipate contemporary events and concerns.

The first characteristic of *Help!* which stands out is that it displays a world being transformed by a process of globalization, as once-distant realms and people now regularly come into contact and grow interconnected to form a single community transcending national boundaries. Released at a time when many Americans had never flown in an airplane or left the vicinity of their upbringing, *Help!* illustrates what was then the peripatetic lifestyle of wealthy jet-setters and would soon become the peripatetic lifestyle of ordinary citizens. The Beatles live in London, but to go on vacation, they can fly to the Austrian Alps for some world-class skiing; when they feel threatened there, John Lennon can rush to a ticket window and request a quick return to "London"; and when even Buckingham Palace does not provide the Beatles with enough protection, they can be whisked off to

---

48. Edward Gross, *The Fab Films of the Beatles* (Las Vegas, NV: Pioneer Books, 1990, 23. Subsequent page references in the text are to this edition.

the Bahamas.[49] It is not entirely without significance that one of the film's songs, "Ticket to Ride" (performed in snowy Austria), describes a disgruntled woman who obtained a "Ticket to Ride" to get "free" from a boyfriend who was "bringing her down"; for the film's narrative celebrates precisely the freedom from permanent confinement in one place that emerged from modern forms of transportation.[50]

Indeed, it is striking to notice just how many methods of traveling are featured in the film. True, people at times rely upon the ancient and not particularly far-ranging techniques of running (in the case of one character, assisted by crutches) and swimming (including a swimmer attempting to cross the English Channel who humorously crops up in unexpected locations), but one also observes Paul McCartney riding a horse, two scientists pushing a baby carriage, and characters traveling by means of bicycles, sleds, skis, a horse-drawn carriage, a ski lift, cars, an ice cream truck, a tank, an elevator, a train, an inflatable boat, a yacht, a dirigible (the Goodyear Blimp), and airplanes. Forms of long-distance communication are featured as well, ranging from books and newspapers to billboards, walkie-talkies, radios, televisions, and telephones (even used by the Beatles to communicate from one end of their room to another). Further, though they are not used in the film, the Beatles posed for the cover of its soundtrack album using semaphore flags as another means of communication. (They originally spelled out "HELP," but it was changed to the incongruous "NUJV" because the photographer thought it looked better.)

As a consequence of this enhanced ability to travel and communicate, cultures from different parts of the globe can now interact in new and stimulating ways. The ring that sets the film's plot in motion was sent to Ringo Starr by a female fan in a far-off country (clearly India, though the region where

---

49. *Help!* (United Artists, 1965).

50. John Lennon and Paul McCartney, music and lyrics, "Ticket to Ride" [song], *Help!* (United Artists, 1965).

the ring and the villains come from is identified only as "the East") who in a previous era would never have been aware of, or able to mail a package to, a British musician. In their London homes, the Beatles can enjoy reading an American comic book, *Superman's Pal Jimmy Olsen*, fleetingly seen in the background. The leader of a bizarre Hindu cult, Clang (Leo McKern), is twice observed politely conversing with a Christian cleric, once with an Orthodox priest sitting nearby; later, he and his followers construct a temple in the Bahamas. To obtain information about their plight, the Beatles go to an Indian restaurant in London that is, with one exception, staffed by British workers pretending to be Indian. In one particularly cross-cultural scene, an escaped tiger from India, raised in a Berlin zoo before being moved to London, is subdued by the sound of Britishers singing the "Ode to Joy" from the *Ninth Symphony* of German composer Ludwig van Beethoven.

The hope had been that such heightened contact between people from different cultures would inspire better under-standing and peaceful co-existence, but as *Help!* demonstrates, it can also lead to violent conflict. In previous centuries, four British musicians would have nothing to fear from an Indian cult; the two groups would probably know nothing about each other and, even if news about one group somehow reached the other, it would require a rare, difficult, and time-consuming journey for one group to actually encounter the other. By the 1960s, however, members of such a cult can easily learn about the Beatles by watching them on film, as occurs in the scene that accompanies the opening credits, and if so inclined, they can purchase plane tickets and travel to London to meet them. Furthermore, if they have some reason to strongly dislike the Beatles, they can attempt a violent attack against them.

This is all true, one might say, but *why* would such a cult feel animosity toward some western musicians? An answer to that question brings up the aspect of *Help!* that today seems most prophetic. Literally, as the McGuffin to keep the story going, the ring received and worn by Ringo is coveted by the Indians, who need it to complete the ritual sacrifice that is central to their religion; and after Ringo has worn the ring long enough to qualify as a sacrificial victim, they shift from attempting to seize the ring to attempting to kill Ringo. However, as they are more and more exposed to the technology and culture of Europe and America, one might imagine that these cultists would become more westernized, more secular, and less inclined to cling to ancient beliefs and customs, diminishing their desire to attack the Beatles. They would be emulating, in other words, the character Ahme (Eleanor Bron), who while officially a member of the cult has now, clearly, rejected their doctrines, looks comfortable in western clothes and settings, and happily intervenes again and again to save Ringo and the other Beatles from the machinations of her ostensible leader. Obviously the screenplay's authors, Marc Behm and Charles Wood, thought that the modern-day persistence of such antiquated beliefs was implausible and, solely seeking to create an amusing fantasy, envisioned this cult as exactly the sort of silly villains that their fantastic story required.

However, as the film unfolds, we observe the other cultists, despite their increasing familiarity with western ways, actually becoming more fanatical, not less fanatical, about their religion; and in keeping with the plot's escalating action, this inadvertently illustrates exactly what has happened throughout the world during the last fifty years. As people in Asia and Africa were increasingly exposed to secular western cultures, followers of certain religions outside of that milieu often responded defiantly, growing more fiercely devoted than ever before to age-old beliefs, and in some cases they grew determined to defend those beliefs with violent attacks on the Americans and Europeans perceived as threats to their religions.

In a nutshell, then, *Help!* may be the first film that depicts westerners being repeatedly victimized by homicidal terrorists motivated by intense devotion to a religion associated with Asia—the phenomenon which has recently dominated the news, and one that was rarely if ever anticipated in other science fiction works. True, the film features terrorists from an offshoot of Hinduism, not Islam, but there are real-life Hindu terrorists who have resorted to violence (though their activities, so far, have been confined to the Indian subcontinent). And while a few of Clang's assaults upon the Beatles might look farcical—a magnetized elevator, or a lavatory hand drier powerful enough to suck in Ringo's arm—some of them—like firing a bazooka at a tank, setting off piles of explosives, or releasing poisonous gas—are, when viewed today, uncomfortably reminiscent of actual terrorist attacks that have been widely reported in the mass media.

What makes the cultists so dangerous in *Help!*, and what makes actual terrorists so dangerous today, is that despite their ongoing devotion to an ancient religion, they have access to, and are willing to employ, advanced scientific technology. Thus, while Clang and his associates sometimes brandish traditional weapons like swords, they also fire guns, use chain saws, drive cars, pilot airplanes, and communicate with walkie-talkies. And the Beatles are vulnerable to this mechanized mayhem, in part, because they themselves are dependent upon advanced technology: unwilling to prepare their own food, they rely on vending machines in their home; unwilling to walk up a stair-case, they take an elevator; unwilling to dry their hands with paper towels, they walk to an electronic hand drier. All of these habits provide openings for violent assaults upon Ringo and his ring.

Thus, we can fully grasp precisely why the Beatles are in such dire straits: globalization has made them easily accessible to foreign opponents, radicalized those persons to the point where they wish to violently attack westerners, and provided them with sophisticated technological tools to make them formidable foes. This is the situation that contemporary residents of America and Europe find themselves in, as members of extreme Islamic cults communicate by means of the Internet and gather advanced weaponry in preparation for their next act of terrorism.

However, science is also a menace to the Beatles, and to modern citizens, in a second way; for it is not merely the devices invented by scientists, but the scientists themselves, who may become threats. In the film, their efforts to remove Ringo's ring lead the Beatles to two British scientists, Foot (Victor Spinetti) and Algernon (Ray Kinnear), who immediately begin to covet the ring for themselves because of its amazing properties. Soon, then, the Beatles are facing attacks from two fronts, as the scientists join the cultists in launching their own violent efforts to obtain the ring. In some respects, Foot is precisely what John calls him—the standard "mad scientist" of old science fiction films, given to muttering that possession of the ring would enable him to "rule the world." However, there is also something distinctly modern about these scientists' motives. They constantly complain about the inadequate financial support they receive from the British government, and the second-rate equipment they must rely upon—Foot observes that one device "would work if the government would spend some more money"—and their desire for the ring at times seems less a quest for power and more an effort to garner more funding; Algernon jokes that Foot "is out to rule the world—if he can get a government grant," and Foot at one point says he might "interest the military" by seizing and showing them the ring.

Now, could it possibly be that actual scientists might be tempted, like Foot and Algernon, to launch violent attacks against innocent civilians simply to get more money from their government? It has already happened. In 2001, after the World Trade Center was destroyed, a second instance of terrorism soon captured everyone's attention: somebody was mailing powder carrying the deadly disease of anthrax to various parties in an obvious and sometimes successful effort to kill them. After considering other suspects, investigators eventually identified the culprit: an American scientist named Bruce E. Ivins, who as *The Los Angeles Times* noted "stood to gain financially from massive federal spending in the fear-filled aftermath of those killings" because he was "listed as a co-inventor on two patents for a genetically engineered anthrax vaccine" and "listed as a co-inventor on an application to patent an additive for various biodefense vaccines."[51] In other words, Ivins set out to murder innocent people as part of a scheme to get the government to provide more generous subsidies for his research—which is precisely why Foot and Algernon were willing to murder Ringo to obtain his ring. Granted, Ivins's plot may represent the only example to date of a working scientist who turns to terrorism, but with seemingly increasing numbers of scientists falsifying research findings in efforts to boost their reputations and enrich their bank accounts, one cannot discount the possibility that, in hard economic times, other scientists may also resort to violence if it seems likely to be profitable. And *Help!* was perhaps the first film to predict such activities.

Considering what the film has to say about globalization and its threats, we may be able to interpret what was previously regarded merely as random absurdity: the fact that *Help!* concludes by announcing, "This film is respectfully dedicated to the memory of Mr. Elias Howe who, in 1846, invented the sewing machine." Figuratively, one might say that advanced means of transportation and communication have, in effect, sewn together different parts of the world to form one vast tapestry, making Howe's sewing machine a metaphor for the process that threatened the Beatles' lives. But the invention also represents a more literal milestone in the history of technology: while machines had previously become part of everyday life, they had been devices that users understood and could, if necessary, construct or repair. The sewing machine may be the first machine that people regularly brought into their homes and used every day without really understanding how it worked; and while making advanced technology available to people without a scientific background has proved a boon in many respects, it also opened the door to the true problem of terrorism: that

51. David Willman, "Suspect Stood to Gain from Anthrax Panic," *The Los Angeles Times*, August 2, 2008, A1; also available at http://articles.latimes.com/2008/aug/02/nation/na-anthrax2 .

people like Clang, without knowing how to build or fix advanced weapons, can readily obtain those weapons and figure out how to use them to deadly effect. That is, if the fanatics seeking the ring had relied only on swords, the Beatles would have had little to worry about; it is resources like explosives, bazookas, powerful magnets, and a shrinking serum that make them a genuine menace. Similarly, while we can now take precautions to ensure that terrorists with box cutters cannot commandeer an airplane, experts in counter-terrorism constantly worry that terrorists will obtain and use biological, chemical, or even nuclear weapons against perceived foes. It has happened at least once—the sarin gas attacks on Japan's subways in 1995, a real-life replay of one of Chang's attacks—and may happen again at any time.

One final question: if *Help!* indeed accurately predicted the plight that citizens confront today, does it also say anything about possible solutions? The film does offer answers to the problem of terrorism, but these are not necessarily reassuring.

First, people who feel threatened can, like the Beatles, seek and obtain "protection," though this may prove ineffectual. In the film, the soldiers recruited by Superintendent Gluck of Scotland Yard (Patrick Cargill), even as they surround the Beatles with tanks, do nothing to prevent an attempt to blow up the Beatles by means of explosives placed in an underground tunnel; later, by allowing the Beatles to get ahead of them while on a walk, the soldiers leave them exposed to another attack. Although the white-uniformed Bahaman soldiers, despite their comically small numbers, are able to round up at least some cultists, they also fail to rescue Ringo from a final effort to make him their victim. Similarly, today's celebrities are always accompanied by trained bodyguards; increasing numbers of government officials and presidential candidates are continuously guarded by the Secret Service; and ordinary citizens, at least when traveling by air, are protected by security personnel at airports and armed air marshals who travel in plain clothes on many flights. All these precautions, however, did not prevent Umar Farouk

Abdulmutallab from attempting to blow up an airplane landing in Detroit.

Second, potential victims may be saved if there is a double agent within the terrorists' ranks, working to thwart their plans. Though Ringo and the other Beatles did nothing to bring about this fortuitous situation, they are rescued, time and again, simply because Clang's associate Ahme is secretly on their side and regularly intervenes to protect them. In real life, government agents constantly strive to infiltrate terrorist groups to gain information about, and prevent, ruinous attacks. For example, attempts by four would-be terrorists to bomb New York synagogues failed because an FBI informant had joined the group and made the authorities aware of their plans. However, governments are not always able to plant such informants, as evidenced by successful attacks by terrorists with no traitors in their midst.

Third, in some situations, ordinary citizens may be able to fight back against terrorists. In the film, after passively allowing themselves to be the targets of innumerable attacks throughout the film, the Beatles finally take George Harrison's advice and go on the offensive, as they actively seek out the cultists' transplanted temple in the Bahamas while riding bicycles (perhaps signaling an impulse to become less dependent upon modern technology) and participate in partially successful plots to trap their foes by having other members of the group disguise themselves as Ringo. In real life, on September 11, 2001, one hijacked airplane intended to demolish the White House instead crash-landed in a field because the plane's passengers, alerted to what was going on elsewhere by cell phones, rose up against the terrorists and prevented the attack (albeit at the expense of their own lives).

Fourth, if all else fails, people may have to rely on sheer dumb luck to be rescued from terrorist attacks. In the film, since Ahme knows nothing about Foot and Algernon's efforts to obtain the ring, their attacks must be thwarted in this serendipitous fashion: when Foot brandishes a gun, it doesn't go off, and when the scientists deploy their "relativity condenser" to slow down the Beatles, its excessive use of electricity blows the "royal fuse" and shuts down the equipment.[52] And after Clang finally figures out that Ahme is working against him, captures her, and prepares to sacrifice Ringo, the hapless Beatle is spared by an implausible stroke of luck: the ring, which has stubbornly remained on his finger throughout the film despite vigorous efforts to remove it, suddenly falls off, meaning that he can no longer be sacrificed, and when Clang instead finds himself wearing the ring, he comically becomes the intended victim. Some actual terrorist efforts have been unsuccessful for similar reasons; thus, the only reason why that airplane landed safely in Detroit is that Abdulmutallab, fortuitously, proved clumsily unable to detonate the explosives he was wearing.

One final strategy for avoiding terrorism is illustrated not by *Help!* but by what happened to its stars after making that film. One reason why the Beatles had so effectively portrayed victims in *Help!* was that they themselves, during its production, actually felt like victims; John famously complained that he had been made "an extra in my own film" and that the film was entirely "out of our control" (cited in Gross 23, 24). Consequently, despite a contractual obligation to make a third film, the Beatles effectively refused to do so, ending their careers as film actors: in 1966, they began rejecting a series of scripts especially prepared for them; agreed to support the creation of an animated film, Yellow *Submarine* (1968), in the mistaken belief that it would be acceptable as their third film; and ultimately arranged for footage filmed for a proposed television documentary to be refashioned as a feature film, *Let It Be* (1970), to provide the promised third Beatles film without their having to actually make a film. Furthermore, during their 1996 world tour, the Beatles famously failed to appear at a scheduled event hosted by the First Lady of the Philippines, Imelda

---

52. One reliable expert on the Beatles, Mark Lewisohn, called the device a "Relativity Cadenza" in *The Complete Beatles Chronicle* (1992; London: Hamlyn, 2003, 188); however, when I viewed the film, the word sounded more like "condenser," and that does make more sense.

Marcos—because they had never agreed to do so—prompting the government to retaliate by, among other things, refusing to provide protection against a violent, angry mob as they were leaving the country, effectively exposing them to a form of government-sponsored terrorism.

Then, as a result of this and other unpleasant developments during that tour (such as American demonstrations protesting John Lennon's comments about the Beatles and Jesus Christ, accompanied by death threats) the Beatles refused to tour again. By withdrawing from filmmaking and touring, the Beatles were essentially protecting themselves by "cocooning," limiting themselves to the comforting confines of their homes and recording studios—until John, long after the Beatles' breakup, chose to enjoy the freedom of New York City, happily walked around without bodyguards, and consequently became the target of a deranged assassin who had just flown in from Hawaii, tragically illustrating the dangers of contemporary life that he and the other Beatles had long avoided. And many ordinary citizens, fearful of terrorism and other threats, are now responding, as the Beatles responded, by declining to travel and spending most of their time at home.

Thus, the ultimate irony of globalization may be that many people, feeling that the risks outweigh the benefits, will refuse to take advantage of its many opportunities for cross-cultural interaction and choose to live as their ancestors were forced to live, constantly confined to the small, homogeneous regions where they reside. The only difference is that today, such cocooned individuals can employ improved communication systems to stay in touch with the world by means of television, radio, cell phones, and the Internet. And one thing they can do on their computers, of course, is to watch downloaded footage from *Help!* and perhaps find a special relevance to their cloistered, anxiety-ridden lives in the lyrics of its title song:

> And now my life has changed in oh so many ways,
> My independence seems to vanish in the haze.

But every now and then I feel so insecure,
I know that I just need you like I've never done before.[53]

Whether we will really receive needed "help" to deal with the insecurities of our changed contemporary lives remains to be seen, but at least watching this uniquely prescient film can entertainingly and incongruously make all of its tragic aspects briefly seem more like a comedy.

---

53. John Lennon and Paul McCartney, music and lyrics, "Help!" [song], *Help!* (United Artists, 1965).

11. WHERE NO MARKET HAS GONE BEFORE: "THE SCIENCE-FICTION INDUSTRY" AND THE *STAR TREK* INDUSTRY

In 1953, the ever-prescient Hugo Gernsback wrote an editorial for his magazine *Science-Fiction Plus*, "The Science-Fiction Industry," which began by conventionally summarizing the recent expansion of science fiction in books, magazines, television, comic strips, and films. However, after discussing "what may be termed as the 'two dimensional' aspect of science-fiction: the printed word, radio and television, and the film," Gernsback added that "in recent years, a new form has been added: *the third dimensional world of science-fiction.*" He elaborated:

> These new three-dimensional forms of science-fiction which are now beginning to swamp our stores consist of toys, games, gadgets, scientific instruments of all kinds, wearing apparel for youngsters, and countless other constantly-evolving, ingenious devices.
> Space helmets of every description, space-suits, space guns, space shooting ranges, Space Cadet modelcraft, space viewer picture guns, "Buck Rogers Sonic Ray Gun," "Official Space Patrol Watch," "Space

Patrol Monorail Train," "Meteor Express" (imported), dozens of space rockets and space ships—these are only a small part of the large catalog of this type of merchandise now to be found in thousands of stores.

Remember, this is only a modest beginning.... So far, little has been produced for the youngsters from ten years upward. This easily may become the most lucrative three-dimensional market.

While he proceeded to optimistically predict more sophisticated—and more educational—products of this kind, Gernsback clearly was willing to accept such materials as an integral part of the science fiction field, which in tandem with its other forms "will certainly play an impressive role in the future."[54]

Gernsback's assertion that the science fiction merchandise of the 1950s represented only a *"modest beginning"* may qualify as his most accurate prophecy, for new science fiction films and television series today invariably engender huge numbers of the sorts of products he discussed—not only toys and games for children, but souvenirs and collectibles for adults as well. (The related phenomena, not further discussed here, are "original" works based on products, featuring characters from toys and video games, like the *Transformers* movies, and works created primarily or solely to serve as the basis for marketing activities, like the Masters of the Universe cartoons and films.) Indeed, the descriptive phrase Gernsback proudly coined—"The Science-Fiction Industry"—might be used by a critic today to epitomize everything that is wrong with modern science fiction.[55]

---

54. Hugo Gernsback, "The Science-Fiction Industry," *Science-Fiction Plus*, 1 (May, 1953), 2. Later page references in the text are to this edition.

55. There were several commentaries on this theme during the 1990s, the most extensive being Christina Sedgwick's "The Fork in the Road: Can Science Fiction Survive in Postmodern, Megacorporate America?," *Science-Fiction Studies*, 18 (March, 1991), 11-52. Different perspectives on these concerns can also be found in the essays collected in Gary Westfahl,

The situation could be described in this way: in the beginning, or at the core, there may be a worthwhile original work; but postmodern megacapitalism, determined to exploit that work to a maximal extent, replicates the work in all conceivable ways and attaches its name and images to every imaginable piece of merchandise that might be successfully foisted upon easily duped consumers. As a result, while there remain a few valuable works that critics might profitably examine, these are now surrounded by masses of overt and covert "products" that critics should unhesitatingly ignore.

But an alternative view might be offered. Consider the mock commercial on one *Saturday Night Live* episode farcically presenting "action figures" based on characters in the film *Philadelphia* (1993). "Nobody discriminates against me!" a little plastic Tom Hanks exclaims as he blasts away with a rocket launcher at a little plastic Jason Robards, Jr. In the comic incongruity of these toys, and in the impossibility that such toys would ever actually be marketed, one observes an important principle: all sequels, spinoffs, tie-ins or merchandise based on a given novel, film, or television series *must*, at least in a small way, derive from and build on some real aspect of the original work. One cannot market action figures based on a serious adult film, just as one cannot market, say, expensive designer jewelry based on underground comic book characters. Thus, all products that emerge from or accompany a given work, no matter how repugnant or exploitative they may seem, can correctly be interpreted as outgrowths of and responses to that work—even as *commentaries* on that work. From this perspective, critics might profitably analyze not only an original work, but also all the products inspired by the work, in order to better understand it.

To test this hypothesis, one might logically turn to the largest science fiction industry of them all—the innumerable offsprings of the television series *Star Trek* (1966-1969). But to understand

George Slusser, and Eric S. Rabkin's critical anthology *Science Fiction and Market Realities* (Athens: University of Georgia Press, 1996).

this phenomenon, one must consider the story of how all these products came to be, and the two very different ways that the *Star Trek* universe expanded beyond its original parameters.

At first, while it was on NBC, the official exploitation of *Star Trek* was surprisingly minimal, even by the standards of the time. James Blish wrote three collections of stories based on *Star Trek* episodes; Gold Key produced a *Star Trek* comic book; Mack Reynolds wrote a juvenile *Star Trek* novel, *Mission to Horatius* (1968); and Stephen Whitfield, drawing heavily upon interviews with *Star Trek* creator Gene Roddenberry, produced a celebratory look at the series, *The Making of Star Trek* (1968), crediting Roddenberry as co-author. And that was about it.

In the 1970s, even as reruns of *Star Trek* episodes proved amazingly popular in syndication, products based on the series remained limited in extent. Blish wrote nine more volumes of *Star Trek* stories; with the publication of the twelfth volume, completed by his wife J. A. Lawrence after Blish's death, all 78 episodes had been immortalized in story form. Blish also contributed an original *Star Trek* novel, *Spock Must Die!* (1970), often (and erroneously) described as the first *Star Trek* novel. After the Saturday morning cartoon version of *Star Trek* (1973-1975) was launched, Alan Dean Foster generated ten volumes of stories based on its twenty-two episodes. David Gerrold, who wrote scripts for the original and animated series, published two books about the series, *The World of Star Trek* and *The Trouble with Tribbles* (both 1973), and a few other books about *Star Trek* appeared. Marvel tried its own *Star Trek* comic book, without much success, and *Star Trek* "Fotonovels"—featuring stills from series episodes with added dialogue balloons to tell stories in comic-book form—appeared in 1977. A few items of merchandise reached the stores; in the 1970s I was given plastic toy replicas of a *Star Trek* phaser, tricorder, and communicator, and I received a birthday card that included detachable, cardboard Vulcan ears. Nevertheless, given the enormous and enduring popularity of *Star Trek*, all of this represented a rather restrained exploitation of the series. It was not until 1980, after the appearance of the first *Star Trek* film, *Star Trek: The Motion Picture* (1979), and after Pocket Books launched its series of original novels, that the marketing of *Star Trek* started moving at warp-speed, further strengthened by ten later movies to date and the four successor series, *Star Trek: The Next Generation* (1987-1994), *Star Trek: Deep Space Nine* (1993-1999), *Star Trek: Voyager* (1995-2001), and *Star Trek: Enterprise* (2001-2005).

However, during the early years of official inactivity, the fans of *Star Trek* were far from idle. As described in Jacqueline Lichtenberg, Sondra Marshak, and Joan Winston's interesting book, *Star Trek Lives!* (1975), the series from the beginning attracted unusual numbers of extremely dedicated fans—and, for a science fiction series, an unprecedented number of female fans. While the series was being filmed, many people asked to visit the set; one visitor, Bjo Trimble, soon became a leading force in early *Star Trek* fandom. Fans carried on enormous letter-writing campaigns to keep the series on the air; and the cancellation of the series in 1969 did nothing to diminish their interest.

Fascinated by the series and its characters, but tired of watching the old episodes, fans began writing their own *Star Trek* stories, published only in crude amateur fanzines; some of the best of these later appeared in Marshak and Myrna Culbreath's anthologies, *Star Trek: The New Voyages* (1976) and *Star Trek: The New Voyages 2* (1978). Most stories, predominantly written by women, focused on two themes: the erotic appeal of the Vulcan Mr. Spock; and the strong emotional bond between Spock and Captain Kirk. *Star Trek Lives!* includes passages from one amateur novel, Diane Steiner's *Spock Enslaved*, where Spock and Kirk visit a planet resembling ancient Rome and Spock is sold into slavery:

> "Now," Octavian continued, "it dawns on us that I have bid the highest price ever paid for a slave, without even seeing what I paid for." The guests laughed.
> "Strip him!" Octavian ordered suddenly.

Spock stood frozen in mid-breath, unable to believe what was happening to him. His guards moved quickly, pulling off his shirt and undershirt, then proceeded to remove the rest of his clothing. Spock closed his eyes, forcing all the resistance from his muscles, as he tried to fight down his rising rebellion. He thought of Kirk, who was counting on him, and of what might befall the Captain if he didn't control himself. The guards had completed their task.

"Your money was not wasted, Prefect," Cornelius said appreciatively.

Octavian chuckled. "I had no doubts of it, Cornelius. But see for yourself."

Trying to endure this treatment to prevent Kirk from being harmed, Spock nevertheless rebels, and Octavian decides to punish Kirk. Soon, the injured Kirk is returned to Spock's cell:

"Captain?" Spock called. There was no response from Kirk. "Captain! Jim!"

Kirk seemed to pull himself together slowly, like a reluctant dreamer coming from sleep, then pulled back slightly, still steadying himself against the Vulcan's strength, to meet Spock's worried eyes. What Spock saw there was nearly enough to make him drop his gaze. For he had never seen such a terrible expression on Kirk's face, such naked hurt in his eyes in all the time he'd known him. There was a pain in them beyond anything physical Spock could see had been done to him. It cut into the Vulcan like someone running a knife through his heart.[56]

In these scenes of the naked, humiliated Spock and Spock's emotional reaction to Kirk's injury, the sexuality of Spock,

56. Cited in Jacqueline Lichtenberg, Sondra Marshak, and Joan Winston, *Star Trek Lives!* (New York: Bantam Books, 1974), 243, 245.

and the powerful bond between Kirk and Spock, come to the surface more than in the original series.

Fans did not limit their activities to writing stories: they painstakingly sewed their own *Star Trek* costumes, fabricated Vulcan ears, and built their own replicas of *Star Trek* insignias, phasers, and equipment, so they could attend conventions dressed as their favorite characters. Original drawings, paintings, and sculptures of the *Star Trek* characters were displayed and sold at every convention. (Trimble's *The Star Trek Concordance* [1976] features several pages of fan art.[57]) In the early 1970s, some fan created a crude *Star Trek* computer game that spread to every college campus in the nation; I recall playing it. The player's task was to employ a limited amount of phaser blasts and photon torpedoes to destroy an attacking Klingon ship, aided by informative comments from other crew members. Since I could never accomplish the task, my games always ended with the destruction of the *Enterprise* and the message, "A Captain Kirk you're not!" A later version involved more participation from other *Star Trek* regulars. And, as conventions of *Star Trek* enthusiasts became regular activities, another type of *Star Trek* game became standard: the *Star Trek* trivia contest, in which fans were asked to identify, for example, the exact beverage that the alien child in "The Corbomite Maneuver" (1966) offered Captain Kirk.

None of these stories, artworks, or games were created or sanctioned by the companies that owned the rights to the series; none of them emerged because of any desire for financial gain. Rather, they spontaneously grew out of the overpowering fondness that many fans felt for *Star Trek*, a fondness that could not be satisfied by endlessly watching reruns or reading adaptations of the episodes. This suggests one conclusion: viewing the many "tie-in" products—novelizations, comic books, games, toys— that seemingly accompany all major films, one logically regards them not as the results of any natural demand, but instead as

57. Bjo Trimble, *The Star Trek Concordance* (New York: Ballantine Books, 1976), 19-31.

products being foisted by greedy exploiters on a gullible, brainwashed public conditioned to purchase such extraneous detritus whenever they are commanded by the Powers-That-Be. However, no advertising masterminds or corporate executives were responsible for the first, unofficial marketing of *Star Trek*, which was an entirely consumer-created phenomenon. Surely, then, there is sometimes a natural, unmanipulated desire for stories, objects, or games based on popular films or television programs, and perhaps in some cases such products in fact represent a classic market response to legitimate demand.

As indicated, the official marketing of *Star Trek* belatedly—but wholeheartedly—took off in the 1980s. A complete description of all modern products would demand an article in itself, but a brief summary might be attempted. The first six films, all episodes of the first series, and the original series pilot were made available as videocassettes, and all of these, along with the later films and all episodes of the later four series, were later released as DVDs. In print, there have been literally hundreds of novels featuring *Star Trek* characters, some adaptations of movies or series episodes, but most of them original novels; a series of novels for younger readers featuring cadets at Starfleet Academy; an unauthorized parody series, *Star Wreck*, which generated at least six volumes; and a third comic book, produced by DC Comics, that lasted longer than previous versions. A small library of books *about Star Trek* have appeared, not only predictable items—guides to all series episodes, books about making the series and films, memoirs of cast members — but also reference books purportedly written by and for inhabitants of the future world of *Star Trek*, including Stan Goldstein and Fred Goldstein's *Star Trek Spaceflight Chronology* (1980), Jeff Maynard's *Star Trek Maps* (1980), Shane Johnson's *Mr. Scott's Guide to the Enterprise* (1987), and Rick Sternbach's *Star Trek: The Next Generation: U.S.S. Enterprise NCC-1701-D Blueprints* (1996).

Beyond celluloid and print productions, a number of products based on *Star Trek* have been marketed. For young, presumably male children, toy stores have recently featured a number of "action figures" (dolls) of the heroes and villains of *Star Trek: The Next Generation* and *Star Trek: Deep Space Nine*, as well as replicas of the starship *Enterprise*, its bridge and transporter room, and a Romulan warship. For children who do not want to play with dolls, there have also been plastic replicas of *Star Trek* paraphernalia—phaser guns, tricorders, communicators, and insignias—for full-scale play-acting. Games based on *Star Trek* include the one to be assembled from Bruce Nash and Greg Nash's *The Star Trek Make-a-Game Book* (1979), the Super Nintendo video game in which players get to "command the *Enterprise*" (as one advertisement puts it), and many later video games, usually featuring the voices of original series actors, designed for more sophisticated game systems.

For adults, especially those with a lot of disposable income, there have been "collector plates" featuring the starship *Enterprise* and its crew to be purchased at an exorbitant price and carefully preserved in hopes that later enthusiasts will be willing to pay an ever more exorbitant price for these "Limited Edition" items. (An advertisement in the April 10, 1994 issue of *Parade,* for example, announced "a compelling new issue" of "Brilliantly conceived and masterfully executed" collector plates from "The Hamilton Collection" based on the first six *Star Trek* films—for $35.00 each.[58]) The home shopping network QVC, while devoting two hours to "The Star Trek Universe," offered viewers a number of expensive products, including a *Star Trek* titanium necklace ($51.00), a clock with a picture of the cast of *Star Trek: The Next Generation* ($53.75), and Captain Kirk and Captain Picard "Autograph Plaques" ($125.00 each). There was even, for several hundred dollars, a deluxe chess set with pieces that looked like the heroes and villains of *Star Trek*.

For those with less money to spend, new *Star Trek* calendars have appeared every year. And the coffee cups—how could

58. "To Save the Future, They Must Rescue the Past," Advertisement for the collector plate *Star Trek IV: The Voyage Home*, *Parade*, April 10, 1994, 21.

I forget the coffee cups? For several years my sister, Brenda Bright, recalling my ancient fondness for the first series, would find a new one to send as a Christmas gift; my favorite one shows the *Enterprise* apparently soaring through a quadrant of empty space—but when you pour hot liquid into the cup, a Romulan warship, previously employing the "cloaking device," suddenly materializes. (For Christmas, 1999, however, Brenda found a more upscale substitute gift: a framed envelope, signed by William Shatner and Leonard Nimoy, featuring the *Star Trek* postage stamp, stamped on its first day of issue.)

With all these products and merchandise available, the unofficial marketing of *Star Trek* largely came to a halt. As committees were established to oversee the regular production of polished *Star Trek* novels, there was no longer much interest in crudely printed amateur efforts, and most of those stories could not appear as part of the official series. (Lichtenberg's Kraith stories, for example, could not be published because they violated too many established facts of the *Star Trek* universe; and the makers of *Star Trek* novels, vigilantly seeking to ensure that their products were acceptable to juvenile readers and their parents, would never sanction the barely concealed eroticism of a novel like *Spock Enslaved*.) Similarly, amateur artworks could not compete with the more attractive and authentic-looking products that professionals could produce, and no one would want to play a primitive computer game like the *Star Trek* game when more sophisticated games for the latest consoles were available. In sum, the official marketplace of *Star Trek* generally destroyed its unofficial marketplace.

There is, however, one prominent example of an unofficial expansion of the *Star Trek* universe that continued to flourish after 1979—the so-called "slashzine" cult. The premise advanced by these fans is that Kirk and Spock were in fact homosexual lovers, and many new stories have been written and have circulated among fans that explicitly depict such a relationship. As their most striking and creative effort to advance their thesis, members of the cult have cleverly re-edited footage from the original series to make it appear that Kirk and Spock are embracing, or looking at each other with longing eyes; similar scenes can also be observed in doctored photographs. Clearly, this is one form of fondness for *Star Trek* which could never be satisfied by the sanitized novels and products available in the marketplace, and the expressions of this movement, unlike others, surely endured because, in this case, none of the official products could replace them.

One reaction to these stories and videos would be that a strange fringe cult inappropriately seized upon a work of popular culture and distorted it to reflect their own peculiar priorities—an example of the process of "excorporation" described in John Fiske's *Understanding Popular Culture* (1989). Yet there have been many popular films and television series in the past thirty years, and few of them have been singled out for such treatment. Perhaps something about the series invited the slashzine reading of *Star Trek*; after all, traces of such eroticism can be detected in some early fan fiction, like the aforementioned *Spock Enslaved*. In fact, this cult may represent an extreme but defensible interpretation of *Star Trek* and its complex emotional undercurrents.

Consider this hypothesis about the hidden structure of the original *Star Trek* series. Despite their relationship to science fiction, most episodes actually adhere more closely to the patterns and themes of the romance novel. James T. Kirk (William Shatner) is the Heroine—young, beautiful, impetuous, and highly emotional. Dr. Leonard McCoy (DeForest Kelley) is the Boy Next Door—affable, down-to-earth, comforting, but not very romantic and, overall, rather boring. Mr. Spock (Leonard Nimoy) is the Mysterious Stranger—dark, exotic, and forbidding, somewhat cold and distant but nonetheless fascinating because there are hints of powerful passions concealed by his stoic exterior. Kirk the Heroine is basically drawn to Spock, despite the danger and mystery, though there are times when the coldness of Spock drives Kirk to the familiar company of McCoy. And, as Kirk cannot decide between Spock and McCoy, the two suitors compete for Kirk's affections in an overtly polite but sometimes petulant and mean-spirited manner.

Without undertaking a full analysis of the series, one can locate many aspects of various episodes that would support this interpretation. The essentially womanly character of Captain Kirk emerges time and again: in "Balance of Terror" (1966), as Kirk reluctantly takes the *Enterprise* into battle with the Romulans, he is tormented by the thought that this action might actually *kill* somebody, and spends considerable time worrying about this possible consequence; but of course a real man—say, John Wayne playing a general in a World War II movie—would order his men into a battle for a good cause without worrying about possible casualties. There is also one startling pattern: if Kirk is in fact the *hero* of *Star Trek*, his main activity should be *rescuing people from danger*—that is what heroes are supposed to do. But many episodes are built upon precisely the opposite situation: *Kirk is in danger, and he must be rescued.* Kirk is stranded on a hostile planet, so Mr. Scott (James Doohan) must locate him and transport him back to the safety of the Enterprise; Kirk and the *Enterprise* are about to be destroyed, so Scott and Spock must hastily repair the engines to save him and his crew; Kirk is dying of a rare disease, so McCoy must devise some treatment to save his life. In other words, Kirk is repeatedly cast in the role of the Heroine in peril who must be saved by a male Hero. Perhaps the most revelatory episode is the last one filmed, "Turnabout Intruder" (1969), in which a vengeful woman takes mental control of Kirk's body. Portraying Kirk with the mind of a woman, William Shatner changed his acting style remarkably little; the episode displays only a slightly exaggerated version of the way Shatner had always played Kirk. "Turnabout Intruder" was appropriately the last *Star Trek* episode, since it finally revealed the true nature of Kirk: he is a turned-about intruder, a man trapped in a woman's role.[59]

---

59. A rejoinder to this interpretation would be that Kirk regularly has affairs with beautiful women, marries a Native American woman in "The Paradise Syndrome" (1968), and meets a former lover and his now-grown son in *Star Trek II: The Wrath of Khan* (1982). However, as one convention

All I am expounding here is what might be termed a *structural* interpretation of *Star Trek*, noting that Kirk seems to take on the functions of a romance-novel heroine and that Spock and McCoy take on the functions of romance-novel suitors. One can accept this reading without imagining that there was any conscious or unconscious effort to depict Kirk and Spock as actual homosexual lovers. Nevertheless, given these patterns in the series episodes, this would be a *logical extension* of the relationship shown there. (Of course, the slashzine cult has largely ignored the possibly erotic relationship of Kirk and McCoy, but the sexuality of the Boy Next Door in romance fiction is often minimized, since his role is to essentially serve as a sexless alternative to the overtly sexual Mysterious Stranger.)

There are, then, lessons to be learned from the slashzine cult and the other official and unofficial expansions of the *Star Trek* universe. The various products, official and unofficial, that have grown out of the original *Star Trek* series allow critics to understand the essentially three-fold nature of that series and the three corresponding reasons for its appeal.

First, in the second series *Star Trek: The Next Generation*, one sees what could be termed the official interpretation of the original *Star Trek*, as developed and approved by creator Gene Roddenberry: that it was a serious dramatic series that employed the devices of science fiction to focus on and explore a number of important human questions and concerns—something like *Masterpiece Theatre* with special effects. Casting a British Shakespearian actor, Patrick Stewart, as the second *Enterprise* captain was one clear sign of this desire to provide the *Star Trek* universe with an aura of respectability.[60] Unlike the hot-headed

---

of the romance film, a heroine may in the course of the film be seen in the company of many suitors, but her true feelings are revealed by the man she accompanies in the final frame. And how do most *Star Trek* episodes end? With Kirk talking to Spock, or Kirk standing between Spock and McCoy.

60. As are, more broadly, the frequent references in *Star Trek: The Next Generation* to the works of William Shakespeare, extensively documented in several essays that appeared in the Spring, 1995 issue of *Extrapolation*.

and violent Captain Kirk, Picard insists that all conflicts can be resolved by calm conversation and patient diplomacy; and episodes religiously steered away from any sorts of violence—phaser guns and photon torpedoes are simply not the way that mature people settle their disputes. Here, no one can deny that *Star Trek: The Next Generation* is legitimately building on one aspect of the original series, which did pay more attention to character development and important social issues than other television series of its day, and which did offer several episodes, like "Errand of Mercy" (1967), "The Omega Glory" (1968), and "Let This Be Your Last Battlefield" (1969), that were overt anti-war statements. And the various upscale products based on *Star Trek* that I mentioned—the collector plates, plaques, and chess sets—similarly draw upon this sense of dignity and serious purpose to effectively enshrine the original series as an expression of the finest aspects of the American character.

However, in the old and new computer games, the action figures of Picard and his crew, and the models of the *Enterprise* and toy phaser guns for children, we observe another aspect of the original *Star Trek* series that was slighted in its second version: that it was a juvenile adventure series, rooted—like much science fiction—in nineteenth-century stage melodrama, a galactic game of Cowboys and Indians with the virtuous Captain Kirk of the *Enterprise* blasting away with photon torpedoes at the evil Klingons or Romulans. Oddly enough, toys based on the second *Star Trek* series recall the atmosphere of the first series, with its uninhibited violence, recurring phaser battles, and fist-fights. But these toys are, then, legitimately building on another aspect of the first *Star Trek* series, one that many commentators found lacking in *Star Trek: The Next Generation*, which was often lambasted as boring and slow-paced in contrast to the violent and colorful original series.

Finally, in some of the more exuberant fan fiction of the 1970s and in the later slashzine cult, we observe a third aspect of the original series—that it was a drama with flimsily concealed and highly convoluted erotic undercurrents largely (but not entirely) focused on a structural but concealed romantic relationship between Kirk and Spock. And this is another element that could not be found in *Star Trek: The Next Generation*; for all of its purported maturity and freedom from network censorship, the series was on the whole surprisingly chaste. The best illustration of this shift in mood would be the character designed to replace Spock—the android Data (Brent Spiner). Unlike the adult and often tormented Spock, Data is an eternal child, cheerful and optimistic, approaching each new experience with joy and curiosity, and utterly lacking in strong internal conflicts. Even the loss of his virginity in the first season episode "The Naked Now" (1987) did not alter his essential innocence. In keeping with this childlike atmosphere, *Star Trek: The Next Generation* initially featured a young boy as a regular character (though the role of Ensign Wesley Crusher [Wil Wheaton] was later eliminated). Also, while *Star Trek: The Next Generation* delved a few times into the repressed romantic feelings of Picard and Dr. Beverly Crusher (Gates McFadden), and William Riker (Jonathan Frakes) and Deanna Troi (Marina Sirtis), such intimations of hidden eroticism are completely absent in most episodes; and certainly, these relationships are not as interesting or as foregrounded as the Kirk-Spock relationship in the original series. Commentators who have bemoaned the absence of action and violence in *Star Trek: The Next Generation* have failed to announce its corresponding absence of underlying sexuality—but that may be another reason why the second series generally did not attract the type of obsessive fans who attached themselves to the first *Star Trek*.[61]

61. Interestingly, there are signs that Rick Berman, who inherited control over *Star Trek* after Roddenberry's death, was aware of these deficiencies in *Star Trek: The Next Generation* and attempted to correct them in the successor series he helped to create. *Star Trek: Deep Space Nine*, *Star Trek: Voyager*, and *Star Trek: Enterprise* all offered milieus that were less sanitized and less civilized than that of *Star Trek: The Next Generation* (Quark's bar in the first series, for example, also serves as a brothel), and all series feature more stories with conflict and violence. And, in the ambivalent sexuality of Dax in *Star Trek: Deep Space Nine*, a woman who

Decades ago, when Gernsback first noted and embraced science fiction merchandise, he believed that such items would eventually serve as another way to achieve one major goal of science fiction—providing scientific education for youngsters. He predicted "the more serious 'Scientific Instruction' branch of the industry" may someday have a "boom" and envisioned products like "Knockdown astronomical telescopes," "scale models (for home assembling) of the solar system," "Space rockets...which actually can ascend (by compressed air)," and "Scale models of space ships, complete with all interior instrumentation" (2). In this respect, of course, Gernsback's prophetic vision was inaccurate; but if young people are not being educated by the modern products of science fiction, critics who examine them may be educated in a different manner—as this cursory examination of the *Star Trek* industry demonstrates.

As I argue elsewhere, good literary critics, like good scientists, should always be interested in examining new data, even if it appears unpromising at first glance; and the modern tendency of narrative works to inspire hoards of subsidiary products, whatever negative effects it might have, also creates new and relevant data. When discussing computer games based on Larry Niven's Ringworld novels, Frederik Pohl's Heechee series, Piers Anthony's Xanth novels, and Frank Herbert's Dune novels—often produced in close consultation with the authors—Clyde Wilcox and Kevin Wilcox note that these games "In some ways...serve as additional sequels to the original novels."[62] The release of any major film today may be accompanied by a novelization, comic book, toys, games, and collectibles. And

---

combined her personality with that of a male alien, and in hints of a lesbian relationship between her and Kira, we see the sorts of concealed eroticism seen in the original *Star Trek*. These series, then, are following the lead not of *Star Trek: The Next Generation*, but of the first series and the products that sprang from it.

62. Clyde Wilcox and Kevin Wilcox, "New Gateways to Adventure: The Creation and Marketing of Science Fiction Computer Games," *Science Fiction and Market Realities*, 199.

while nothing has emerged to rival the size and impact of the *Star Trek* cult, smaller groups of fans devoted to other films and television series are creating their own marketplaces of amateur work; there was once, for example, a considerable body of underground literature featuring characters from the television series *Beauty and the Beast* (1987-1990). When marketers watch a forthcoming film trying to think of profitable products to accompany its release, and when devoted fans create their own stories and artifacts, they are in effect functioning as literary critics, trying to locate and emphasize key elements in those works. To be sure, the resulting products may be arbitrary and meaningless—just as some scholarly analyses may be obtuse or irrelevant; but the possibility exists that such products may reveal a certain shrewdness in evaluating their works.

In addition, even if certain items of merchandise do not perfectly reflect the character of the original narrative, they might be fruitfully examined as a potential *influence* on the continuing film or television series they derive from. Consider the action figures of characters in *Star Trek: The Next Generation*. As noted, Captain Picard and his crew engaged in precious little action during the course of their series, but the later films have been noticeably different in this regard: in *Star Trek: Nemesis* (2002), for example, Picard can be observed brandishing and firing a phaser and punching out an opponent. While a producer's desire to foreground violence in a film for mass audiences cannot be discounted as an explanation, one could also argue that, after two decades of appearing in toy stores as an action figure, Captain Picard was finally inspired to start behaving like one.

For critics of *Star Trek* in all its incarnations, then, I submit that the *Star Trek* industry requires, and will reward, serious scholarly attention. Gene Roddenberry came to believe, and wanted the world to believe, that *Star Trek* was a series that appealed to the highest and most admirable elements in human nature—concern for important social and human issues and a desire for meaningful stories and complex characterization.

But the series also appealed to some baser elements in human nature: a simplistic fondness for the clarity and simplicity of black-and-white, melodramatic conflict and the resolution of disputes with fistfights and ray guns; and a need for expressions of repressed and socially unacceptable erotic passions. Those who expanded and marketed the *Star Trek* universe, therefore, may have understood the original series better than its creator.

12. A CIVILIZED FRONTIER: MICHÉLE BARRETT AND DUNCAN BARRETT ON *STAR TREK*

For most readers, exploring Michéle Barrett and Duncan Barrett's *Star Trek: The Human Frontier* (2001) will prove an entertaining and enlightening journey.[63] The authors bring to their work a refreshing admiration and respect for their chosen subject, a determination to appreciate the various *Star Trek* series and films for what they are—rather than chastising them for what they are not—and some of their book's most effective moments come when they gently refute the unduly harsh criticisms of other scholars. Their observations are usually worthwhile and unobjectionable, if not always surprising, and they strive to explain themselves in clear, polished prose, making *Star Trek: The Human Frontier* an unusually readable text. If I found its omissions and silences ultimately more provocative than its statements, that in itself might be regarded as one of the book's many virtues.

To summarize its contents: determined to "interpret *Star Trek* in a historical, cultural context" (5), the Barretts begin, in a section entitled "The Starry Sea," by analyzing the relationship between *Star Trek* and nautical literature, making

---

63. Michéle Barrett and Duncan Barrett, *Star Trek: The Human Frontier* (London: Routledge, 2001). Later page references in the text are to this edition.

thought-provoking connections to Herman Melville's *Moby Dick* (1851), Jules Verne's *Twenty Thousand Leagues under the Sea* (1870), C. S. Forester's Horatio Hornblower novels, and Joseph Conrad's *The Nigger of the "Narcissus"* (1897). The second section, "Humanity on Trial," characterizes *Star Trek*—particularly *Star Trek: The Next Generation* (1987-1994)—as an extended examination of the basic nature of humanity, a classically modernist concern, employing to good effect devices like courtroom trials, conflicts between alien species, the splitting of individuals into two identities, and the gradual "humanization" of the android Data (Brent Spiner) and (in *Star Trek: Voyager* [1995-2001]) the former Borg Seven of Nine (Jeri Ryan). The final section, "Exhuming the Human," argues that the two series following *Star Trek: The Next Generation*—particularly *Star Trek: Deep Space Nine* (1993-1999)—move beyond modernism into more postmodernist territory, displaying new interests in irrationality, religion, and insanity, and utilizing the figures of the shapeshifter and the symbiont to explore issues of personal identity and sexual ambiguity. All points are supported by detailed discussions of selected episodes and films.

To summarize its two major omissions: first, notwithstanding the value of its genuinely illuminating references to nineteenth-century nautical literature, *Star Trek: The Human Frontier* displays a startling inattentiveness to the literature manifestly more closely related to the series, science fiction. While several paragraphs are devoted to Verne, only *Twenty Thousand Leagues under the Sea* is addressed, and not always in a manner that inspires confidence in the authors' knowledge of Verne—since the name of his viewpoint character is alternately rendered as Aronnax and Aronax, and since at one point the authors appear to mistake Aronnax for Nemo in a reference to "Aronnax's motives for giving them hell" (38-39). H. G. Wells warrants only a single mention, and giants of the field like Isaac Asimov, Arthur C. Clarke, and Robert A. Heinlein—or if you prefer, giants of the field like Philip K. Dick, Stanislaw Lem, and Ursula K. Le Guin—are completely ignored. Except for books with titular references to *Star Trek*, science fiction criticism also is generally neglected.

Second, despite an announced focus on all *Star Trek* series and films, this book has relatively little to say about the seventy-nine episodes of the original series (1966-1969); if there is some perceived need to discuss the key characters of Captain Kirk (William Shatner), Mr. Spock (Leonard Nimoy), or Dr. McCoy (DeForest Kelley), the authors typically prefer to discuss one of the films featuring those characters. Something about the original series seems to disturb or disorient the Barretts, leading them to avoid that subject as much as possible and to speak tersely and dismissively when it cannot be avoided.

To argue that these omissions are significant, one could first note that the later *Star Trek* series were heavily influenced by the original *Star Trek*, which in turn was heavily influenced by twentieth-century science fiction. In support of the latter claim, we know from Stephen Whitfield and Gene Roddenberry's *The Making of Star Trek* (1968) that creator Roddenberry's "interest in science fiction dated back to his junior high school days when a classmate lent him a battered copy of *Astounding Stories*."[64] One episode, Gene L. Coon's "Arena" (1967), was based on a published story by Fredric Brown, and seventeen episodes were written or co-written by writers who had previously published science fiction stories or novels (Jerome Bixby, Robert Bloch, Max Ehrlich, Harlan Ellison, George Clayton Johnson, Richard Matheson, Jerry Sohl, Norman Spinrad, and Theodore Sturgeon). If we include the three episodes written or co-written by lifelong fan and future author David Gerrold, that means that over one-fourth of the original series's episodes emerged from writers steeped in the traditions of science fiction literature.

In addition, despite the efforts of later series to establish their own distinctive identities, the original *Star Trek* has remained a dominating presence in all regions of the burgeoning *Star*

64. Stephen Whitfield and Gene Roddenberry, *The Making of Star Trek* ((New York: Ballantine Books, 1968), 31.

Trek universe. Characters from the original series made guest appearances on *Star Trek: The Next Generation*, *Star Trek: Deep Space Nine*, and *Star Trek: Voyager*; episodes of those series were obliged to work within the parameters of concepts established in the 1960s, such as the Federation of Planets, the Prime Directive, the mirror universe, and the Vulcan, Klingon, and Romulan cultures; and episodes repeatedly redacted or referenced plots from the original series.

For these reasons, the origins of several aspects of later *Star Trek* series interesting to the Barretts can be traced back to the science fiction that preceded the original series and/or to the original series. Three common tropes in science fiction—the god-like alien judging the human race, the shapeshifter, and the character split into two personalities—first entered the *Star Trek* universe by means of episodes from science fiction writers (respectively, "Arena," based on Brown's story, Johnson's "Man Trap" [1966], and Matheson's "The Enemy Within" [1966]). Other episodes of the original series, including "The Alternative Factor" (1967), "Metamorphosis" (1967), "Return to Tomorrow" (1968), "By Any Other Name" (1968), and "Turnabout Intruder" (1969) addressed in various ways issues of personal identity. However, except for "The Enemy Within," none of these episodes are in the index of *Star Trek: The Human Frontier*, even though the Barretts might have fruitfully related them to their exegeses of episodes from later series instead of neglecting them, one assumes, on the grounds of seeming simple-mindedness.

One could also argue that the decisions to ignore science fiction and minimize references to the original series weaken the Barretts' case, by leading them to unwise speculations and arguable assertions while also depriving them of helpful evidence. For example, the Barretts unpersuasively theorize that *Star Trek*'s "warp drive" derives from the ancient nautical meaning of "to warp," to pull a ship by a cable (12-13), although it actually emerged much earlier in science fiction to describe the idea of bending or "warping" space, a pattern of usage so endemic in the genre that by 1954, in Chapter Seven of Heinlein's *Starman Jones*, the hero can knowingly rebuke a colleague who speaks of a "space warp" by saying, "Oh no, not a space warp. That's a silly term—space doesn't 'warp' except in places where *pi* isn't exactly three point one four one five nine two six five three five eight nine seven nine three two three eight four six two six four three three eight three two seven, and so forth—like inside a nucleus."[65] While discussing the *Star Trek: Deep Space Nine* episode "Far Beyond the Stars" (1998)—which argues poignantly that the *Star Trek* universe in fact is an outgrowth of 1950s science fiction, though the Barretts miss that point—the authors posit that the female science fiction writer named K. C. Hunter might refer to long-time *Star Trek* writer D. C. Fontana; however, given that Hunter is a 1950s writer who collaborates with her husband, she almost certainly represents C. L. Moore, wife and writing partner of Henry Kuttner.

As a few examples of neglected supporting evidence, the Barretts' extended discussion of nautical metaphors in *Star Trek* does not mention Sturgeon's episode "Shore Leave" (1966), and their discussion of the importance of World War II to *Star Trek* ignores the episode "Balance of Terror" (1966), which was little more than a thinly disguised World War II submarine drama. With minimal evidence on hand, other than blatant references in the film *Star Trek: First Contact* (1996), to support their claim that Melville's "sea fiction had had such an influence on the conception of the *Star Trek* series" (177), the Barretts are driven to a questionable argument that an obscure Melville reference to underground passages between bodies of water somehow means that he originated the concept of the wormhole (35)— when they might have better supported the idea by discussing Spinrad's episode "The Doomsday Machine" (1967), wherein a captain obsessed with attacking the immense alien vessel that destroyed his starship perfectly recalls Captain Ahab. While correctly noting that Roddenberry actively sought to down-

65. Robert A. Heinlein, *Starman Jones*, 1953 (New York: Dell Publishing, 1967), 78.

play the importance of religion, they fail to employ scintillating supporting evidence from the conclusion of the episode "Obsession" (1967), when Spock upbraids Scott for exclaiming "Thank heavens" by replying, "Mr. Scott, there was no deity involved; it was my cross-circuiting to B that recovered them."[66]

In sum, one could readily assemble a considerable amount of ammunition in order to assail *Star Trek: The Human Frontier* for its shoddy, inadequate research regarding important aspects of *Star Trek*'s development. Still, although gathering such evidence might be justified as a stimulating exercise, I do not wish to advance that argument—choosing instead to appreciate the book for what it is, rather than chastising it for what it is not. Yes, *Star Trek: The Human Frontier* might have been a better book with more references to science fiction and more references to the seminal original series, but it is also a perfectly good book without those references; the authors may be neglecting other productive contexts, but they make *Star Trek* perfectly comprehensible within the contexts of their own choosing. What the Barretts' book unintentionally but powerfully demonstrates, then, is the triumph of *Star Trek* over its own origins.

In the beginning, *Star Trek* was a series continually assembled in haste, largely relying, like most programs of its era, on scripts and stories submitted by independent writers to achieve its demanding quota of twenty-six episodes per season. While Roddenberry struggled valiantly to maintain a sense of overall logic and purposefulness to his series, its cohesiveness inevitably suffered in light of the incessant need to find a script, any decent script, and start filming it next Monday. Some signs of sloppiness and incongruities were inevitable: intending basically to validate the integrity and judgment of Captain Kirk, the series nevertheless filmed an episode ("Errand of Mercy" [1967]) that presented Kirk as a belligerent fool; determined, as the Barretts correctly note, to minimize religion as an outmoded belief system, the series nevertheless filmed an episode ("Bread

66. "Obsession," *Star Trek* (New York: NBC-TV, December 15, 1967).

and Circuses" [1968]) with a subplot featuring sympathetic Christians (first called "sun worshippers," later clarified to mean "son worshippers"). They were undoubtedly the best scripts available at the moment, and there was no time for revisions. Overall, then, it is understandable why some scholars might choose to avoid the original series as crude, inconsistent, weak in overall vision, and a bit messy to deal with—resembling in these ways, as it happens, the science fiction literature of the 1930s, 1940s, and 1950s that the series sprang from.

Yet over the years, as Roddenberry came to appreciate what *Star Trek* had come to mean for so many people, he resolved to do it better the next time, with the results of that resolution visible in *Star Trek: The Next Generation.* The juvenile elements of violence and melodramatic conflict were virtually eliminated; episodes were produced more slowly and more carefully so as to unfailingly reflect the series' humanistic philosophy and background; efforts were made to emphasize literary references and discussions of serious issues. The series also benefitted from changes in the television industry that led producers of dramatic programs to rely almost exclusively on teams of in-house writers, rather than free-lancers, making it much easier to achieve a smoothly flowing and unified series. *Star Trek: The Next Generation* and other later series are thus easier to approach as *texts*, the clear products of single authorial voices (first Roddenberry, later Rick Berman and other like-minded producers) operating within their own, self-devised, cultural and literary frameworks.

Star Trek: The Human Frontier signals the success of all these efforts. *Star Trek* has uplifted itself; it has transcended its seedy roots in science fiction magazines and the chaos of television programming of the 1960s, and it has transformed itself into a body of works that can be understood without reference to their origins, a body of works that can be plausibly likened to the plays of William Shakespeare (as in a special issue of *Extrapolation*), to classics of nineteenth-century nautical literature (as in this book), or to any number of other distinguished texts to be identified and discussed by future scholars. In fact, the progress of *Star Trek* to this status invites comparison to the story of science fiction itself—a literature that similarly strived to uplift itself and has similarly succeeded in making itself comprehensible without reference to its origins. There is thus an eerie resonance between the Barretts' belated discovery in 2001 that "the central preoccupation of *Star Trek*" is the question, "what does it mean to be human?" (viii) and Brian W. Aldiss' belated discovery in 1973 (seemingly unknown to the Barretts) that science fiction can be defined as "the search for a definition of man."[67] Just as the Barretts feel free to analyze *Star Trek* without learning anything about its gritty origins, contemporary science fiction scholars similarly feel free to discuss Iain M. Banks in the context of Jean Baudrillard without learning anything about the old space operas that to knowledgeable readers lurk as influences underneath his Culture novels. Depending upon one's critical stance, this state of affairs might be criticized or lamented, but one can also argue for its inevitability and even its desirability.

Still, I must confess that the new, improved *Star Trek* described so affectionately by the Barretts is for me far less intriguing than the raw, rough-hewn *Star Trek* that I first encountered as a teenager, and there are signs that even those who originally refashioned *Star Trek* to appeal to the sophisticates are growing bored with their handiwork—inasmuch as episodes of the most recent *Star Trek* series, *Enterprise* (2001-2005), and J. J. Abrams's new *Star Trek* movie (2009), both invite consideration (even more than *Star Trek: Voyager*) as a visceral repudiation of the polished, literate universes of *Star Trek: The Next Generation* and *Star Trek: Deep Space Nine* and an effort to return *Star Trek* to its primal, inchoate roots in science fiction literature. *Star Trek* itself, in other words, may be newly committed to exploring frontiers rather different than those examined by Michéle and Duncan Barrett.

67. Brian W. Aldiss, *Billion Year Spree: The True History of Science Fiction*, 1973 (New York: Schocken Books, 1974), 8.

13. MONKEY MYTHOLOGY; ERIC GREENE ON *PLANET OF THE APES*

First books should always be treated with special kindness; and, since Eric Greene's *"Planet of the Apes" as American Myth: Race and Politics in the Films and Television Series* (1996) is apparently his first book, I am tempted to say nothing but kind things about it. And that would not be difficult. The author has studied his subject well: he has watched all of the *Apes* films, television programs and cartoons; he has read all of the novelizations, magazines, and comic books; he has researched the original screenplays and rejected story treatments; he has interviewed several of the films' creators and performers; and he has examined a wide range of commentaries and critical studies. In addition to providing a wealth of information about these texts, Greene develops and supports a persuasive argument that the five *Apes* films represent first covert, then overt, reflections on American racial politics, as they argue for peaceful racial harmony but remain convinced that continuing conflict cannot be avoided. His interpretations of individual stories are generally sound, there are no significant errors, and he more than succeeds in demonstrating that the *Apes* saga merits critical attention. The book completely achieves its announced objectives and might even serve as a model for other scholarly studies of its kind.

Why, then, do I find myself ambivalent about this book?

My reason may be parochial: while Greene fruitfully connects the *Apes* films to political and racial issues, scientific thought and research regarding humans and primates, and other films and popular entertainment of their period, he fails to place these works in their most obvious context, that of science fiction.

To be sure, he states several times that they are science fiction; he is not afraid to speak its name. But he approvingly quotes *Planet of the Apes* director J. Franklin Schaffner to the effect that making a science fiction film was the least of his priorities;[68] his few general comments about science fiction are banal; and except for two references to Vivian Sobchack's *Screening Space: The American Science Fiction Film* (1987), he does not make use of any criticism focused on science fiction. (Robert Holdstock's *The Encyclopedia of Science Fiction* [1978] is listed in the bibliography, but it is hard to say how that was helpful to him.) Tellingly, the Library of Congress subject headings listed for the book do not mention science fiction, only motion pictures, television, race relations, and politics. Thus, scholars looking for studies of science fiction will not find this book; literally, science fiction critics are not part of its intended audience.

No one has argued that science fiction films should only be examined by science fiction critics, and no one could object to the attentions of a critic as respectful and diligent as Greene. It should only be noted that, when science fiction is placed in a different context, something is gained, and something is lost.

On the positive side, a new perspective can bring new insights, or new appreciation for previously marginalized works. The science fiction community has tended to enthusiastically praise the first film, *Planet of the Apes* (1968) (aside from some carping about its scientific logic, as in John Brosnan's *Future Tense: The Cinema of Science Fiction* [1978]), to be less enthusiastic about the next two films, *Beneath the Planet of the Apes* (1970) and

---

68. Eric Greene, *"Planet of the Apes" as American Myth: Race and Politics in the Films and Television Series* (Jefferson, North Carolina: McFarland Publishers, 1996), 28. Later page references in the text are to this edition.

Escape from the Planet of the Apes (1971), and to utterly disdain the last two films, *Conquest of the Planet of the Apes* (1972) and *Battle for the Planet of the Apes* (1973). This consensus opinion within the field is logical, since the first three films are most obviously in dialogue with science fiction, recalling many of its themes and texts, while the last two films largely lack those resonances. But to Greene, viewing the films as cultural artifacts, the first three films represent an incomplete, perhaps unconscious, effort to grapple with the vexing problems of American race relations, whereas in *Conquest* and *Battle*, the creators recognized their true subject and dealt with racial issues in a more forthright and satisfying manner. Certainly, Greene's long and sympathetic analyses of the neglected final films constitute one of his major contributions.

However, by not considering the *Apes* films as science fiction, Greene's argument is deprived of certain nuances. When Greene quotes the first film's comment that, while "all apes are created equal," "some apes...are more equal than others," he misses the allusion to George Orwell's *Animal Farm* (1945) and hence the possibility that, among other things, the film reflects an old preoccupation of science fiction cinema, opposition to communism (though he does detect such a subtext in *Beneath*). Discussing at length the final glimpse of the Statue of Liberty emerging from a barren landscape, Greene seems unaware that this has long been a standard icon in science fiction, dating back at least to the February, 1941 cover of *Astounding Science-Fiction*, and that the film thus evokes a tradition of post-holocaust fiction where the end of human civilization may be viewed as a beneficial cleansing and opportunity for new beginnings (what Brian W. Aldiss alternately terms the "cozy catastrophe" or "delightful doomsday"). In fact, while Greene calls the *Apes* films "dystopian and apocalyptic" (23), one can see the first film's conclusion as a happy ending: the human race has gotten what it deserved; it has been replaced by a better, if not perfect, ape society; and Charlton Heston's Taylor may be sinking to his knees because he can finally, shorn of futile ambitions, enjoy some rest, perhaps to drift into serene senility like the hero of George Stewart's *Earth Abides* (1949), watching a new civilization emerge and accepting his inability to bring the old one back. The bomb-worshipping mutants of *Beneath*, and the time-travel paradoxes implicit in *Escape*, also suggest connections to earlier science fiction that Greene never discusses.

In addition, recognizing that the genre can serve many purposes other than political commentary, science fiction critics rarely feel compelled to find explicit references to contemporary events and concerns at every point in the texts they examine; but Greene is driven to do exactly that, sometimes with infelicitous results. Consider the book's weakest passage, when Greene attempts to explain "one of the most complicated references in the *Apes* series" (129), the fact that mutant humans travel in school buses to attack an ape village in *Battle*. After devoting two pages to dubious interpretations that are clearly implausible even to their author, he lamely concludes that "Even unclear allegory may be evocative" (131). But why insist that this is an allegory? Given the theme of education that Greene correctly discerns in the film, the school buses may have simply been thrown in to emphasize the point; searching for specific connections to conflicts about school busing for integration is demonstrably fruitless. There is further wasted effort when Greene ponders the racial implications of the skinlessness of the mutants in *Beneath* (66-67); isn't "shock value" explanation enough?

Finally, insisting that the films offer serious commentary on serious issues, Greene fails to appreciate what may be the most charming aspect of the *Apes* series (and much science fiction): their spirit of humor and playfulness. After quoting a few jokes from the first film, Greene rushes to explain their serious import (35-36); he does not discuss the funniest scene in the entire film, the "see no evil, hear no evil, speak no evil" tableau, apparently because he finds no political subtext in it; and while he notes that the third film is "lighter in tone" than its predecessors (71), that considerably understates the fact that film is for much of its length played as a comedy. It is strange and unfortunate that his indefatigable search for Apesiana did not lead him to the *Mad* magazine parody of the first four films, "The Milking of the Planet That Went Ape" (in issue 157, March, 1973), for it would have provided amusing support for his thesis of a racial subtext in the films; for example, in the parody of *Conquest*, a white man defends the status of apes, declaring "we must *perpetuate* slavery! We have always *needed* slaves, and we always *will!*" An African-American then addresses the readers: "Ever get the feeling you're in the *wrong movie?*"[69] More broadly, while he documents America's ongoing fascination with the *Apes* universe, he ultimately fails to account for it: surely, people do not wear ape masks or collect *Apes* memorabilia only because they support the films' advocacy of racial justice or see its characters as wonderful vehicles for political commentary, but more because they are delighted with the sheer *otherness* of beings that are somewhat like humans and somewhat like apes, the same reason why people wear Vulcan ears and Klingon masks. Even if not a stimulating basis for critical inquiry, this source of the *Apes*' appeal should be explored.

Having described and praised the book's virtues, and having demonstrated that I know a few things about its subject that the author does not know, I have fulfilled the traditional purposes of a scholarly review. As I said, the book accomplishes its own goals, and it should not be criticized for failing to accomplish other goals. Still, since this will likely be the only scholarly study of the *Apes* phenomenon for a long time (perhaps for all time), I do wish that Greene had slightly expanded his agenda, perhaps adding a chapter where he pondered other contexts for these films, and other explanations for their popularity. And I hope that my saying these things does not seem unkind.[70]

69. Arnie Kogen, writer, Mort Drucker, artist, "The Milking of the Planet That Went Ape," *Mad*, No. 157 (March, 1973), 11.

70. A new version of this book might also fruitfully extend Greene's argument to the most recent additions to the series, Tim Burton's *Planet of the Apes* (2001) and Rupert Wyatt's *Rise of the Planet of the Apes* (2011).

14. THE ODYSSEY CONTINUES: THE RELEVANCE OF *2001* RESOUNDS IN 2001

It is the only film about space travel that is regularly chosen by critics as one of the ten best films every made, a film that continues to fascinate audiences and provoke lengthy discussions over thirty years after its initial release in 1968. And, even though Stanley Kubrick's *2001: A Space Odyssey* has now become officially outdated as an accurate prediction of humanity's future, it remains a film with much to say about what humans are and where we are going.

2001 has been analyzed countless times, and no single theory can hope to explain all of its mysteries to everyone's satisfaction. Still, most would accept that there is one unifying theme in the film, what could be called the Standard Interpretation, involving humanity's development and the use of tools. By adding a wrinkle or two to the Standard Interpretation, one can argue that *2001*, despite its apparently excessive optimism about human progress into space, correctly predicted why space travel would prove so awesomely difficult and presented its own ambitious solution.

* * * * * * *

In the film's opening "Dawn of Man" sequence, the problem

facing our ancient ancestors, it seems, is that they do not under-stand how to use tools, dooming them to lives of constant hunger and fear. Then, the alien monolith appears and enlightens one member of their band, named Moon-Watcher in the noveliza-tion of the film by Arthur C. Clarke (who also collaborated with Kubrick on the screenplay). He figures out how to use an animal jawbone as a tool, kills a pig, leads a successful bone-wielding assault on a rival tribe, and triumphantly throws his bone into the air. Then, a famous jump cut replaces the bone with a futur-istic spaceship. The bone was our first tool; the spaceship, our very latest tool. The trouble is, as the film will demonstrate, tools can only take people so far, demanding the appearance of a new monolith to advance humanity to the next level.

However, one could complain that this Standard Interpretation is incomplete, on the grounds that the monolith was surely teaching those prehistoric man-apes something else as well. Consider: we first see Moon-Watcher using the bone all by himself; but later, Moon-Watcher and his entire band collec-tively descend on their opponents, bones in hand, to drive them away. It is hard to believe that the monolith simultaneously gave everyone in the tribe the same idea to use bones as weapons, inspiring a spontaneous joint attack. Instead, Moon-Watcher must have been able to use language effectively to explain to his comrades how to use bones, and how to work together to overcome their rivals.

Did the monolith, then, also grant prehumans an enhanced ability to communicate, advancing them from expressive grunts and groans to a genuine language? While there is no specific evidence to suggest that shift, the visible progression from indi-vidual action to group action in the film conveys that definite improvements have occurred in people's ability to work cooper-atively, improvements that demanded complex language skills. (It is also significant that, after the soaring bone is replaced by a soaring spaceship, we immediately observe, within the space-ship, a third soaring object—a pen belonging to Dr. Heywood Floyd [William Sylvester], floating in the weightless compartment, which is both a tool and an instrument to communicate by means of language.)

The key events of the opening scenes further illustrate both the power and the danger of these new talents. With the capacity to create tools and communicate complicated ideas, humans can become masters of their environment (as shown when they slaughter the pig)—but they can also misuse these skills to kill other humans (as shown when they bludgeon one member of the opposing tribe). When the film leaps into the world of 2001, subsequent events will reveal the same drawbacks when humans rely solely upon tools and language to accomplish their goals.

* * * * * * *

During the next sections of the movie—Floyd's journey to the monolith on the Moon, and the Jupiter expedition of David Bowman (Keir Dullea) and Frank Poole (Gary Lockwood)— here is a game to play if you are watching the film for the sixteenth or sixtieth time: count the number of tools displayed on the screen. From the straws and scrapers employed during the film's meals to the elaborate spacesuits donned for extra-vehicular activities, humans in space are constantly accompanied by tools—necessarily so, of course. On a warm summer's day on Earth, it's still possible for people to strip down and briefly enjoy life without clothes or tools in the manner of our distant ancestors. But to survive in space, you constantly need special equipment to provide you with oxygen, protect you from the deadly vacuum, eat your food, and walk upright in weightlessness. Even though they are essential, one notices, as another motif, the negative effects of tools. The eating utensils are awkward. The stewardess' shoes for weightlessness demand a slow, ungainly style of walking. And the spacesuits are clumsy and make people unrecognizable, which makes the scene where the visitors to the lunar monolith are photographed so amusing—why take a picture when no one will ever know that it was you inside of that spacesuit?

As people in space constantly rely on tools, they are also constantly communicating—in person and by radio, television, film, and written messages—and communication is the other recurring motif in the main part of the film. Everyone, it seems, is always talking to everyone else on a fairly regular basis. Yet this communication is consistently stilted or ineffectual. Most of the conversations are consistently banal compendiums of clichés. Floyd must intently study an interminable list of instructions to use the zero-gravity toilet—another of the film's deliberate jokes. A conversation between Floyd and the Russians at the space station comes to an awkward halt due to security concerns. After Floyd delivers a stunningly insipid speech to residents of the lunar base, it is laughable to hear him lauded for his excellent work. And on his birthday, Poole receives an expensive, but vacuous, phone message from his parents. Commentators often note how detached from each other the characters in *2001* seem to be; to a large extent, they have discovered that language can at times become only a matter of formula and ritual, something that hinders communication more than enhancing it.

All these problems with tools and language are insignificant, but a major crisis eventually ensues involving the computer HAL 9000, the brains of the spaceship *Discovery* and, in effect, humanity's ultimate tool. As such, despite its miraculous abilities, HAL is also a fatally flawed tool, as it reaches the decision that the only way to ensure the success of the mission to Jupiter is to kill all of its crew. Virtually by definition, this is not a well-designed piece of machinery.

Yet HAL's murderous mistake also reflects, again, a problem in communication, as is better explained in Clarke's novel and the film's sequel *2010: Odyssey Two* (1982). HAL's original programming included the lethally contradictory instructions to keep the mission a secret from the crew, tend to all of their needs, and ensure that the mission is completed. HAL's creator recommended against these instructions, but his advice was ignored, and Bowman and Poole were handicapped in their efforts to deal with HAL because they were not told the real reason they were going to Jupiter. If there had been better communication between HAL, his programmers, the ground crew, and the *Discovery* astronauts, in other words, the entire situation could have been avoided. Instead, just as in the film's opening sequence, a combination of misapplied tools and misapplied communication skills has led to both an astounding technological advance and a series of homicides.

* * * * * * *

So, if inherent limitations in the use of tools, and in the use of language to communicate, are causing problems in humanity's world of 2001, what is the solution? First, humans must be weaned away from their reliance on tools and language, which defines what happens in the final scenes of the film. Bowman turns off HAL, depriving himself of an important tool, and in approaching the monolith orbiting Jupiter he uses only the absolutely essential spacesuit and his space "pod." Once through the Star Gate, and lodged for many years in an elaborate mansion, he is systematically stripped of all of his tools. First, he sits in his space pod within a spacious room. Then, the space pod vanishes and he walks around the room in his spacesuit. Next, his spacesuit is replaced by a black robe as he sits and eats a meal, dropping and breaking a glass. The fourth Bowman lies in bed, clad only in a white covering and completely without tools. Finally, he appears as the Star Child, a huge, naked fetus.

Along with tools, language is removed from the picture: while Bowman disables HAL, the computer's articulate language slows down and regresses to a childish song, "Daisy" (which involves tools, by the way—a "horseless carriage" and "a bicycle built for two").[71] Then, a videotape comes on to explain the purpose of the mission: to investigate an alien monolith, its "origin and purpose still a total mystery." And, after the words "total mystery"—an apt preview of what Bowman is about to

---

71. *2001: A Space Odyssey* (MGM, 1968).

experience, perhaps—not another word is spoken in the entire film.

Now completely deprived of tools and of language, Bowman becomes the Star Child, floating in orbit around the Earth. He no longer needs tools to survive in the vacuum of space, since his embryonic new body seems invulnerable, and he no longer needs language to communicate, since his large, knowing eyes suggest new telepathic powers. (This is more clear in the novel,[72] where the Star Child immediately employs his new abilities to destroy all of Earth's nuclear weapons with a single thought.) The use of tools and language allowed us to advance from prehuman to human; but to advance to a superhuman level, we must develop spectacular new mental abilities to transcend our reliance on such crude mechanisms to control our environment and communicate with others.

* * * * * * *

This is all well and good, one might say, as a vision of humanity's eventual future in space, to be achieved either through millennia of natural evolution or accelerated genetic engineering. But this is hardly helpful advice for the men and women now engaged in the practical business of maintaining and expanding the human presence in space. To them, the film might seem only a utopian dream of tremendous space advances standing in stark contrast to the dismally minimal progress evident in our actual 2001. Still, there are relevant lessons to garner from the film for the NASA engineers and mission specialists of today.

First, before criticizing what *2001* got wrong, one must celebrate what it got right. Even after thirty years of additional experience, the equipment that Kubrick imagined would accompany humans into space still looks absolutely authentic, even if frustratingly beyond current budgetary constraints. More impressively, *2001* perfectly reflects the *rhythms* of space activity. On

72. Arthur C. Clarke, *2001: A Space Odyssey* (New York: Signet Books, 1968).

the one hand, to get anything done in the vacuum and weight-lessness of space, an astronaut must engage in a long series of incremental steps, executed slowly and painstakingly. On the other hand, something can go horribly wrong in an instant, demanding immediate, accelerated action. The first time Bowman goes outside to replace that piece of equipment, the task demands many careful actions, accomplished with meticulous care; when Poole goes out to do the same thing, HAL cuts his air hose and sends him hurtling through space in an instant. Bowman takes several minutes to prepare for his perilous lurch into the airless airlock; the actual journey takes less than ten seconds. To prepare new astronauts for both the slow-motion rigor and sudden perils of extravehicular activities, a screening of those scenes from *2001* might serve well as an introductory orientation.

Acknowledging its accuracy in predicting the ambience of space, NASA has paid tribute to *2001* in a noteworthy, though unacknowledged fashion. Everyone recalls the tremendous publicity when the prototypical space shuttle, which never entered space, was named *Enterprise*, to honor the starship of the television series *Star Trek*; but no one noticed that one shuttle in the actual fleet was named *Discovery*, to honor the space-ship of *2001*. Yes, NASA officially maintains that the shuttle was named after one of Captain Cook's ships, but someone in NASA's corridors of power was surely thinking in part of *2001* when that name was originally chosen.

While the name might have seemed inauspicious, in light of what happened to the crew of Kubrick's *Discovery*, it was another space shuttle, *Challenger*, that actually ended up killing its crew—for two reasons that might have been anticipated after a screening of *2001*. First, there was a problem with faulty tools: the o-rings used in the fuel tanks were not designed to function properly in cold-weather conditions, leading to that fateful explosion. Yet there was also a problem in faulty communication: at least one person who worked for the company that manufactured the tanks understood the danger, and he attempted to warn those responsible for scheduling shuttle launches. Yet his concerns never reached the proper level of authority. The commission that investigated the *Challenger* disaster thus was obliged to recommend both changes in the design of the fuel tanks and improvements in communication between the various entities involved in shuttle flights.

Perhaps the same two problems are continuing to hinder humanity's efforts to expand into outer space. Are we really using the right tools to get there—large, chemical-fuel rockets? Probably not, most experts would agree. Yet what are the alternatives? Over the years, hundreds of people have presented their own plans for new approaches to space travel that would be more safe, efficient, and economical than our present-day vehicles. The vast majority of these people, undoubtedly, are dead wrong—but one of them may be right, and that right idea simply hasn't been properly communicated.

It is finally important to recognize that the film was not so far off the mark in its prediction of human advances into space by the year 2001. Today, we actually have a functioning space station, though it is not nearly as large and attractive as Kubrick's spinning wheel. And while humans haven't been to the Moon for quite a while, returning there and establishing a few bases, as were seen in the film, is certainly something that could be done now, given the institutional will and resources. What seems hopelessly idealistic, in light of current progress, is what happens in the film *eighteen months* after the discovery of the lunar monolith in 2002 and 2003—namely, a manned flight to Jupiter in a huge, nuclear-powered spaceship. Such an expedition would seemingly take us decades, not months, to achieve. Yet, we must remember what inspired that mission in the film— new and indisputable evidence of intelligent alien life elsewhere in the universe.

Today, humanity is in fact progressing on two fronts towards indisputable evidence of alien life, if not intelligent alien life, elsewhere in the universe. As scientists continue to examine old and new Martian meteorites, suggestive signs of alien microbes may be supplanted by hard, undeniable evidence. And, with the Galileo space probe lingering in orbit around Jupiter and the Cassini space probe having just left its vicinity, additional data may emerge proving that there is a liquid ocean beneath the ice of Europa, making it a likely home for alien life. (Also, as it happens, Europa was the world chosen by the monoliths as the cradle for a new alien civilization in the first sequels to *2001*, the novel *2010: Odyssey Two* and film *2010: The Year We Make Contact* [1984].) With several months to go, it remains possible that 2001 will go down in history as the year in which humans first learned, beyond any doubt, that we are not alone in the universe. And it remains possible that the electrifying news will inspire a crash program to send humans to investigate the distant world where that alien life exists. Perhaps, then, *2001: A Space Odyssey* will turn out to have been an accurate prediction of humanity's future after all.

15. *2010*: THE YEAR WE LOWER OUR EXPECTATIONS

Almost by their nature, sequels tend to attract less attention than original works. Thus, while the arrival of the year 2001 brought many tributes to the celebrated film and novel *2001: A Space Odyssey* (1968) and learned considerations of the contrast between Arthur C. Clarke and Stanley Kubrick's predictions, and the realities, of that year, it is not surprising that no one to date in the year 2010 has stepped forward to offer a similar celebration of Clarke's 1982 sequel to that story, *2010: Odyssey Two*, which was filmed two years later by writer-director Peter Hyams as *2010: The Year We Make Contact* (1984). Commentators may be particularly inclined to overlook those works because, more so than most sequels, *2010* may be regarded as a genuine trivialization, even a repudiation, of the expansive vision of the original epic; furthermore, while both the 1968 film and novel can be admired as milestones of the genre, most would dismiss *2010: Odyssey Two* as one of Clarke's lesser works, while Hyams's film was universally derided as vastly inferior to Kubrick's masterpiece. Nevertheless, the manner in which Clarke chose to extend his most famous story, generally replicated by Hyams, can (like the original *2001*) inspire some ruminations about both its failures, and its successes, as a forecast of humanity's current situation.

The premise of the sequel appears to represent a spectacular failure in prophecy, although there are illuminating undercurrents in its story. In 2010, a still-antagonistic United States and Soviet Union, puzzled by the mysterious loss of communication with the spaceship *Discovery* just as Dave Bowman was preparing to investigate an immense monolith orbiting Jupiter, are separately preparing missions to investigate what happened, a task rendered more urgent by recent findings that *Discovery*'s orbit is rapidly deteriorating, meaning that the craft may soon crash into Jupiter. The problem is that the Russians can get there in time, but they lack the expertise to reactivate the *Discovery*, revive the disabled computer HAL 9000, and obtain essential data; the Americans can do all these things, but their preparations are taking longer and their spaceship will not be able to reach *Discovery* before it is destroyed. The solution, devised by opening a private channel of communication between Heywood R. Floyd and a Soviet colleague, is for the two hostile nations to work together to launch a joint mission using the Soviet spacecraft and a combined crew of Soviet cosmonauts and American scientists.

Now, in the early 1980s, when President Ronald Reagan's bellicose rhetoric was making the Cold War seem more entrenched than ever, it was certainly reasonable to predict that the conflict between the United States and Soviet Union would endure well into the twenty-first century, and while Clarke posited only low-level tensions, Hyams's screenplay envisioned the United States and Soviet Union about to go to war due to a crisis in Honduras, driving the American and Soviet crew members apart. No one at the time, it seems, was capable of imagining that, less than a decade later, the Soviet Union would collapse, the United States and a now-independent Russia would drift toward a wary but peaceful partnership, and the main threat to American security by 2010 would not be a nuclear-armed Soviet Union, but rather stateless terrorists committed to spectacular acts of mass destruction.

Still, two aspects of this scenario are arguably predictive. Although Clarke did have the precedent of the one-time Apollo-

Soyuz rendezvous in 1975, he correctly realized, one might say, that the two major spacefaring nations would be driven into a more formal partnership, which is certainly the case today, with active Russian participation in the construction and occupation of the international space station and American astronauts regularly traveling to the station in Russian *Soyuz* spacecraft. This collaboration, though, was not inspired by any pressing concern as in the novel, but more by economic realities. (Even in 1982, Clarke and other science fiction writers had still not grasped that the staggering costs of space travel would dominate all decisions about such initiatives.)

The timing of the second mission to Jupiter is also intriguing. Given that science fiction has typically been optimistic about rapid advances in space travel, a sequel to a story about a mission to Jupiter, taking place about eight years after its launch, would presumably envision that, by that time, humans would have ventured even farther away from Earth. Instead, we learn that by 2010, the Soviet Union is finally ready for its first Jupiter mission while the United States has not yet completed preparations for a second Jupiter mission. Choosing one's words carefully, one could say that *2010* correctly predicted that there would be no significant progress in human space exploration between 2001 and 2010.

However, since only eighteen months elapsed between the lunar monolith's signal to Jupiter and the successful launch of the *Discovery*, why would it take eight years to simply repeat the job? True, Clarke undoubtedly posited this long gap between the missions solely so that his sequel's title could reverse the final two digits of "2001" and thus resonate with the original title. Nevertheless, even if inadvertently, the story does suggest that, paradoxically, doing something a second time in space might require more time and effort than doing it the first time—which is precisely what the United States has actually discovered in contemplating a second effort to reach the Moon. As Jerry Pournelle reported in his anthology *The Endless Frontier, Volume II* (1982):

In spring of 1980 I had an astonishing experience: one of the highest officials of NASA solemnly informed me that the United States could not put a man on the Moon within ten years.

"But," spluttered I, "we did it in eight, starting from a lot less in 1961. Surely we can do better now?"

"No."[73]

Reflecting the same realities, when President George W. Bush finally made an official proposal to return to the Moon, his 2005 initiative called for the first flight to occur a full fifteen years later, in the year 2020. With those plans now being abandoned by President Barack Obama, it remains unclear when humans might again walk on the Moon, but it will manifestly require more than a decade to move from the drawing board to a countdown, even though we once did it more quickly. And *2010: Odyssey Two* may represent the first anticipation of the counterintuitive principle that a repeated space mission might involve more preparation time than the original mission.

Other aspects of the storyline of *2010* range from the plausible to the impossible. It was hardly prophetic of Clarke to envision Jupiter's moon Europa as a potential abode of life (with exotic beings described at length in the novel, though mostly ignored in the film), since it was already known in 1982 that the world possessed a vast underground ocean of liquid water, an obviously promising environment for life to develop; but ongoing investigation has made it more and more reasonable to assume that, if there is indeed life to be found elsewhere in the Solar System, Europa represents the best place to look for it. However, the way that the monolith builders make the moon more hospitable for its embryonic species—transforming Jupiter into a star—would appear to be well beyond the ability of both human and alien engineering, for the process would require increasing

73. Jerry Pournelle, "Introduction: The Insurmountable Opportunity," *The Endless Frontier, Volume II*, edited by Jerry Pournelle with John F. Carr (New York: Ace Books, 1982), 1.

the mass of Jupiter to about sixty to eighty times its current mass. And, since Jupiter already represents about 77% of the total mass of the Solar System outside the Sun, it is clear that obtaining sufficient mass to cause this transformation would be extraordinarily challenging, to say the least. Clarke assumes that his unseen aliens have the ability to somehow materialize innumerable monoliths that rain on Jupiter to boost its mass to the necessary level, but one cannot begin to calculate just how many of these would be required to equal sixty times the current mass of Jupiter. If the goal was simply to provide Europa with a steady source of heat so as to facilitate the sustained evolution of its inhabitants, it would have been far easier for the aliens to move the moon closer to the Sun, or for that matter, to construct a million waterproof nuclear-powered furnaces and drop them into its oceans. However, as a testament to Clarke's general credibility as a scientific prophet, it is amusing to note that in 2003, when NASA decided to send its aging, dysfunctional *Galileo* space probe plunging into Jupiter's atmosphere, there were crazy internet rumors that NASA had filled the probe with nuclear bombs designed to ignite Jupiter and turn it into a star, an idea that was surely inspired by Clarke's sequel.

What commands the most attention in *2010: Odyssey Two*, though, is its striking and disappointing reconstruction of the original story's transformed Dave Bowman, the Star Child. To briefly recapitulate the original narrative, the first stage of the monolith builders' plan was to uplift some terrestrial primates to the status of intelligent beings by granting them the ability to use tools, a skill that inexorably drove humans from adapting bones as clubs to constructing spaceships (as conveyed by the film's famous jump cut). But tool-making, by the year 2001, had reached the limits of its usefulness: all the innumerable tools surrounding and employed by the characters in that year have clearly had the effect of making people more and more like machines, as evidenced by the film's wooden acting and banal dialogue, and the most advanced tool humans have devised, the computer HAL 9000, is revealed to be significantly flawed, inasmuch as it goes insane and murders all but one member of the *Discovery*'s crew. Thus, it is now time for the second phase of the aliens' plan: to uplift humanity to a new, higher level of superhumanity which will no longer require them to employ tools. Thus, after Bowman (Keir Dullea) disables the homicidal HAL, he is taken by the aliens to a faraway apartment with furniture suggesting an era prior to the Industrial Revolution; he is stripped of his tools—his spacecraft and spacesuit; and he is transformed into a naked, fetus-like being that can survive in the vacuum of space. Clarke's novel further informs us that this first representative of the new species also has vast psychic powers, which he employs to instantly disintegrate each and every one of Earth's nuclear weapons—tools which he finds particularly objectionable. And the logical way for this story to continue would involve the Star Child raising other humans to this new stature and working with them to forge a new, super-human civilization.

2010: Odyssey Two, however, completely changes the story. The mission of the monolith builders is no longer to find promising species and to first make them intelligent, and to later make them superintelligent; rather, they simply wish to forge intelligent species and then to periodically check on their progress to ensure that they have not developed so badly as to require what Clarke terms "weed[ing]," or extermination.[74] They transformed Bowman not to become the first representative of *homo superior*, but rather to serve as a sort of errand boy who will assist them by conducting an ethereal survey of human civilization in the early twenty-first century and by overseeing activities involving their new interest, uplifting the promising beings of Europa to intelligence. As to why humanity no longer requires a second evolutionary leap forward, it turns out that tool-making actually remains a valuable and helpful activity even for species that are conquering space; for the characters in the second novel and film are more rounded and eloquent,

74. Arthur C. Clarke, *2010: Odyssey Two* (New York: Del Rey/Ballantine Books, 1982), 265.

indicating that tool-using humans are really not becoming like machines. In addition, the apparently-errant computer HAL is rehabilitated as a victim of human error (conflicting instructions), and once the problem is resolved, the computer is again a flawless, perfectly functioning companion who ably helps his human mentors escape from the vicinity of Jupiter before it becomes a star. As additional evidence that intelligent beings will always make use of tools, *2010: Odyssey Two* and Clarke's two later sequels—*2061: Odyssey Three* (1987) and *3001: The Final Odyssey* (1997)—indicate that the advanced aliens who manipulated humanity, although said to have first adapted to mechanical bodies and later to have evolved into beings of pure energy, will still construct and employ tools, most conspicuously the monoliths themselves, eventually characterized in *3001* as very advanced but deteriorating computers.

The sequel's new, diminished vision of future human progress, I would argue, represented Clarke's accurate anticipation of evolving attitudes both within and outside of science fiction. Many science fiction stories in the pulp magazines of the 1930s expressed boundless optimism about humanity's glorious future; as one example, I recall John W. Campbell, Jr.'s Arcot, Wade, and Morey stories, which begin (in "Piracy Preferred" [1930]) with scientists on Earth combating an aerial pirate and conclude (in *Invaders from the Infinite* [1932]) with its heroes freely traveling through the entire universe, slightly stressed because their discovery of "Cosmic Power," enabling them to do anything they want to do with a single thought, has rendered them the effective masters of the cosmos. A youthful Clarke read such grandiose adventures and absorbed their attitudes; thus, in *Against the Fall of Night* (1953) and its revision *The City and the Stars* (1956), there are intimations that humans in the far future have moved on to bigger and better things, leaving behind a few remnants of their former selves on a mostly deserted Earth, while *Childhood's End* (1953) more vividly describes humanity's future transformation, supervised by alien conquerors, into an immensely powerful group intelligence which effortlessly demolishes its home planet before traveling out into space to fulfill its superhuman destiny. *2001: A Space Odyssey* seems very much in the same tradition, for just as the ancient Moon-Watcher learned how to use tools and would then "think of something" that allowed his species to conquer the Earth, Bowman's Star Child, having mastered his new mental powers, is clearly poised to similarly "think of something" that will allow his new species to conquer the universe. And around the time Clarke was writing *2010*, such bold dreams of almost unlimited human progress had not yet gone out of fashion, as evidenced, for example, by George Zebrowski's *Macrolife* (1979), wherein human space colonies evolve into a group intelligence that expands throughout the entire cosmos.

However, *2010: Odyssey Two* suggests that Clarke was sensing a coming shift in attitudes and felt the need to recalibrate the original story's grand ambitions to better accord with the actual human aspirations he was expecting in the year 2010. Thus, in his sequel to *2001*, humans now see themselves as destined merely to muddle on, more or less as we are, with our major challenge being to simply stay alive in a universe of potentially inimical forces which include both the unseen aliens—who may resolve to "weed" us out of existence—or their machines, the monoliths—which might drift toward a similar decision as they degenerate into senility. Even when leaping forward a thousand years for his final sequel to the original story, Clarke only imagined a humanity that has managed to conquer its own solar system and to develop a few new technological tricks, such as a device that connects everyone's minds to a sort of super-internet. And such modest hopes for the future have gradually come to dominate science fiction, which now features few if any stories envisioning an entire universe dominated by human beings and instead has largely settled into a consensus, *Star Trek*-like future of humans joining forces with some aliens and battling against other aliens while slowly expanding only throughout our own galaxy. Meanwhile, outside of science fiction, even these predictions seem overly bold, as public opinion has moved away from a more subdued optimism about human space conquests to obsessive worries about a dangerous universe about to effect our extinction by means of an asteroid impact, alien invaders, absorption into a visiting black hole, or other cosmic catastrophes featured in alarmist documentaries. When Obama announced that he was cancelling projected efforts to first revisit the Moon and later reach Mars in favor of vague hopes to inspire private enterprise to reignite the space race—a decision made in the year 2010— it was simply one more sign that humans no longer expect, or desire, to fulfill the old dreams of science fiction and someday conquer the universe.

Thus, Clarke's *2010* might finally be viewed as a prophecy of humanity's steadily diminishing hopes for the future, as it endeavors to invalidate one of science fiction's boldest visions of human transcendence and substitutes a prediction of perpetual human stagnation, distinguished only by the most timid sorts of advances. No other work of science fiction, then, has more provocatively or correctly suggested that the year 2010 would find humanity firmly entrenched in an era of lowered expectations.

16. THE ENDLESS ODYSSEY: THE *2001* SAGA AND ITS INABILITY TO PREDICT HUMANITY'S FUTURE

In a literary marketplace where sequels to successful works are almost inevitable, it is not surprising to find that one of the grandest and most evocative epics in the history of science fiction has so far generated, by one count, no fewer than nineteen sequels involving four different authors. What *is* surprising is that, despite these various efforts to continue this story, it remains conspicuously incomplete—for reasons that convey important messages about the inherent limitations of its genre whenever it attempts to predict the eventual future of the human race.

I am referring to Stanley Kubrick's film *2001: A Space Odyssey* (1968),[75] along with the novel of the same name simultaneously written by his co-screenwriter Arthur C. Clarke; for while the hero of its namesake, Homer's Odysseus, did finally reach home after twenty years of warfare and wandering, Kubrick and Clarke's adventure has now reached its forty-second year with no signs that it will ever reach its announced destination.

---

75. *2001: A Space Odyssey* (Metro-Goldwyn-Mayer, 1968).

* * * * * * *

To determine the logical way that the story should have been extended, one must begin by considering the conclusion of the original film and novel. In the more cryptic film, an alien race first places one monolith on the planet Earth four million years ago, and after a brief encounter with a tribe of prehuman primates, the monolith somehow boosts their intelligence so that they now can figure out how to use tools. Soon they are on their way to becoming fully human and conquering their world. Then, in the year 2001, a representative human, Dave Bowman (Keir Dullea), is directed by a second monolith on the Moon to a third monolith orbiting Jupiter, which transports him to a distant world through a hyperspatial Star Gate; and the still-unseen aliens proceed to study this specimen while he lives out his life in order to determine exactly how this species now needs to be further improved. Finally, a fourth monolith transforms Bowman into the Star Child and teleports him back to the vicinity of Earth, where he will presumably deploy his new powers—which include the ability to survive in the vacuum of space without a spacesuit—to make its other humans into superhumans like himself. Thus, as the novel explains, "history as men knew it would be drawing to a close."[76] The novel adds the information that the Star Child begins by noticing Earth's nuclear weapons and, displeased by this discovery, instantly disintegrates each and every single one of them, indicating that these new beings are immensely powerful and that they, if nothing else, strongly abhor violence, a reasonable assumption to make about advanced beings in light of the history of our own civilization. However, no other information about this superhuman race's characteristics and attitudes is provided, only a final comment in the novel that the Star Child "would think of something" to do next (221). A proper sequel to *2001: A*

---

76. Arthur C. Clarke, *2001: A Space Odyssey*, based on a screenplay by Stanley Kubrick and Arthur C. Clarke (New York: Signet Books, 1968), 221. Subsequent page references in the text are to this edition.

Space Odyssey, then, would need to resolve these uncertainties by describing the further exploits of the transformed Bowman and the other members of his new species.

Yet the novel also offers a different perspective on precisely what the aliens were doing, in the distant past and in the early twenty-first century. Clarke's first monolith is explicitly described as a teaching machine: transparent rather than black, it produces throbbing noises to hypnotically attract protagonist Moon-Watcher and the others in his tribe, entices them with images of well-fed primates like themselves to encourage their progress, manipulates their bodies to force them through the motions of productive activities like tying knots and employing rocks as weapons, and chooses the most promising candidates for some additional education. In this version of the story, then, the prehumans had already developed the intelligence to use tools, but simply needed some training in how to use them, which is exactly what the monolith provides to a few of the brightest ones, so that they in turn can communicate their new knowledge to their peers.

In Clarke's first version of the story, Bowman's final encounter with the monolith was also an educational, rather than a transformative, experience. This information is gleaned from what might be regarded as the first sequel to *2001*, Clarke's *The Lost Worlds of 2001* (1972), which mingles nonfictional chapters about Clarke's experiences during the filming of *2001* with narrative chapters providing fictional materials developed to be part of the story that were omitted from the final film and novel. Its last fictional chapter, "Second Lesson," offers Clarke's original description of what happened to Bowman after he emerged from the Star Gate. Finding himself on a seemingly endless black plain, Bowman observes not a monolith but an enormous cube that begins to generate bright lights and a drumming sound. Then,

> the turning wheels of light merged together, and their spokes, fused into luminous bars that slowly receded

into the distance. They split into pairs, and the resulting sets of lines started to oscillate across each other, continually changing their angle of intersection. Fantastic, fleeting geometrical patterns flickered in and out of existence, as the glowing grids meshed and unmeshed; and the hominid watched from its metal cave—wide-eyed, slack jawed, and wholly receptive.

The dancing moiré patterns suddenly faded, and the rhythm sank to a barely audible, almost subsonic, pulsing throb. The cube was empty again; but only for a moment.

The first lesson having been moderately successful, the second was about to begin.[77]

What this Bowman found at the end of the Star Gate, in other words, was another teaching machine—which suggests a different way to interpret what happened to him. If Bowman's final encounter is precisely analogous to the experience of the human ancestors in the novel, one would deduce that contemporary humans already have the ability to become superhuman—but they simply need some additional training to learn how to do it. And, if he was now being educated in how to achieve such a stature, then what happened when the elderly Bowman gestured toward the final monolith was not that he was transformed in the Star Child; rather, his lessons completed, he had finally figured out *how to transform himself* into the Star Child and proceeded to do just that. Afterwards, in the same way that Moon-Watcher and the other trained prehumans had taught the other members of their species how to use tools, the Star Child, having returned to Earth, would in parallel fashion undertake the task of teaching other ordinary humans how to make themselves into superhumans. (And this would explain how the alien manipulators of humanity could undertake to uplift the entire species by means of one advanced individual.) However, as we shall observe,

77. Arthur C. Clarke, *The Lost Worlds of 2001* (New York: Signet Books, 1972), 238.

this story of humanity's further progress is precisely what all sequels to *2001*—with one small exception—have contrived to completely avoid.

* * * * * * *

If one discounts *The Lost Worlds of 2001*—which as noted does little if anything to extend the original narrative—the first person to produce a sequel to *2001* was comic book writer-artist Jack Kirby. After working with writer Stan Lee to create and develop iconic characters for Marvel Comics like the Fantastic Four, the Incredible Hulk, the Mighty Thor, and the X-Men, Kirby had surprisingly defected to its bitter rival DC Comics in 1969. By the time he returned to Marvel in the mid-1970s, other writers and artists had long been handling his original assignments, so he was in need of some new projects; as one of them, Marvel purchased the rights to *2001: A Space Odyssey* and, clearly envisioning this as a fitting challenge for this seasoned creator of epic comic adventures, the company first assigned him to adapt the novel as a large Marvel Treasury Special. Then, he was further asked to write and draw a new comic book which would expand upon and continue Kubrick and Clarke's original story.

As part of his preparation for these tasks, one hopes and assumes that Kirby both watched the film and read Clarke's novel, and his approach to the story may have been inspired by one sentence in the novel about Moon-Watcher's monolith: "Neither it, nor its replicas scattered across half the globe, expected to succeed with all the scores of groups involved in the experiment" (25). So, in the novel at least, there were actually many monoliths in different locations helping many prehuman primates learn how to be fully human; and, analogously, one might further posit that in the future, in addition to the monolith which encountered and captured Bowman, there were other monoliths in other regions of space which came into contact with, and transformed, other astronauts. This was the premise that Kirby relied upon while crafting the first six issues of his new comic book.

The initial, large-sized Marvel Treasury Edition adaptation of the film was basically faithful to its source material, although Kirby did introduce his own distinctive version of the monolith as more squarish in size, with its black surface covered with blue streaks presumably representing the mysterious energy pulsating through the object, and hovering above the ground in defiance of gravity; and to prepare readers for his series, he also explains that Bowman is only the first of many humans who will be transformed into superhumans: "He is to be the first of many 'new ones.' For the monolith knows that there must be more than one new seed to sow the harvest of a new species."[78]

What was disturbing, and what did not bode well for this ambitious project, was that Kirby seemingly failed to grasp certain elements of the film's plot. For one thing, it should have been obvious to any filmgoer that Heywood R. Floyd (William Sylvester) was traveling to the Moon primarily to gather information, not to impart it, yet Kirby believes that Floyd was sent to lead the lunar briefing, not to listen to others; so that, illogically, it is a visitor from Earth who must inform residents of the Moon about the mysterious object that has been discovered buried on the Moon. In addition, Kirby misses the real reason why Bowman, stranded outside his spacecraft by the demented HAL, will find it difficult to re-enter the *Discovery* through an airlock: in his haste to rescue his crewmate Frank Poole (Gary Lockwood), he forgot to put on his space helmet, so he will have to briefly expose himself to the potentially lethal vacuum of space to enter the airlock. Bowman employs the pod's explosive bolts for an emergency exit from the rear, instead of using its front door, solely in order to minimize the time he will be exposed to the vacuum. Yet Kirby numbly draws Bowman wearing his space helmet and presents the re-entry as hazardous only because of the explosive bolts which, if he were wearing

78. Jack Kirby, writer and artist, *2001: A Space Odyssey*, Marvel Treasury Special (New York: Marvel Comics Group, 1976), 71.

a helmet, he would have no need to employ. This suggests that Kirby, unlike Kubrick and Clarke, will not be developing space adventures meticulously based on scientific plausibility, a suspicion validated by later issues of the comic book which would feature three battles with evil, humanoid aliens and an improbable swarm of destructive meteoroids.

The first issue's story, "Beast-Killer," introduces the character who will eventually bear that name; although he is said to be living in the "Miocene Age"[79]—roughly three to five million years ago, close to the era of the film's Moon-Watcher, four million years ago—he is nevertheless drawn to appear like a human being, not an apelike hominid, undoubtedly a concession to readers who can better sympathize with characters resembling themselves. Like Moon-Watcher, he has been communing with a mysterious monolith that he calls the "stone-spirit" (3), which has taught him how to use a wooden club, but this proves an inadequate tool in hunting and killing large animals when he must pause to fend off other jealous humans seeking the animal and the insufficiently wounded animal is able to run away and escape. He then visits the monolith, touches it to mentally communicate the problem, and is resultingly taught how to build a better killing instrument, a stone knife. After successfully killing a saber-tooth tiger with this new weapon, Beast-Killer has the additional idea of placing such a blade on a longer stick and constructing a spear; he throws the spear, and in the very next panel, recalling the famous jump cut in *2001* from bone to spaceship, we see an astronaut in the year 2001, stranded on an asteroid, who is tossing an ancient alien artifact in frustration.

Woodrow Decker, said to be a direct descendant of Beast-Killer, is frustrated because he and another astronaut, assigned to search for signs of alien life in the asteroid belt, have found precisely the sort of the evidence they were seeking, but their

79. Jack Kirby, writer and artist, "Beast-Killer," *2001: A Space Odyssey*, No. 1 (December, 1976), 3. Subsequent page references in the text are to this edition.

spacecraft has been destroyed, so they will never be able to tell others about their discovery. After a red creature with tentacles emerges from the alien debris to attack and kill his colleague Mason, a fleeing Decker encounters another hovering monolith, which dispatches him on a long voyage through space and brings him to a bucolic field, where a lad named Bill greets him and urges Decker to walk with him toward a nearby house. As he walks, Decker rapidly ages and finally collapses, whereupon another monolith appears to transform him into a fetus-like Star Child—although Kirby as noted prefers to call these beings "the New Seed"—who promptly embarks upon a cosmic journey.

This story set the pattern for the comic's next two stories: Kirby will retell the story of the original film and novel with new characters, though he leaves out the Heywood R. Floyd episode of a future man traveling to a second monolith which guides another human to a third monolith, to be eventually transformed by a fourth monolith. Instead, there is first a prehistoric human who is trained or made more intelligent by a monolith, and then there is an abrupt transition to a future human who is transported to an alien realm by a second monolith and transformed into one of the New Seed by a third monolith. The other differences are that, to meet the different demands of the comic book medium, Kirby will contrive to introduce as much action and violence as possible—in the first issue, a battle between prehistoric humans and a struggle with an exotic monster—and instead of having the transported astronauts finding themselves alone in an earthlike environment, Kirby will introduce other human companions who are presumably alien constructs, again in the interest of keeping the story lively with some conversation. Further, while Kubrick and Clarke's Star Child returned to Earth to contemplate his home planet, each of Kirby's New Seeds, like Decker, "answers the call of the beckoning cosmos" (31) and travels into deep space—suggesting that beings who can survive in the vacuum of space would probably prefer to live in space, their natural home, instead of enduring the confining gravity of a planetary surface. Kirby finally provides his superhumans with another human trait—curiosity about their universe—since the third New Seed, in "Wheels of Death," is said to embark upon his journey through space because he is "eager—impatient to thrive and discover."[80]

Interestingly, in the Kirby comments that fill up the first issue's page of "Monolith Mail" which obviously cannot yet feature any readers' letters about the just-published comic book, the writer-artist indicates that he has no real intention of ever taking the story much further than the original film and novel:

> Yes, the New Seed is the conquering hero in this latest Marvel drama. Why? Because he has staying power, that's why. He will always be there in the story's final moments to taunt us with the question we shall never answer. The little shaver is, perhaps, the embodiment of our own hopes in a world which daily makes us more than a bit uneasy about our future.[81]

Kirby thus states out loud what will emerge as one major reason why the sequels to *2001: A Space Odyssey* can never say very much about humanity's successors—because from a human perspective, the nature of superhumanity is a "question we shall never answer." He is instead inclined, or obliged, to present his New Seed as little more than a metaphor for something that is quintessentially human:

> In short, the New Seed is no more than the spirit of our own self-belief, our own confidence in the stubborn rationale which has brought us from the caves to condominiums in the suburbs. Somehow, at the very edge of group destruction, history gives evidence of a persistent proclivity on the part of human beings for

80. Jack Kirby, writer and artist, "Wheels of Death," *2001: A Space Odyssey*, No. 4 (March, 1977), 31.

81. Jack Kirby, "Monolith Mail," *2001: A Space Odyssey*, No. 1 (December, 1976), 19. Subsequent page references in the text are to this edition.

keeping mind—and whatever else matters—on a even keel.

The New Seed merely says that we can still do it. We can keep the environment *and* ourselves running into the distant future. We can, someday, knock off our hostilities and concentrate together on the great mystery of the stars. (19)

If Kirby believed that readers would be content with a continuation of *2001* that never advanced beyond the creation of one New Seed after another and presented the new beings only as enigmatic representatives of human stick-to-it-ivity, he would soon find that he was mistaken, and that he would be asked to actually say something substantive about what these new beings were like and what they would be doing. But for now, Kirby had a plan, and he would follow that plan in the next five issues.

The novelty in the second issue's story, "Vira the She-Demon," is that it is a prehistoric *woman* at an unspecified prehistoric time, named Vira, who finds a monolith and, inspired by the encounter, figures out that she can disguise herself as a god and thus be worshipped, fed, and sheltered by her fellow humans; then, a female astronaut exploring Ganymede, Vera Gentry, survives a battle with sinister green-skinned aliens in flying saucers and is taken by a monolith through space to enjoy a relaxing swim with old neighbors before becoming Kirby's second New Seed.[82]

Then, in the two-part story that appeared in the third and fourth issue, "Marak!" and "Wheels of Death,"[83] a warrior who lived 200,000 years ago converses with an old man who

---

82. Jack Kirby, writer and artist, "Vira the She-Demon," *2001: A Space Odyssey*, No. 2 (January, 1977).

83. Jack Kirby, writer and artist, "Marak!," *2001: A Space Odyssey*, No. 3 (February, 1977). Note: on the cover, the title is given as "Marak the Merciless," but I am regarding the title presented on the first page of the story as definitive.

has been getting ideas from a monolith; taken to the monolith himself, Marak receives a vision that he must seek out a warrior queen named Jalessa. Training his men to ride on horses and inventing the wheel, Marak takes his army to her kingdom and meets Jalessa, who is also being assisted by a monolith; they conclude that they are destined to work together to further advance humanity, and a romantic relationship is implied but not specified. Then, in a space station orbiting Mars, commander Herbert Marik orders his crew to abandon the station because it is about to be destroyed by a swarm of huge meteoroids; remaining in the station himself, he finds a monolith which takes him to a meeting with Jalessa—presented as a reunion—in an idyllic kingdom before becoming the third New Seed. The added element in this adventure is that, like the original monolith in Clarke's novel which carefully selected the brightest prehumans to receive its training, Kirby's monoliths, it is suggested, are not assisting whatever random humans come in contact with them, but are rather making a deliberate effort to seek out and uplift only the most promising candidates.

In the two-part story in the fifth and sixth issues, "Norton of New York 2040 A.D." and "Inter-Galactica: The Ultimate Trip,"[84] Kirby alters his pattern by eliminating the prehistoric prelude and simply telling the story of a future man's encounters with monoliths. New Yorker Harvey Norton loves visiting "Comicsville" where he can act out being a superhero with realistic props and live actors, but a monolith intrudes upon the scripted action to begin the process of encouraging him to abandon a society obsessed with illusory experiences in order to become an astronaut who will have actual adventures in outer space. Specifically, Norton later finds himself attempting to rescue a yellow-skinned alien princess from fellow beings seeking to capture her by fleeing with her on a journey that

84. Jack Kirby, writer and artist, "Norton of New York 2040 A.D.," *2001: A Space Odyssey*, No. 5 (April, 1977); Jack Kirby, writer and artist, "Inter-Galactica: The Ultimate Trip," *2001: A Space Odyssey*, No. 6 (May, 1977).

takes them to another galaxy; besieged by her would-be captors, the princess escapes by means of a teleportation device but Norton is trapped in rubble, whereupon the familiar monolith appears to first refashion him into a genuine superhero and then to transform him into another New Seed.

In this story, Kirby is perhaps providing interesting commentary on the mentality of readers who love comic books and gently suggesting that they may be devoting too much of their lives to their fantasies—a surprising message to detect in a comic book—but he again is doing nothing to advance his story, and some readers were visibly becoming impatient. "I'm hoping #3 doesn't end like the first two. I suggest having different endings," wrote one reader in the fifth issue's letter column.[85] More complaints emerged in the "Monolith Mail" of the sixth issue: "I don't believe readers are going to get too excited reading a variation of the same story every issue." "Where is this comic going?" "Is there any long-range plan in mind for this book?" All the unnamed editor could say in response was to urge the comic book's readers to be "patient."[86]

Finally, instead of concluding with the transformation of a future human into a New Seed, the story in the seventh issue, "The New Seed," actually begins with such an event and then follows the evolved Gordon Pruett on his cosmic voyage through space. While the New Seed finds the experience pleasurable— he "begins to know the joy of pursuing the comets and racing meteors in their fiery flights"—he primarily devotes his time to examining the many worlds he encounters, including a barren, lifeless planet, a world with prehistoric creatures, and a world with stunning advanced technology.[87] But the New Seed lingers

85. Sam Powell, letter, "Monolith Mail," *2001: A Space Odyssey*, No. 5 (April, 1977), 19.

86. Mike Underwood, Sam Hays, and Mark Boersma, letters, "Monolith Mail," *2001: A Space Odyssey*, No. 6 (May, 1977), 19.

87. Jack Kirby, writer and artist, "The New Seed," *2001: A Space Odyssey*, No. 7 (June, 1977), 7. Subsequent page references in the text are to this edition.

at one devastated "planet of smashed cities" in order "to marvel at the folly which could generate such massive and complete destruction" (11). Sadly observing bands of desperate survivors fighting with each other to survive on the dying world, the New Seed is particularly moved by the senseless murder of a man and a woman, and he thinks to himself "Life must be perpetuated. Though I could not involve myself in their destiny, I can act when it no longer exists. I can claim what remains" (27). Taking the glowing life-energy of the couple, he transports it to a hospitable but lifeless planet and leaves it there to begin the evolution of life: "A quest is fulfilled...a mission completed. A billion years will pass before lovers may live again to test the whims of fate..." Then, the New Seed again flies away to seek the answer to "the why of being," while wondering, "What if it turned out to be merely—simple?" (31)

Out of all the works that have purported to continue or revisit the story of *2001: A Space Odyssey*, "The New Seed" might claim to be its only genuine sequel, since it alone tells the story of what happens to a representative of superhumanity after his creation. But it is also an unfinished sequel: if the first version of the story ended with the birth of the superhuman, "The New Seed" limits itself to telling about his early childhood, as he experiences his first journey through space and takes his first actions to improve the cosmos. We learn that Kirby's New Seed, like the novel's transformed Bowman, despises violence, and although he feels bound by some curious prohibition against intervening in the "destiny" of other living creatures, he is committed to doing what he can to preserve and extend life in the universe—another logical deduction to make about the priorities of a superhuman being. However, in seeking to assist in the creation of other species that resemble the being that he used to be, the New Seed is conspicuously neglecting the development of his own species—in a way, he is anticipating Clarke's coming transformation of the Star Child into an "errand boy" instead of the progenitor of a new race—and is further illustrating another strategy to avoid fully developed depictions of superintelligent beings: to envision them as being primarily focused on, or even obsessed with, the activities of less advanced species, thus shifting attention away from humanity's successors back to humanity, or to species at the same level as humanity.

It is particularly incongruous that each New Seed goes off by himself or herself, when we would assume that members of a new, superintelligent species would more naturally wish to come together in order to collectively progress toward whatever they might be capable of achieving. After all, when his encounter with the monolith was over, Moon-Watcher did not embark upon a solo quest across the Earth to learn more about his planet and to test his new powers; instead, he remained with the other members of his tribe and assisted them in becoming the masters of their immediate environment. Kirby's new beings, if they are never in contact with each other, will obviously be limited in how they can develop and grow.

Whether further Kirby adventures involving the New Seed would have gone on to address these issues in an intelligent manner seems unlikely, but as it turned out, he never even made an attempt to do so, as the final three issues of *2001: A Space Odyssey* instead lurched in an entirely new direction. It is reasonable to guess that as readers grew frustrated with a story that did not seem to be going anywhere, the sales of the comic book dramatically declined—leading to a spirited in-house discussion about what might be done to revive the series. Given that the overwhelming majority of successful comic books have featured superheroes, the answer would have been obvious: *2001: A Space Odyssey* must shift its focus to the action-packed adventures of a superhero.

Thus, the story in the eighth issue, "The Capture of X-51," first describes a secret military effort to develop intelligent, powerful robots; however, since most of them go "berserk" and become destructive,[88] the scientists are inevitably obliged to

88. Jack Kirby, writer and artist, "The Capture of X-51," *2001: A Space Odyssey*, No. 8 (July, 1977), 3. Subsequent page references in the text are to

activate the self-destruct mechanism implanted in each model, and it is decided to abandon the entire project. But one scientist, having grown especially attached to model X-51, gives him a human face, removes his explosive device, and sets him free—whereupon he is puzzled to find that everybody in the world seems determined to destroy him.

When the robot is captured and his face is removed, the monolith does make a brief appearance on the story's very last page to free him, indicating that it has some interest in the robot's survival and development—indeed, we are told that the monolith "is destined to serve him" (31)—but the story otherwise has nothing to do with preceding versions of the *2001* story. In fact, to most commentators, the lethal malfunctioning of the computer HAL 9000 in the original film and novel—the most advanced tool humans had ever crafted—apparently serves to illustrate that tool-building is ultimately limited in its value, requiring another leap forward in the evolution of humanity in order for the species to keep progressing while abandoning the use of tools. So it is fitting that immediately after we see Bowman turning off HAL—symbolically recognizing that such constructs are not a promising avenue for advancement—he is taken to another world to be transformed into a super-human being. In light of all this, it is indeed strange to posit that the monoliths would at some point lose interest in the creation of New Seeds and instead focus their attention on attempting to foster a form of machine intelligence as a promising new direction for the advancement of life. Still, a robot with super-strength and the power to defy gravity, initially named "Mister Machine," did enable Kirby to fill the pages of the eighth issue with scene after scene of spectacular violence, which was presumably the point.

In the ninth issue's story, "Mister Machine," the robot gets his face back and does some more fighting while again briefly communing with the monolith, which tells them that he should

------

this edition.

"not seek destiny," but rather allow destiny to "find me—and lead me to my destined path."[89] However, this elaborate exercise in boosting reader interest had the opposite effect on this comic book reader, and I never bothered to purchase—and still have not read—the tenth and final issue of *2001: A Space Odyssey* which again featured the character of Mister Machine in an adventure named "Hotline to Hades."[90] (Online sources indicate that the monolith does not even make a token appearance in the issue, which would render the story a sequel to *2001* only in its venue's title.) Then, completely abandoning the pretense that this new story arc had anything to do with Kubrick and Clarke's original epic, Marvel ended the *2001* comic book and instead launched a new title—*Machine Man*—to feature the further adventures of this new superhero, now given a slightly different name and presented without any references whatsoever to alien monoliths. While this comic book was abandoned by Kirby after the ninth issue and only lasted for ten more issues, the character has continued to resurface at times in the Marvel universe, but there is no reason for anyone interested in the story of *2001: A Space Odyssey* to examine his further exploits.

* * * * * * *

While Jack Kirby was laboring to extend the saga of *2001*, its co-creator Arthur C. Clarke was, by his own report, getting ready to retire. Newly prominent because of the success of *2001: A Space Odyssey* and appearances as a commentator during television coverage of Apollo missions to the Moon, Clarke had obtained a then-impressive one-million-dollar advance to write three unrelated novels, which turned out to be *Rendezvous with Rama* (1973), *Imperial Earth* (1975), and *The Fountains of Paradise* (1979), and upon completing them Clarke had

89. Jack Kirby, writer and artist, "Mister Machine," *2001: A Space Odyssey*, No. 9 (August, 1977), 22.

90. Jack Kirby, writer and artist, "Hotline to Hades," *2001: A Space Odyssey*, No. 10 (September, 1977).

announced that he would write no more novels. Yet fascinating data about Jupiter's moons garnered in 1979 from the *Voyager* space probes gave Clarke some ideas for a sequel to *2001*, which he originally wrote up as a film scenario; but when his agent responded that it would be more immediately profitable to first make the story a novel, Clarke set to work, and in 1982, *2010: Odyssey Two* was published and became a best-seller.

More so than most science fiction writers, Clarke had previously dealt with the topic of humanity's future evolution. In his first novel, *Against the Fall of Night* (1948, 1953), later revised as *The City and the Stars* (1956), there were intimations that the vanished human race of the far future had advanced to some higher level, leaving behind only a few remnants of ordinary humanity in the Earth cities of Diaspar and Lys. But he directly described the transition from humanity to superhumanity in *Childhood's End* (1953), wherein aliens resembling devils, called the Overlords, conquer the Earth in order to prepare humanity for the next step in the evolution of intelligent beings, merging into a group mind. The only surviving representative of the human race does not find his successors to be a pretty sight:

> They might have been savages, engaged in some complex ritual dance. They were naked and filthy, with matted hair obscuring their eyes. As far as Jan could tell, they were of all ages from five to fifteen, yet they all moved with the same speed, precision, and complete indifference to their surroundings.
>
> Then Jan saw their faces. He swallowed hard, and forced himself not to turn away. They were emptier than the faces of the dead, for even a corpse has some record carved by time's chisel upon its features, to speak when the lips themselves are dumb. There was

no more emotion or feeling here than in the face of a snake or an insect.[91]

The Overlord has to remind the man that "You are not watching human children" and that "They have no more identity than the cells in your own body. But linked together, they are something much greater than you" (202, 203). This new collective being soon demonstrates its powers by transforming itself into pure energy and destroying the planet Earth before leaving to pursue its superhuman destiny.

Evidently, Clarke himself was rather disquieted by the logic that drove him to this vision of humanity's future, prompting him to precede the novel with an unusual note—"The opinions expressed in this book are not those of the author" ([4])—as if to reassure readers that he really did not believe that anything like this would ever happen. And this might be one reason why, in crafting a sequel to *2001: A Space Odyssey*, he would not address the disquieting question of how humanity might actually progress in the future and would instead take the story in other directions in order to avoid that issue.

Of course, the original story had always involved two races which had advanced beyond humanity—the Star Child, and the unseen aliens who had created the monoliths to improve humans—and *2010: Odyssey Two* for the first time offers some description of the latter beings. In their physical nature, they have undergone a transformation not unlike that observed in *Childhood's End*, albeit by means of a lengthier process:

And now, out among the stars, evolution was driving toward new goals. The first explorers of Earth had long since come to the limits of flesh and blood; as soon as their machines were better than their bodies, it was time to move. First their brains, and then their

---

91. Arthur C. Clarke, *Childhood's End* (1953; New York: Ballantine Books, 1967), 202-203. Subsequent page references in the text are to this edition.

thoughts alone, they transferred into shiny new homes of metal and plastic.

In these, they roamed among the stars. They no longer built spaceships. They *were* spaceships.

But the age of the Machine-entities swiftly passed. In their ceaseless experimenting, they had learned to store knowledge in the structure of space itself, and to preserve their thoughts for eternity in frozen lattices of light. They could become creatures of radiation, free at last from the tyranny of matter.[92]

However, it does not seem that these aliens have evolved into a group intelligence, although Clarke leaves some room for ambiguity; for after several times experiencing what he termed the "presence" of "a vast mentality, an implacable will" (176), the transformed David Bowman

realized that more than one entity was controlling and manipulating him. He was involved in a hierarchy of intelligences, some close enough to his own primitive level to act as interpreters. Or perhaps they were all aspects of a single being.

Or perhaps the distinction was totally meaningless. (198)

The other point Clarke stresses about these aliens involves their overriding mission, which has been subtly but significantly altered from what one would have inferred from the original story:

When they looked out across the deeps of space, they had felt awe, and wonder, and loneliness. As soon as they possessed the power, they set forth for

---

92. Arthur C. Clarke, *2010: Odyssey Two* (New York: Del Rey/Ballantine Books, 1982), 266-267. Subsequent page references in the text are to this edition.

the stars. In their explorations, they encountered life in many forms and watched the workings of evolution on a thousand worlds. They saw how often the first faint sparks of intelligence flickered and died in the cosmic night.

And because, in all the Galaxy, they had found nothing more precious than Mind, they encouraged its dawning everywhere. They became farmers in the fields of stars; they sowed, and sometimes they reaped.

And sometimes, dispassionately, they had to weed. (265)

While broadly congruent with the behavior observed in the original novel and film, this new description of the aliens' motives has two novel aspects that were neither explicit nor implicit in this sequel's predecessors. First, we learn that the aliens are sometimes displeased with the results of their interventions and will consequently take action to eliminate the species that they have transformed; thus, they are not always benefactors and might in some cases function as a race's enemies. As shall be seen, the idea that the aliens might be regarded as inimical to human survival will be amplified in future sequels.

Second, the aliens are now depicted as being exclusively concerned with ensuring that the transition from non-intelligence to intelligence is achieved; nothing is said about a further desire to boost already intelligent beings to a higher level of intelligence. It is in this way that Clarke's sequel spectacularly betrays the promise of the original film and novel; for in changing David Bowman into the fetus-like Star Child, Clarke is now asserting, the aliens actually were in no way seeking to advance humanity beyond its current level. Instead, they had entirely different motives. Furthermore, since later sequels to *2001: A Space Odyssey* will mirror *2010: Odyssey Two* in declining to portray the transformed Bowman as a representative of a new superhuman species, and will offer no other depictions of such a new species, the saga henceforth will deal with the subject of humanity's future only in an indirect manner. That is, since the aliens who constructed the monoliths are clearly much more advanced than humans, any information that is presented or implied about their nature and behavior may be interpreted as a provocative suggestion, or even a prediction, of what humanity's nature and behavior might someday become.

In effecting this expedient demotion of the Star Child, the question that Clarke had to confront was this: if not to serve as the vanguard of a new species, why *did* the aliens transform Bowman into this novel and more powerful creature? The prosaic answer given in *2010: Odyssey Two* is that Bowman "was being used as a probe, sampling every aspect of human affairs. The control was so tenuous that he was barely conscious of it; he was rather like a hunting dog on a leash, allowed to make excursions of his own, yet nevertheless compelled to obey the overriding wishes of his master" (168). In other words, instead of bothering to return to the Solar System to assess the results of their labors, the aliens decided to make Bowman into an ethereal superman so that he could examine everything and report back to them. Given that the aliens are said to be made of pure energy with the apparent power to communicate, and even travel, faster than the speed of light, the reason why they would need this sort of errand boy to undertake a survey of Earth and its environs is not immediately clear; but Clarke will resolve the issue in later sequels by claiming that Bowman has really only been in contact with and controlled by the monolith, functioning as an automatic machine on its own, and not with its alien makers themselves.

Clarke also takes steps to reduce the powers and abilities of the transformed Bowman, further diminishing his significance. In the first novel's concluding pages, he had been portrayed as an almost omnipotent free agent, who decides that he does not like nuclear weapons and accordingly is able, by the pure power of thought, to eliminate all of them in an instant. But this Bowman, under the firm control of the unseen aliens, is variously described by Clarke as a "puppet" (178), a "tool" (198), and a "pet dog" (189, 271); he is dispatched to Earth simply to observe and report back on how humanity has evolved since the intervention of the monolith, although he indulgently makes side trips to visit his mother and an old girlfriend. And his reduced powers are limited to the ability to mentally throw a switch of sorts and prematurely detonate one atomic weapon which is launched at him. Thus, this Dave Bowman is far removed from the infant superman observed at the conclusion of the original novel and film.

After examining humanity on the planet Earth, Bowman is next sent to Jupiter, where he discovers two forms of alien life: balloon-like creatures in the upper atmosphere of Jupiter, not unlike those observed in Clarke's novella "A Meeting with Medusa" (1971), and a variety of creatures coming into existence in the underground seas of the moon Europa, though these tend to quickly become extinct due to constantly changing conditions. Concluding that the Jovians do not have the potential to be intelligent, whereas the Europans do, the aliens develop and implement a bold plan: to transform Jupiter into a star, which will destroy its indigenous life but provide Europa with a regular source of heat and energy to allow its promising creatures to evolve and develop into intelligent beings. A secondary motive is to provide humans with amenable new worlds to inhabit, perhaps providing some modest assistance in further human advancement, as is conveyed in the eleven-word message that the aliens send to humanity after Jupiter becomes a star: "ALL THESE WORLDS ARE YOURS—EXCEPT EUROPA. ATTEMPT NO LANDINGS THERE" (277). Perhaps, then, even if the aliens are no longer perceived as interested in taking direct action to further improve the species they have uplifted to intelligence, they may be willing to do other things that would assist in the process—in this case, providing some interesting new environments that might contribute to humanity's evolutionary progress. Still, the lengthy descriptions of the life-forms on Europa and Jupiter—which Clarke deemed important enough to repeat, almost verbatim, in his other two sequels to

2001—clearly indicate that the aliens' main interest at this point is their new project, not the species they had previously uplifted to intelligence. In fact, one might regard the aliens' "gift" of the Jovian moons to humanity basically as a bribe, to induce them to stay away from Europa in exchange for several other attractive worlds.

There is another way in which Clarke, rather subtly, is undermining one of the implicit messages in the original film. Anyone evaluating Stanley Kubrick's *2001: A Space Odyssey* might reasonably draw these conclusions: the director did not select actors who were particularly talented; he provided them with dialogue that was mostly banal or bureaucratic, and not very much of it; and he made no effort to urge those actors to deliver those lines with any special force or conviction. And while these judgments do apply to other performers in the film, they seem especially true regarding the actor portraying Heywood R. Floyd, the unheralded William Sylvester. However, since these are not observations that one would make about other Kubrick films, it is logical to assume that there was a deliberate intent behind this apparent dereliction of directorial duty. Specifically, the argument would go, the film is designed to show us that, in the millions of years since Moon-Watcher's first use of tools, human beings have gradually grown so dependent upon their advanced mechanical tools that they have started to become like machines themselves, incapable of any genuine communication or emotional responses—as is reflected in their superficial conversations and bland demeanors. Bowman's decision to disable HAL and eliminate the influence of this advanced tool, and his immediate transformation from a stiff, spacesuited figure into a rounded, superhuman fetus, then, signal an evolutionary move away from a mechanical lifestyle and back toward true, full-blooded humanity, albeit at a new level of intelligence and abilities.

In the novel that Clarke produced to accompany the film, Floyd was no better developed than in the film, but at that time, he was still writing with relative indifference toward deep characterization. Perhaps in response to repeated criticisms, however, the later Clarke worked harder to make his characters seem like real, complex people; so, in elevating Floyd to the status of protagonist in *2010: Odyssey Two*, he unsurprisingly strived to reshape the previously-nondescript Floyd into a nuanced and communicative person who enjoys warm relationships with his second wife, young son, and scientific colleagues and responds with strong emotions to various events in the course of the novel. Yet, if humans in the twenty-first century, surrounded by various sorts of intricate machinery, are in fact capable of retaining their humanity in the manner of the reinvented Floyd, then there would seem to be no real need for our race to undergo any further evolutionary development—which would explain and justify the new indifference of the monolith builders to that issue. The same problem is even more evident in the film based on *2010* that was released two years later.

* * * * * * *

Even if Clarke's sequel lacked the epic scope and *gravitas* of *2001: A Space Odyssey*, it still struck Hollywood producers as sufficiently appealing as to merit a film version—Clarke's original plan—and after Stanley Kubrick declined an offer to become involved with the project, the film was assigned to writer-director Peter Hyams, who thus became the third author to wrestle with the problem of how to best continue the original story. Predictably—since Hyams, unlike Kubrick, had never been noted for his daring or originality—his screenplay for the film, retitled *2010: The Year We Make Contact* (1984), for the most part closely adhered to Clarke's novel.[93] However, Hyams did add some distinctive elements of his own to the story, which generally function to take it even further away from the promise of the original film's and novel's conclusion.

For one thing, while Kubrick seemingly sought out undis-

---

93. *2010: The Year We Make Contact* (Metro-Goldwyn-Mayer, 1984).

tinguished actors to play their parts with a limited emotional range, Hyams strived to cast his film with talented and expressive performers. Thus, even though William Sylvester was still active and presumably available, he chose to recast the part of Heywood R. Floyd with a more renowned and respected actor, Roy Scheider; and two other cast members, John Lithgow and Helen Mirren, had been or would be nominated for an acting Academy Award (like Scheider). Hyams is also visibly anxious to take advantage of these performers' skills in order to depict fully rounded characters; thus, while he does omit some events from Clarke's novel, he retains and gives ample attention to Floyd's close relationships with his family, including a long series of scenes showing Floyd playing with his son that have no counterpart in the novel, and Scheider, as is his habit, regularly displays strong emotional reactions (unlike Sylvester). As for the other American astronauts voyaging to Jupiter, computer expert Dr. Chandra (Bob Balaban) is provided with an appealing back story, displaying a tendency to form emotional relationships with computers that provides him with an unusually strong motivation to revive and rehabilitate his former creation and associate, HAL 9000, while engineer Walter Curnow (John Lithgow) is made endearing by means of his amusing reluctance to travel through outer space from the Russian spacecraft *Leonov* to the abandoned *Discovery*.

In addition, although Kubrick and Clarke's screenplay provided a minimal amount of dialogue, usually of a routine or superficial nature, Hyams's screenplay offers almost nonstop conversations that at times become intimately personal. This approached is signaled by the way that Hyams' film begins: whereas *2001: A Space Odyssey* opened with a long sequence depicting prehuman primates who had no dialogue at all, *2010: The Year We Make Contact* begins, like Clarke's novel, with a lengthy conversation between two contemporary humans— which is not enlivened by the facts that it takes place in the novel setting of a large radio telescope and that the speakers, Floyd and Russian scientist Dimitri Moisevitch (Dana Elcar), spend much of their time shouting at each other from different levels of its staircase until they ultimately get close enough for normal conversation. In other words, in this film, unlike *2001*, the only barrier to true communication between human beings is excessive distance. The rest of the film is also characterized by almost constant conversations between the American and Russian crew members on board the *Leonov*, so much so as to force the revived HAL (again voiced by Douglas Rain) to alter his manner of communication: although he spoke in slow and measured tones in the original film, as if recognizing that the laconic Bowman and Poole were by no means anxious to speak, the HAL of this film is obliged to talk more quickly in order to get a word in edgewise while in the company of Hyams's chatterboxes. In these ways, then, the film makes it clear, even more so than Clarke's sequel, that people of the early twenty-first century are both highly emotional and effectively communicative, apparently requiring no evolutionary improvements in order to recapture their basic humanity.

It is only natural, in a sense, that a writer-director without Kubrick and Clarke's singular agenda would opt for full-bodied characters who do a lot of talking, which is the usual pattern in popular films, and it is also a justifiable change given that Clarke's own sequel, which Hyams is adapting, moved in this direction as well. What is more surprising that this writer-director did not take advantage of opportunities for other crowd-pleasing developments that were contained in *2010: Odyssey Two*. Specifically, even though the film's new subtitle—*The Year We Make Contact*—announces that the story will focus on an encounter with alien life, that aspect of the novel is strangely downplayed in the film. True, the American-Soviet mission to Jupiter does send a probe down to Europa where there are said to be signs of organic life, and the apparently intentional destruction of the probe indicates that the beings behind the monolith do not want humans to have any contact with beings on Europa; and true, the film retains (with additions to be discussed) the final message from the aliens that could also be regarded as humanity's first contact with an alien intelligence. Still, as is not the case in the novel, the variegated creatures of Europa described in the novel are never observed, and the balloon-like lifeforms that the transformed Bowman discovers floating in the vast atmosphere of Jupiter are entirely omitted. A filmmaker, one might think, would seize upon Clarke's intricate descriptions of these beings as a chance to enthrall audiences with bizarre images of exotic aliens, persuasively rendered with the best special effects available—an attraction that the original *2001: A Space Odyssey* briefly contemplated but did not provide. Yet it seems that Hyams did not want to deal with, or be troubled by, the challenge of representing actual alien beings; perhaps he was uncomfortable with the whole idea of special effects, since his scenes of spacecrafts, astronauts, and Jupiter, in contrast to the brilliantly meticulous work overseen by Kubrick for the original *2001*, are conspicuously inferior and never quite realistic. Kubrick's film, even today, can trick viewers into imagining that they are watching footage of actual space vehicles and space travelers, but audiences watching *2010: The Year We Make Contact* will always be aware that they are watching a movie with second-rate special effects.

One might defend Hyams, though, by arguing that he had an agenda of his own, one that made the absence of aliens and his unconvincing special effects perfectly appropriate; for apparently, Hyams wished to depict the aliens who made the monoliths as maintaining an overriding interest in human progress, if not human evolution, even as Clarke was indicating that they were now shifting their attention to another, embryonic intelligent race. As noted, Hyams does retain a minimal reference to their desire to protect the emerging inhabitants of Europa by having them destroy the Russian probe, as is also indicated by the aliens' message to humanity; Floyd's closing voiceover does mention the anticipated appearance of intelligent Europans— "Someday, the children of the new sun will meet the children of the old. I think they will be our friends"; and the film's final image, a monolith standing in shallow water on the surface of Europa, indeed suggests that they will soon be advancing the Europans in the same way that they once advanced Earth's prehumans. Yet for the most part, Hyams keeps his attention, and the attention of his aliens, squarely on humanity and its representatives; in fact, in his major revision of Clarke's story, he emphatically suggests that the monolith builders are transforming Jupiter into a star primarily in order to assist a human race seemingly hell-bent upon its own destruction.

That is, while Clarke's *2010*, reflecting the political climate of the early 1980s, does convey that American-Soviet relations in the early twenty-first century remain rather tense, somewhat problematizing the careful negotiations that lead to a joint Soviet-American expedition to investigate what happened to the *Discovery*, Hyams's screenplay adds the element of a calamitous crisis: as the *Leonov* approaches Jupiter, the United States and Russia become enmeshed in an escalating military dispute in Honduras, which leads to provocative incidents, casualties, a break in diplomatic relations, and an order from authorities on Earth that the three Americans on the mission must leave the *Leonov*, which is Soviet territory, go to the abandoned American spaceship, the *Discovery*, and have no further contact with their former crewmates. Matters have grown so grim that characters openly wonder if Earth will still be there when they are ready to return, anticipating a devastating nuclear war between the superpowers. Fortunately, though, it seems that humanity's alien mentors have been monitoring the situation, and by means of forceful intervention they seek to resolve the dispute before it leads to a ruinous global war—apparently reasoning that the spectacular transformation of Jupiter into a star, which will make the moons of Jupiter amenable to human habitation, will provide humans with several new worlds to inhabit and thus eliminate any motive for conflicts over territories on Earth. That this, and not the development of intelligent life on Europa, is the major motive behind their action is made explicit in the seven new words that Hyams adds to his otherwise-slight alteration of Clarke's original eleven-word message from the aliens to Earth:

ALL THESE WORLDS
ARE YOURS EXCEPT
EUROPA
ATTEMPT NO LANDING THERE
USE THEM TOGETHER
USE THEM IN PEACE

And immediately thereafter, duly chastised and humbled by this extraordinary gesture and sage advice, the leaders of the United States and the Soviet Union, Floyd tells us, "perhaps [...] learned something because they finally recalled their ships and their planes," bringing the crisis to an end.

Needless to say, the story's original vision of a threatened humanity that requires a further evolutionary leap is now being reinterpreted in a genuinely trivial manner. In Hyams's world-view, the problems facing the human race today are not deeply ingrained issues like an overreliance on tools, an inability to feel genuine emotions, or an absence of meaningful communication; rather, humans all just getting a little uptight because we're all crammed together on the planet Earth, and if we all just get some more places to live, which will take the form of the newly hospitable Jovian moons, then everything will be all right. And, if our alien manipulators' major concern is to ensure that the humanity they once crafted survives its latest catastrophe, it makes perfect sense for Hyams's film to omit depictions of aliens and render outer space in a slipshod manner—because the focus of his story, basically, is almost entirely on planet Earth.

If this statement seems extreme, consider another significant difference between the original film and Hyams's sequel: except for the prologue involving humanity's ancestors on the plains of Africa, four million years ago, not a single moment of *2001: A Space Odyssey* takes place on Earth: the modern story begins with Floyd in space, on the way to the space station and later the Moon, moves on to the crew of the *Discovery* already in space and on their way to Jupiter, and concludes with the Star Child hovering above the planet. Our only glimpses of the future Earth during the film come in brief videophone or television transmissions. Since the protagonists of the film are spending all of their time away from their home planet, the implicit message would appear to be that in the twenty-first century, humanity's natural home is no longer Earth, but rather outer space; and one often-overlooked aspect of Bowman's transformation, as noted earlier, is that as the Star Child, he can now survive in the vacuum of space without a spacesuit, making this new being perfectly suited for perpetual life away from planetary surfaces. In contrast, *2010: The Year We Make Contact* begins with an extended depiction of Floyd's pleasant life on Earth in the year 2010, including an expansive look at his attractive home, and concludes with a series of images of familiar Earth landmarks and a scene showing Floyd and his family sitting on the beach before that final glimpse of the surface of Europa. In this film, then, the implicit message is that humanity's natural home, in the past and in the future, remains the planet Earth.

Overall, then, one can say that Hyams has weakened Clarke's story with a trite overlay—a simplistic call for world peace as the once-enigmatic aliens' chief motive—and with a conservative argument to the effect that humanity does not really need to evolve or move away from its home planet. However, as if to compensate for the banality that has ensued in his film, the writer-director does provide his film with some concluding comments from Floyd, obviously crafted with great care, that belatedly provide a few interesting ideas and represent Hyams's only noteworthy additions to the overall narrative of *2001*.

Speaking to his son as he begins his voyage home, Floyd first contemplates the amazing event he has witnessed and says that "We have seen the process of life take place" in the birth of a new star and the creation of newly habitable planets. He then speculates that "Maybe this is what happened on Earth millions of years ago." While he immediately adds that "Maybe it's something completely different," Floyd is basically theorizing that perhaps, something resembling the amazing transformation of Jupiter also occurred in Earth's past. Now, persons familiar with the previous film and movie might argue that Floyd is simply making an incorrect guess about the unseen aliens' earlier actions, since the first film indicated that their only intervention in Earth's history involved boosting our intelligence, not altering our environment. However, there is actually nothing in the *2001* saga to invalidate Floyd's hypothesis. Perhaps, indeed, the appearance of the monoliths in Africa four million years ago did not represent their first good deed on our behalf; perhaps, indeed, they also visited our planet much earlier and carefully shaped the solar system so as to ensure that it would include a suitable star with an orbiting planet perfectly situated and perfectly equipped first for the development of life, and later for the development of intelligent life.

Floyd's theory is defensible because it is soundly based upon an analogy between what he has observed in 2010—which was cosmic engineering on a vast scale—and what the unseen aliens might have done in Earth's distant past. And if Floyd is correct, the pattern of alien intervention into the evolution of other beings would not involve the two-step pattern apparently presented in *2001*—first, finding suitable candidates and raising them to intelligence, and later, raising them to a higher level of intelligence—but a different two-step pattern: first, an alteration in the physical environment of a suitable planet so as to increase the chances that promising beings might emerge there (their unknown actions long ago in the solar system, the transformation of Jupiter into a star so as to make Europa fully habitable); and second, an alteration in the resulting beings' mental makeup so as to make them truly intelligent (the monolith's education of Moon-Watcher and his tribe on Earth, the placement of the monolith on Europa presumably to someday perform the same service for the Europans), with some ongoing monitoring to ensure that the uplifted species remains alive during the sorts of crises that typically afflict a developing civilization. If nothing else, this idea represents a fuller and more cohesive way to reinterpret the aliens' entire agenda, and it is a conceit that might have led Clarke, or someone else, to craft not a sequel to *2001: A Space Odyssey*, but a prequel, describing the spectacular stellar or planetary changes made by ancient aliens in order to lay the groundwork for the development of the prehuman primates that they would return to educate in the prologue to the original novel and film.

In keeping with the notions that the aliens may have been responsible for creating the human environment, and are maintaining an active interest in our progress, Floyd concludes his remarks with a novel description of the monolith builders: "You can tell your children of the day when everyone looked up and realized that we were only tenants of this world. We have been given a new lease—and a warning—from the landlord." In Clarke's vision, the advanced aliens were busy travelers who planted monoliths in various suitable locations and then hurried on to other tasks, never lingering to assess the fruits of their labors or to check on the progress of the uplifted species. Justifying their singular intervention into a specific crisis in the year 2010, Hyams instead portrays the aliens as the "landlords" of Earth (and presumably other inhabited worlds), who like terrestrial landlords keep a constant eye on their property and take immediate action if there is some threat. Floyd's reference to a "new lease" might refer to the fact that the aliens' deeds have prevented the Earth from being destroyed, thus renewing humanity's occupation of that planet, or he might be thinking about the new habitable worlds that are now open to human occupation. His comment about "a warning," however, is less clear. Perhaps, Hyams's Floyd feels humans are being warned that, if they misbehave again, their alien overseers might not be around, or might not be inclined, to save them a second time; or perhaps, in keeping with Clarke's comment that the aliens sometimes "had to weed," Floyd fears that if humans keep behaving badly, their "landlord" might decide to evict them— which would effectively mean exterminating them—although there is nothing else in the film to support the sense, which will emerge more clearly in Clarke's later sequels to *2001*, that the aliens might be more sinister than benign.

Finally, Floyd's speech includes a provocative comment about the monolith: "I still don't know really what the monolith is. I think it's many things—an embassy for intelligence beyond ours, a shape of some kind for something that has no shape." Here, Floyd—and Hyams—are definitely guilty of mixing metaphors, since whereas a landlord has power over a tenant, a nation with an embassy in another country is merely endeavoring to maintain communication with a presumed equal; but this alternate image does comfortingly suggest that, before they do anything rash, the aliens may at least consult with humanity. And calling the monolith "a shape [...] for something that has no shape" may represent Hyams's watered-down version of the fleeting observation in *2010: Odyssey Two* that the monolith was an extra-dimensional object ("How obvious, now, was that mathematical ratio of its sides, the quadratic sequence 1:4:9! And how naive to have imagined that the series ended there, in only three dimensions!" [149]).

Overall, however, a few good ideas as its coda do not serve to make *2010: The Year We Make Contact* a good movie, and although (according to the Internet Movie Database) the film did make more money than it cost to make, its overall box office earnings of around forty million dollars—much less than *2001: A Space Odyssey*, even if one does not take inflation into account—were surely considered disappointing, which would provide one explanation as to why the other two sequels to *2001* that Clarke would go on to write were never adapted as films.

* * * * * * *

By Clarke's own report, he had first planned to wait for new data about the Jovian system from the Galileo space probe, due to arrive around 1990, before returning to the *2001* saga, but when the *Challenger* disaster indefinitely postponed its launch, he decided to proceed without any new information; a cynic might note that completing and publishing *2061: Odyssey Three* earlier than planned, in 1987, when memories of the previous book and its film adaptation were still fresh, would seem to make better business sense as well. Certainly, it is the book in the series that seems to contribute the least to the ongoing story, heightening suspicions that Clarke was primarily doing it for the money.

To best convey its relative emptiness, one might point out that for much of the length of *2061: Odyssey Three*, it appears that Clarke has entirely forgotten about the monoliths, the transformed Dave Bowman, or any alien efforts to intervene in the development of advanced life; the topics simply do not come up as Clarke crafts another sedate space adventure involving Heywood R. Floyd. Although he is an elderly man in the year 2061, he nonetheless accepts an invitation from a billionaire to accompany other celebrities on a voyage in his private spaceship, named the *Universe*, to rendezvous with Halley's Comet, which is again approaching Earth in that year. In the meantime, Clarke employs the theory, presented in a 1981 article, that gas giants like Jupiter might have cores of solid diamond in order to generate some melodramatic hijinks: having discovered that a fragment from Jupiter's core, which shattered when that planet became a star, has landed on Europa to provide the moon with a mountain made out of diamonds, dubbed Mount Zeus, a diamond manufacturing company has conspired to plant an agent on a spaceship traveling in Jovian space, and that agent hijacks the ship and forces it to land on Jupiter, presumably in an effort to obtain access to the moon's enormous deposits of valuable diamonds. Although the agent is soon killed, bringing an end to the company's scheme, the disabled spaceship is stranded on Europa with a crew in need of rescue, which humanity seeks to effect as quickly as possible, since they are worried about how the unseen aliens might react to this conspicuous violation of their express orders. As the only suitable spacecraft in the vicinity, the *Universe* is asked to abandon its study of Halley's Comet and rush to Europa in order to retrieve the crew members before anything happens.

In the midst of all of these goings-on, only Floyd seems to recall that there was once a man named Dave Bowman who had somehow been transformed into an ethereal representative of those aliens, and after discussing matters, the people on board the *Universe* agree that it might be a good idea for Floyd to send a radio message to Bowman, explaining the whole situation. The only immediate response to the message is that Floyd has a dream in which he sees the monolith, and he is never contacted by Bowman. But Clarke, in the next-to-last chapter of his novel, finally provides readers with a glimpse of what he has been up to since the end of *2010: Odyssey Two*.

First, expanding upon what was said at the end of the second novel, Clarke explains that Bowman has been allowed to bring the deceased HAL into his company as a second, disembodied errand boy for the monolith. Then, in response to the immediate crisis, they decide that since Floyd's grandson is now an adult member of the crew that landed on Europa, it would be helpful to create a duplicate of Floyd as serve as a third ghostly companion who can attract his grandson's attention in order to give him an important message: that his crew needs to move away from a dangerous position in order for the ship with Floyd on board to safely pick them up.

While they are explaining all of these matters to their new friend, Bowman and HAL first provide some more information about the monolith:

> It is a tool, serving many purposes. Its prime function appears to be as a catalyst of intelligence [....] we can tap its memories—or some of them. In Africa, four million years ago, it gave a tribe of starving apes the impetus that led to the human species. Now it has repeated the experiment here—but at an appalling cost.

When Jupiter was converted into a sun so that this world could realize its potential, another biosphere was destroyed.[94]

After Clarke's description of the variegated Jovian lifeforms is repeated, they go on to express the grave concern they are now developing:

> *Something has gone wrong* [....]
> When Mount Zeus fell, it could have destroyed this whole world. Its impact was unplanned—indeed, un-plannable [....] It devastated vast areas of the Europan seabed, wiping out whole species—including some for which we had high hopes. The monolith itself was overturned. It may even have been damaged, its programs corrupted. Certainly they failed to cover all contingencies. (271)

The advanced aliens that created the monolith, and their handiwork, are being diminished in stature, inasmuch as it now transpires that their policy is to place monoliths in various areas where intelligence might develop and then go away, providing no further monitoring of what happens afterward. The monoliths themselves, previously depicted as impervious and flawless, are now susceptible to damage and, as a result, are now seen as being capable of making mistakes. Even before the problem of the huge chunk of diamond colliding with Europa, the monolith's decision to wipe out the Jovians in order to nurture the Europans struck Bowman and HAL as questionable, even ominous, and it has engendered fears about humanity's own eventual fate.

Finally, since they believe that the monolith can no longer be regarded as trustworthy, Bowman and HAL now feel that it has

94. Arthur C. Clarke, *2061: Odyssey Three* (New York: Del Rey/Ballantine Books, 1982), 268. Subsequent page references in the text are to this edition.

become *their* "task to help [the Europans] find their true potential—perhaps here, perhaps elsewhere" (271). And they must work quickly:

> "How much time do we have?"
> "Little enough; barely a thousand years. *And we must remember the Jovians.*" (272)

Their worry, obviously, is that a flawed, malfunctioning monolith might decide, sometime in the future, that some higher purpose requires it to destroy the human race in the same way that it once destroyed the Jovians. In other words, Clarke is building upon the ominous hint in *2010: Odyssey Two*—"And sometimes, dispassionately, they had to weed"—to suggest that the monolith crafted by advanced aliens that was once a friend to humanity might now be evolving into its enemy. And in fact, when Clarke next returns to the *2001* saga, that is exactly what has happened.

* * * * * * *

Clarke took a decade before he published *3001: The Final Odyssey* (1997), perhaps in part because the now-elderly Clarke necessarily was working more slowly, perhaps in part because he wasn't sure who he might employ as its protagonist, given that Dave Bowman had been transformed into an ethereal servant and Heywood R. Floyd had grown too elderly to serve as a hero in any year past, say, 2071. Clarke's ingenious solution was to revive the other hero of *2001: A Space Odyssey*, Frank Poole, last seen as a corpse drifting through interplanetary space near Jupiter. But it was reasonable enough to presume that by the year 3001, if his frozen body was by some happenstance retrieved, the advanced medical science of that time might be able to bring him back to life; and that is precisely how *3001* begins.

As might be expected, Clarke goes on to spend a substantive amount of time acquainting Poole with the technological wonders of another new millennium and saying little about the whereabouts of Dave Bowman and HAL, the monoliths, and the aliens who created them. Still, there is an initial chapter that for the most part repeats the description of the aliens presented in *2010: Odyssey Two*, so that readers immediately know that Clarke has not forgotten them. (Surely, one small factor contributing to the sense that the later two sequels are not going anywhere is Clarke's unfortunate habit of copying lengthy passages from *2010: Odyssey Two* to fill their pages.) Still, there are a few revisions: the monolith builders are now named the Firstborn, confirming that they were indeed the first intelligent species to emerge in the universe, and there are some new concluding paragraphs that set the stage for the eventual appearance of Poole's old comrades:

> [The aliens'] marvelous instruments still continued to function, watching over the experiments started so many years ago.
>
> But no longer were they always obedient to the mandates of their creators; like all material things, they were not immune to the corruptions of Time and its patient, unsleeping servant, Entropy.
>
> And sometimes, they discovered and sought goals of their own.[95]

Thus, when Poole finally encounters Bowman and HAL—now, somehow, combined into one ghostly being called Halman—readers have been prepared for the ominous news that they provide, as reported by Poole:

> The Monolith is a fantastically powerful machine—look what it did to Jupiter!—but it's no more than that. It's running on automatic; it has no consciousness [....]

---

95. Arthur C. Clarke, *3001: The Final Odyssey* (1997; New York: Del Rey/ Ballantine Books, 1999), 5. Subsequent page references in the text are to this edition.

Worse still, some of its systems may have started to fail; Dave even suggests that, in a fundamental way, it's become stupid! Perhaps it's been left on its own for too long—it's time for a service check.

And he [Halman] believes that the Monolith has made at least one misjudgment. Perhaps that's not the right word—it may have been deliberate, carefully considered.... (181)

Further, because Halman now fears that the Monolith may be about to do something very inimical to human interests, he asks Poole to get the scientists of Earth to figure out some way to disable the Monolith. Since it is now being characterized as a sort of computer, scientists of the year 3001 soon devise an appropriate solution: venturing into an ancient vault of stored computer viruses, they extract a suitable weapon, Halman contrives to somehow inject it into the Monolith, and the "fantastically powerful machine" that has loomed over humanity since ancient times is finally turned off, perhaps destroying the being named Halman—since it was in some fashion powered by or contained within the Monolith—but ensuring that humanity will survive for at least another thousand years—the time when Poole and his colleagues anticipate that the makers of the Monolith will find out that one of their machines is no longer functioning and perhaps respond in some threatening manner.

Overall, in a fashion almost unimaginable, the astonishingly advanced aliens that were once depicted as the very pinnacle of evolution have now been effectively reduced to the level of mere humanity. Quite literally, they are now Just Like Us. Like humans, they have constructed an impressively advanced computer (HAL 9000, the Monolith); like humans, they failed to anticipate that this computer would at one point malfunction and become a menace to the beings it was supposed to assist; and like humans, they must now depend upon Dave Bowman to venture into the bowels of the machinery, shut down the faulty piece of equipment, and restore order to the world.

Furthermore, consider what has happened to the original theme of the film. As already explained, the story seems to argue that, after depending upon tools for millions of years to advance them from using bones to using spaceships, humanity has now reached the point where tool-making has taken them as far as it can, requiring the race to evolve beyond the use of these tools of limited value. Now, it transpires in *3001: The Final Odyssey* that even the most advanced of aliens have not risen above the need to build and use tools, and that they also have not risen above the problem of tools that can be misused, or can malfunction, and become inimical to their own interests. Evolution beyond the merely human, in other words, is now not only a topic that is being avoided in this series; rather, the series is now arguing, such evolution would appear to be virtually impossible. No matter how far humans might travel or what incredible technologies they might develop, the story line of *3001* appears to suggest, they will always be, like their alien manipulators, fallible creatures depending upon the unreliable tools they will always need to construct.

However, Clarke does not merely indict the aliens as the builders of bad machines; he is further willing to suggest that they themselves might also be ready to destroy humanity. For there is one specific reason why Halman fears the Monolith is about to become a threat: in the twenty-first century, it will be recalled from *2010: Odyssey Two*, the transformed Bowman returned to Earth to survey his home planet and found any number of festering conflicts and problems that might lead advanced aliens to conclude that the entire species was becoming a failed experiment in need of "weeding." Halman knows that it took about 450 years for his report to reach the entity that is the Monolith's immediate supervisor, so it would take about the same amount of time for that supervisor to relay new instructions to the Monolith, based upon its opinion of that report; and Halman reports, in fact, that the Monolith appears to be receiving a flurry of new instructions, and he fears that those instructions might involve the elimination of the human race. Thus, humanity's problem is not simply that a flawed alien computer might erroneously decide to eradicate their species; the aliens who constructed it, in fact, might coldly resolve to mandate precisely such an action. Thus, while the Monolith might now be "stupid," the aliens might be downright evil.

It should be noted that, in the brief and enigmatic final chapter, Clarke appears to back away from this unflattering portrait of hyper-evolved aliens, since such a being is presumably the speaker who intones these words: "Their little universe is very young, and its god is still a child. But it is too soon to judge them; when We return in the last days, We shall consider what should be saved" (237). One reasonable interpretation of this statement is that it comes from a race of aliens who are as far beyond the aliens who built the monoliths as those aliens are beyond humanity: by this reading, the "they" is humanity, "its god" is the alien race that has been manipulating our species, and while some of the things that advanced race is doing might be questionable, its actions are excused on the grounds that, by the standards of this even more advanced being, the race of the monolith builders is still "a child." Perhaps, then, there is indeed a model for human evolution which inarguably represents a vast improvement upon humanity, though this model is now not the aliens who have been the agents behind events in the *2001* saga, but rather another race that is far, far above them in its powers and wisdom.

3001: The Final Odyssey also contains another idea about humanity's possible advancement, though it is left undeveloped, and that is the combined being named Halman, who blends together human intelligence and machine intelligence. It has been shown, by humans in the twenty-first century and the potentially genocidal monolith builders, that sentient creatures with organic origins are unreliable, and it has been shown, by HAL 9000 and the increasingly suspect monolith, that sentient creatures of mechanical origins are also unreliable. Perhaps, by merging an organic being and a mechanical being, a truly superior sentient creature might be achieved—the ideal of the "cyborg" which has often been celebrated by proponents of the postmodern. Yet just as Bowman himself was never presented as a superhuman successor to humanity in the first two sequels to *2001*, Halman in *3001* is similarly in no way elevated to such a status; in fact, he seems pretty much like Bowman, creating the impression that integrating HAL into his already unemotional personality has really not changed him very much. And, given that the central conceit of this novel is the monolith reconsidered as a fallible computer, it is hard to simultaneously maintain the position that merging a computer with an organic being might in some way improve the species.

And what about the Europans, the promising beings that the monolith builders hoped to raise to intelligence by transforming Jupiter into a star? Might they be developing into beings with even greater potential than humans to achieve some sort of super-humanity? Clarke deflates this possibility as well, since Poole reports that "Though a thousand years is a very short time, one would have expected some progress, but according to Dave they're exactly the same now as when they left the sea" (186). It would seem hard to be optimistic, then, that this race will someday achieve intelligence, let alone a status that transcends human intelligence.

Thus, despite the manifest promise of the fetus-like Star Child at the end of the original film, Clarke has now brought his saga about a prophesied leap beyond the merely human to an effective dead end. The transformed Bowman is not the vanguard of a new superhuman species, but now is only a sort of computer simulation of an ordinary human who is being assigned to perform various chores for an advanced alien species. Although the once-unhinged HAL 9000 was rehabilitated, there is not the slightest hint that machine intelligence represents a path to superhumanity; indeed, with the monolith redefined as an advanced computer that, like the original HAL, has started to malfunction, such a possibility seems specifically precluded. The aliens who built the monoliths are now perceived as beings capable of grievous errors and malicious actions that would result in the destruction, not the nurturing, of other intelligent life, rather diminishing their luster as possible models of humanity's glorious future. The Europans' lack of progress indicates that other species are equally unlikely to achieve a state of superhuman perfection. There is one final hint of the existence of a truly transcendent, unimaginably advanced species, but upon close examination they, too, may turn out to retain the grievous flaws already observed in the other species once thought to have evolved beyond them.

Perhaps, one might argue, all of this in fact is designed to convey an unexciting, but potentially accurate picture of humanity's future. Perhaps, we have already gotten to be as good as we are ever going to get, and we can expect to remain pretty much the same as we are now for as long as our species might endure; and other intelligent beings will similarly cease developing as soon as they attain a stature similar to present-day humanity. And one might concede that this vision of eternal stagnation is just as likely as any other prediction one might make about humanity's future. Yet everything that we know about the human race would appear to undermine this theory; for our history demonstrates that humanity has kept evolving biologically, intellectually, and culturally for millions of years, so it would seem extraordinarily unlikely that we now happen to be living at the precise moment in history when all of that progress is destined to come to a screeching halt. Surely, some sort of further improvement must be on the horizon, and arguing otherwise seems not a reasoned conclusion, but rather a desperate expedient in the face of a fundamental inability to clearly envision precisely what forms that further improvement might take. So it is that, in the course of his three sequels to *2001: A Space Odyssey*, Clarke felt compelled to take his readers further and further away from the subject of future human evolution, even though that was manifestly the central point of the original film and novel.

Still, the expressed concerns in 3001 about what might happen around the year 4001, and the provocative coda suggesting the existence of beings beyond any yet encountered in the series, did provide Clarke with an opening for another sequel, which presumably would again have failed to add much of interest to this deteriorating saga. But instead of taking that step, Clarke resolved to keep the promise implicit in his subtitle—*The Final Odyssey*—and would never return to the world that he and Kubrick had crafted decades ago, and would never allow any other writer to do so. However, even if he never sanctioned another sequel, he did, a few years after the appearance of *3001*, authorize and involve himself in what might be described as a sidebar to the story of *2001*, presented in three volumes that offer another perspective on the possible characteristics of a superhuman race.

* * * * * * *

Having produced only two other novels in the 1990s, the seventy-seven-year-old Clarke made a second announcement, after *3001: The Final Odyssey*, that he would write no more novels (although he again broke this promise and began another one, *The Last Theorem* [2008], which was eventually completed by Frederik Pohl). Yet several other novels had been appearing that prominently displayed Clarke's name as their principal author, followed by the name of one of his so-called "co-authors," who were Gentry Lee, Mike McQuay, Michael Kube-McDowell, and Stephen Baxter. Clarke made little effort to conceal that, in fact, these other men were actually writing these novels, while Clarke generally limited himself to contributing some initial ideas, regular feedback, and an afterword. Since one of these authors, Gentry Lee, had been allowed to produce a three-volume continuation of Clarke's *Rendezvous with Rama*—another saga involving an artifact built by unseen, enigmatic aliens—it was perhaps inevitable that another of Clarke's writing partners might bring up the possibility of continuing the *2001* series in some fashion. And while Clarke held firm to his public declaration that he would never produce another *2001* novel, he was open to the idea of a new story along those lines that would not be directly connected to the *2001* saga.

Thus, to introduce *Time's Eye* (2004), subtitled *Book One of A Time Odyssey*, a brief "Authors' Note" attributed to Clarke and the book's purported co-author and probable sole author, Stephen Baxter, stated that "This book, and the series that it opens, neither follows nor precedes the books of the earlier *Odyssey*, but is at right angles to them; not a sequel or prequel, but an 'orthoquel,' taking similar premises in a different direction."[96] To be specific, Clarke and Baxter would develop the narrative of this new trilogy by again positing the existence of mysterious advanced aliens, represented solely by stark geometric artifacts, who will undertake in the near future to meddle in the affairs of humanity. The difference this time, as Baxter explained in the interview, "A Conversation with Stephen Baxter and Sir Arthur C. Clarke," included as an afterword to *Time's Eye*, is that they would be "assuming an intervention that's hostile from the very beginning" ([365]). Even if it was not a true sequel to *2001*, then, this trilogy would in a way be completing the narrative arc of the series—moving from a first volume and film depicting what seems to be an entirely benign race of manipulators, to later volumes depicting a race that increasingly seems flawed or even potentially inimical, to a final trilogy depicting a race that seems entirely evil.

Crafting a trilogy along these lines, however, did pose some problems for Clarke and Baxter, who were far more scientifically astute, and more principled, than the many lesser authors and filmmakers who had long offered colorful but contrived tales of sinister aliens with awesome scientific capabilities who attempt to invade Earth but are defeated by plucky humans. Naturally wishing to assume that the future evolution of intelligent life would involve both advances in technology and advances in

---

96. Arthur C. Clarke and Stephen Baxter, *Time's Eye: Book One of A Time Odyssey* (2004; New York: Del Rey/Ballantine Books, 2005), [v]. Subsequent page references in the text are to this edition.

morality, they could not posit purely malevolent aliens as the end product of their own extended evolution, and thus as models for what humanity might eventually evolve into, but instead would need to provide some logical reason why advanced aliens might seek humanity's downfall. And the justification developed by the masterful writer who effectively introduced this theme in his *The War of the Worlds* (1898), H. G. Wells—that a once-admirable race might seek to conquer the Earth because their own depleted planet compelled them to covet our lush environment and rich resources—no longer made sense in an era when scientists knew the universe was filled with planets, and when they could readily predict the future development of technologies such as terraforming which could transform barren worlds into paradises, eliminating any reason for an advanced species to take over inhabited planets. In addition, if authors envision truly superior aliens, and not the easily-defeated bumblers of popular culture, they would have to accept the fact that such beings would obviously be capable of eradicating a lesser race like humanity quickly and easily, making it difficult to sustain an extended narrative about their sure-to-be-successful efforts.

To address the first issue, Clarke and Baxter begin by dropping numerous hints in *Time's Eye*, while describing their otherwise-incomprehensible handiwork on the new world of Mir (to be discussed), that these new aliens are far from kindly: one character asks, "Do any of us actually *believe* there can be benevolence behind this meddling?" (111), another speaks of their "cruelty" and "Arrogance" (244), while a third thinks that their artifact is "hovering above them both balefully" (270-271) and opines that they are "not gods" "Because they have no compassion" (267). But only near the end of the book, in the forty-fourth of its forty-seven chapters, do the authors spell out exactly what the aliens—the first intelligent race that emerged in the universe—are up to:

> as they looked ahead, they saw only a slow darkening,
> as each generation of stars was built with increasing

difficulty from the debris of the last. There would come a day when there wasn't enough fuel in the Galaxy to manufacture a single new star, and the last light flickered and died [....]

They returned to their abandoned machines of war. The ancient machines were directed to a new objective: to the elimination of waste—to cauterization, if necessary. The makers saw now that if even a single thread of awareness was to be passed to the furthest future, there must be no unnecessary disturbance, no wasted energy, no ripples in the stream of time.

The machines [....] waited, unchanging, dedicated to a single purpose, as new worlds, and new life, congealed from the rubble of the old.

It was all for the best of intentions. The first ones, born into an empty universe, cherished life above all else. But to preserve life, life must sometimes be destroyed. (353-354)

In other words, to preserve the universe's finite supply of energy as long as possible, and thus to keep themselves alive as long as possible, these aliens, here called "the Firstborn" as in *3001: A Space Odyssey*, had dedicated themselves to wiping out all intelligent species in their own galaxy, since they tended to use up energy at an alarming rate.

In addition, to explain specifically why they feel so driven to survive into the "furthest future," the third book in the trilogy, *Firstborn: A Time Odyssey: 3* (2008), presents a theory developed by the extinct Martian race:

The Martians argued among themselves as to *why* the Firstborn were so intent upon reaching the Last Days.

Perhaps it derived from their origin. Perhaps in their coming of awareness in the First Days they had encountered—*another*. One as far beyond their cosmos as they were beyond the toy universes in which they stored their time-sliced worlds. One who would return in the Last Days, to consider what should be saved.

The Firstborn probably believed that in their universal cauterization they were being benevolent.[97]

This idea of an ultimate über-race that would eventually materialize to pass judgment on the universe, of course, is borrowed from the conceit in the brief final chapter of *3001: A Space Odyssey.*

Despite this elaborate exercise in justification and rationalization, it is hard to dispute that, by any ethical code one can imagine, this behavior by the aliens is immoral. They are precisely equivalent to a man who escapes from a sinking ship, gets on board its single lifeboat, and proceeds to murder any other passengers who attempt to join him, arguing that this represents the best way to prolong the lifeboat's supplies and thus ensure that there will be at least one survivor. That is, simply because they happened to be the first intelligent species to evolve, what gives these aliens the right to conclude that they deserve to be the only intelligent species that remains alive? Beings that genuinely "cherished life above all else," upon noticing that another energy-consuming intelligent race has emerged, might approach the newcomers, school them on the importance of conserving the universe's energy, and then collectively commit suicide, allowing another species to carry on the task of waiting for the "Final Days" until they, too, properly decide to pass the torch to yet another new species and eliminate themselves. Or if, as the Martians speculate, "the universe could only bear one world as populous and energy-hungry as their own, one world in each of the universe's hundred billion empty galaxies, if the Last Days were to be reached" (292-293), then upon the arrival of each new intelligent species, the Firstborn could destroy a

---

97. Arthur C. Clarke and Stephen Baxter, *Firstborn: A Time Odyssey: 3* (New York: Del Rey/Ballantine Books, 2008), 293. Subsequent page references in the text are to this edition.

part of their own population and replace it with representatives of the newcomers, so that when the universe is ending, the super-advanced beings which would appear could be greeted by a world collectively populated by all of one galaxy's intelligent species, not just a world populated by one surviving species.

It is also incongruous that there is never a mention of any efforts by the Firstborn to devise an alternative strategy to meet their goals, such as devising some mechanism that would replenish the universe's supply of energy, tapping some source of energy from outside the known universe, and/or developing innovative techniques that would enable intelligent species to persist with such an amazingly minimal expenditure of energy as to allow for the long-time endurance of several or many races instead of one. Readers might have more sympathy for these implacable aliens if they had been told, for example, that the Firstborn had first devoted countless millennia to a thoroughgoing search for some other solution before finally and reluctantly implementing their policy of galactic genocide. But there are no statements of this kind anywhere in the trilogy.

When one considers how Clarke and Baxter addressed their second problem—providing the Firstborn with a methodology for murder which would fill an entire trilogy—it will become apparent that these advanced aliens are not only the most evil ones yet encountered in any continuation of *2001*, but also the stupidest. (This might also explain why they so quickly began slaughtering other races apparently without pausing to consider other possible courses of action.)

As eventually becomes clear in *Firstborn*, the aliens follow a three-step process whenever they learn about the emergence of another intelligent race, with each step successively illustrated in the three books of the trilogy. As the first step, they make copies of various bits and pieces of the targeted world's past history and put them all together to form a new, amalgamated planet within an especially-created pocket universe that endures for a few centuries before being destroyed. This is essentially the story of *Time's Eye*: United Nations soldiers fighting in

Afghanistan in the year 2037 suddenly find themselves in a world that also includes, among others, australopithecines, the armies of Alexander the Great and Genghis Khan, and a troop of nineteenth-century British soldiers accompanied by a young Rudyard Kipling; and it is their various conflicts, partnerships, conspiracies, and romances that fill up almost all of the volume.

The natural question to ask is *why* the aliens would bother to do this. First, it would all seem to represent an unnecessary expenditure of energy on the part of beings purportedly obsessed with avoiding precisely that, although we are told in *Firstborn* that, according to a Martian scientist, "the energy sums would cancel out" when the universe expired (293). If this is granted, then the aliens are simply employing an energy-neutral method to carefully observe the history of the species they are about to exterminate. This is intimated throughout *Time's Eye* because the ubiquitous artifacts that represent these aliens—not monoliths, but perfect, floating spheres—are universally referred to as "Eyes" and are repeatedly described as somehow watching or observing the novel's characters (19, 90, 191, 227, 249-250, 268, 276, 287, and 297). A character in the second novel, *Sunstorm: A Time Odyssey: 2* (2007), describes this observation as something the Firstborn regard as a painful duty:

> "One thing I'm sure about, though. They *watch*."
> "Watch?"
> "I think that's what Mir was all about. Mir was a montage of all our history, right up to the moment of this—our possible destruction. Mir wasn't about us but about the Firstborn. They forced themselves to look at what they were destroying, to face what they had done."[98]

---

98. Arthur C. Clarke and Stephen Baxter, *Sunstorm: A Time Odyssey: 2* (New York: Del Rey/Ballantine Books, 2007), 198-199. Subsequent page references in the text are to this edition.

But this explanation does not really make any sense; for if the Firstborn were capable of traveling back into the past to select and replicate slices of human history, they were presumably capable of sending Eyes back into those past eras to observe our history as it actually happened, instead of settling for an artificial and possibly unrepresentative summary of our history derived from the juxtaposition of random representatives of various periods and cultures. The aliens' actions, therefore, do not really serve their own interests, but rather serve the interests of an author, Stephen Baxter, with a known fascination with alternate history. So, have you ever wondered who would have triumphed if Alexander the Great had fought a battle against Genghis Khan, with each commander assisted by some nineteenth-century and/or twenty-first-century technology? You can read *Time's Eye* and find out. And while *Firstborn*'s return to Mir does not emulate Garrett P. Serviss to describe *Edison's Conquest of Mars* (1898), there is at least a vignette about Edison's Contact with Mars. As I have argued elsewhere, all of these exercises in alternate history represent little more than authorial game-playing, and not the thoughtful extrapolation of future possibilities that Clarke, and other great science fiction writers, are noted for.[99]

In any event, having temporarily preserved and observed some of Earth's history, the aliens proceed to their usual second step—destroying the intelligent species—by detaching a huge, distant planet from its orbit around another star and sending it crashing into our sun, provoking interior energy fluctuations that eventually cause a sudden outpouring of stellar energy— the "sunstorm" of the second volume—which will devastate Earth and kill all of its advanced life forms. Again, this might be regarded as a maneuver which uses an excessive amount of energy, but Clarke and Baxter anticipate and try to counter that argument: as a scientist explains, "they act with—*economy*. If

---

99   Gary Westfahl, "Greyer Lensmen, Or Looking Backward in Anger," *Interzone*, No. 129 (March, 1998), 40–43.

a star system is giving them cause for concern, they first hit it with a sunstorm. Crude, a blanket blowtorching, but a cheap way of sterilizing an entire system" (*Firstborn* 271).

However, despite their enormous powers, the Firstborn manage to botch the job of slaughtering the human race due to two astounding blunders. First, it transpires that the Firstborn's decision to destroy humanity was not a unanimous one—it was reached "despite some dissension" (*Sunstorm* 184)—and some of those dissenters have apparently been secretly working to prevent the genocide. In *Time's Eye*, they employ one of Mir's Eyes to transport one resident, a twenty-first-century soldier named Bisesa Dutt, back to Earth, where in *Sunstorm* she is able to provide authorities with the vital clue that the sunstorm is not a natural event, but was rather caused by homicidal aliens. Great Britain's Astronomer Royal of the year 2037, Siobhan McGorran, figures out the situation: after asking Bisesa, "Why would they warn any of us—and why *you*?...," she is immediately able to answer her own question:

> Because there are factions among these Firstborn. Because they are no more united and uniform of view than humanity is—why should a more advanced civilization be homogeneous? And because there are some of them, at least, who believe that what is being done is wrong. A faction of them, working through Bisesa, are trying to warn us. (*Sunstorm* 152-153)

Yet this represents a typical error made by scoundrels in popular adventures: allowing a traitorous underling to secretly work against them without being aware of the betrayal. One would imagine that advanced aliens, having reached an important decision, would have the capability and resolve to prevent the opponents of that decision from doing anything to undermine it.

Their second mistake is even more indefensible: having set in motion the events that will cause Earth's doom in the year

2042, they proceed to ignore the planet while, during five years of frenetic work, humanity manages to construct an enormous, ultrathin, and intelligently flexible shield which will provide our planet with sufficient protection against the sunstorm as to prevent Earth's complete devastation, though there will still be catastrophic consequences. If they had been paying attention to this activity, the Firstborn presumably could have destroyed this shield in an instant and thus ensured the extinction of humanity; instead, the work proceeds on schedule and humanity is ultimately saved. In this respect, these aliens resemble the absurd villain of melodramas who places the hero in an inescapable deathtrap, cackles with glee, and then, instead of lingering to watch the hero die, inexplicably leaves to deal with some other business, thus giving the hero an opportunity to devise a way out of the trap. True, we are told in both *Sunstorm* and *Firstborn* that the aliens secretly placed an Eye at a Trojan point near Jupiter in order to observe Earth's destruction, but they obviously were not watching the planet very carefully.

Furthermore, it is evident that the aliens' surefire method of exterminating intelligent life must be counteracted on a fairly regular basis, bolstering the sense that they are fairly incompetent, because they have a third step, a back-up system, in place: according to the same scientist, "But if the sunstorms don't work, if worlds continue to be troublesome, they strike more surgically" (271)—specifically, by transforming an Eye into a so-called "Q-Bomb" of dark energy which is directed to strike the "troublesome" planet and will not only devastate it, but actually remove it from the universe. The menace of such a Q-Bomb, due to collide with Earth in twenty-one months, provides the plot for the third book in the trilogy, *Firstborn*.

Again, however, the Firstborn manage to bungle the job. First, we learn that many millennia ago, a race of intelligent Martians managed to trap an Eye in some sort of force-field, still present to be fortuitously discovered by twenty-first-century humans exploring Mars, before the Martians were exterminated by a Q-Bomb. (This raises any number of questions: how could advanced aliens allow a lesser race to do such a thing? If they wanted to eliminate the Martians, why did they proceed directly to a Q-Bomb instead of unleashing a sunstorm? And if ancient Mars was indeed struck by a Q-Bomb, why did the now-lifeless planet remain in our universe? But one tires of pointing out unresolved issues in Clarke and Baxter's story). Then, Bisesa Dutt is transported back to Mir, where she learns that its universe contains not only an amalgamated Earth, but amalgamated versions of the solar system's other planets, including a patchwork Mars that still includes one intelligent Martian. (But why would the aliens bother to do this, since Mir was ostensibly created only as a way to study Earth's history?) On Mir, Thomas Alva Edison figures out that humans can send a message to Mars—a string of symbols somehow extracted from the force-field the Martians placed around the Eye—by carving immense ditches forming those symbols, filling them with combustible materials, and lighting them on fire so that Martian astronomers can observe them. When the Martian sees the symbols, she realizes that another race needs assistance in fighting the Firstborn and, by means of her advanced science, her "gravitational cage crushed the Firstborn Eye" (294). This for some reason distresses not only the duplicate Eye on the Mir universe's Mars, but also the original Eye trapped on our Mars, causing it to send out a distress signal which, when detected by the Q-Bomb, inspires the intelligent bomb to shift its course away from Earth and instead strike Mars, now perceived as the greater threat. In other words, like the unseen aliens in Clarke's original series, these Firstborn have also constructed a flawed, inept machine, capable of being diverted from its mission by an obvious diversionary tactic.

Like Clarke's *3001: The Final Odyssey*, *Firstborn* concludes by providing an obvious opening for a sequel: Bisesa and her daughter Myra are transported by the Eye to a barren plain, probably Earth in the far future, where they are met by a woman who resembles Bisesa's granddaughter Charlie who tells them, "We call ourselves the Lastborn. We are at war. We are losing

[....] Please. Come with me now" (359). Thus, one can easily envision another trilogy involving an alliance of newer races which would successfully oppose the Firstborn and, one hopes, devise a better way to deal with the problem of the universe's limited supply of energy. But, in light of the mess that the *Time Odyssey* trilogy became, one has to be pleased that no such continuation has so far emerged.

The sad thing about this failed project is that it did have genuinely interesting features. For one thing, *Time's Eye* includes a brief, almost atavistic, remnant of the original story line of *2001: A Space Odyssey*, in that an australopithecine named Grasper was subjected by one Eye to a "probing of her body and mind," designed "only to record her capabilities." However, since "the probing had been clumsy," her "half-formed mind had been stirred," making her "a creature with potential," and "there was no particular reason why that potential had to be realized exactly as it had been before." Then, in a deliberate echo of *2001*, Grasper "hefted the heavy stone in her hand," recognized that she was now "master of the world," and while "not quite sure what to do next," she knew "she would think of something" (361-362). The concept of a new and different form of humanity, this time created not intentionally but accidentally by the always-blundering Firstborn, is fascinating, but while Grasper does briefly reappear in *Firstborn* as a more intelligent being, nothing else is done with the idea.

The Eyes themselves also command attention. Even though we see numerous Eyes throughout the trilogy, we are repeatedly told that "There was only one Eye, though it had many projections into spacetime. And it had many functions" (*Time's Eye* 349); the energies it emits when serving as a transportation device indicate that it, like the monolith, is an object of more than three dimensions; and when the Eye is measured, it transpires that the ratio of its circumference to its diameter is not pi, but exactly three, indicating that it is an object not of our universe. It is incomprehensible that beings intelligent enough to craft such an object could also be stupid enough to make the simple mistakes that doom all of their lethal plans; and it is depressing to speculate that such scientific advances, and such stupid and sinister actions, might be regarded as representing humanity's probable future. And, if authors as astute and capable as Arthur C. Clarke and Stephen Baxter can be driven to such an unlikely and disheartening portrait of the imagined evolution of intelligent life, it indeed suggests that there may be fundamental, and irresolvable problems, in any effort to predict the eventual fate of the human race.

* * * * * * *

As this long odyssey draws to a close, there is only time for a few general conclusions about science fiction's efforts to depict the future of humanity, drawn primarily from consideration of the *2001* saga but with brief sidelong glances at other relevant texts.

The first lesson is the point made long ago by Jack Kirby—that it may be fundamentally impossible for present-day humans to accurately predict the nature of superhumans. Fully recognizing that analogies are both a tool and a trap for prognosticators, one might consider an ant, temporarily endowed with a modicum of intelligence and imagination, who is asked to envision a super-ant. This posited being would no doubt have enhanced abilities to construct larger and more complex anthills, to better locate and retrieve food, to create and nurture a larger number of offspring—in sum, to do everything that an ant does, only in a superior fashion. But could this ant conceive of an advanced creature who could plant crops, devise a monetary system, build a steam engine, or write an opera? In other words, members of the species *homo superior* may indeed be smarter, more powerful, and kinder than we are, but they may also be able and inclined to do things that we cannot begin to imagine. This is why science fiction's best portrayals of intelligences beyond our own may be those stories, such as Stanislaw Lem's *Solaris* (1961) and Terry Carr's "The Dance of the Changer and the Three" (1968), that limit themselves to describing bizarre alien behavior without making any effort to explain it—thus conveying the point that a genuine superbeing would indeed be incomprehensible to present-day humans.

Second, by employing another reasonable but flawed technique for prophecy, extrapolation, writers can ponder how humanity has progressed during the last centuries, posit that those trends will continue into the future, and employ those conclusions as a basis for portrayals of more advanced humans and aliens. Thus, observing that humans have grown less violent over the years, one might logically imagine that a superhuman would be vehemently opposed to violence, like the Star Child at the conclusion of Clarke's *2001: A Space Odyssey* or, for example, the alliance of pacifistic worlds united to prevent conflicts in outer space described by the alien visitor Klaatu in the original version of *The Day the Earth Stood Still* (1951). And, noting that we have become steadily less inclined to kill other animals and more inclined to nurture and protect them, one might logically imagine that a superhuman would be even more interested in preserving and improving lesser forms of life, like Kirby's fifth New Seed, the aliens in Clarke's sequels to *2001*, or the various alien races dedicated to "uplifting" other species to intelligence in David Brin's *Startide Rising* (1983) and its sequels.

Third, if writers feel unable to go beyond such reasonable but unadventurous projections of advanced beings, they may be inclined to simply abandon the effort to depict the successors to humanity. This is what happened in Kirby's comic book series, as he stopped writing about the New Seed and instead began describing the adventures of Machine Man, and what Clarke essentially did in transforming the Star Child from the first representative of *Homo superior* to the monolith's servant. As another example, consider Isaac Asimov, who in the 1980s, like Clarke, returned to his most famous epic and added new volumes to his Foundation trilogy while also connecting the saga to his robot stories. As one new development, *Foundation's*

Edge (1982) introduced as a possible model for human advancement a form of group intelligence on the world of Gaea, creating the possibility that he might conclude the series not only with the predicted reestablishment of the Galactic Empire, but also with a leap forward in human evolution not unlike that observed in Clarke's *Childhood's End*. However, as if unwilling to move in that direction, Asimov also left his narrative unfinished and instead shifted his attention to its back story, concluding the series with two "prequels," *Prelude to Foundation* (1988) and *Forward the Foundation* (1993), that described the life of Hari Seldon, the psychohistorian who had long ago launched the whole saga.[100]

Fourth, as another way to avoid detailed examination of an envisioned superrace, writers may be drawn to what are effectively efforts to change the subject. The most common of these is to convey the impression that advanced beings will be not only concerned, but positively obsessed, with the progress of lesser species in their vicinity of space. This serves to draw attention away from strange beings, who are frustratingly difficult to describe, toward familiar beings, who are easy to describe. Thus, aside from a few generalities, virtually all we are told about the Firstborn in Clarke's *2001* series, and the Firstborn in Clarke and Baxter's *Time Odyssey* trilogy, involves their opinions of humans and similar species and their interventions

---

100. In "What Science Fiction Leaves Out of the Future, #2: The Day After Tomorrow," *The Internet Review of Science Fiction*, March, 2009, at http://www.irosf.com/q/zine/article/10528, I also discuss how Asimov's Foundation series and other science fiction epics tend to remain incomplete and look backward, probably because writers are unwilling to explore the issue of humanity's eventual destiny. In that article I further acknowledge (as I should also acknowledge here) that George Slusser has previously analyzed this phenomenon in his own distinctive fashion, most thoroughly in "Dimorphs and Doubles: J. D. Bernal's 'Two Cultures' and the Transhuman Promise," *Science Fiction and the Two Cultures: Essays on Bridging the Gap between the Sciences and the Humanities*, edited by Gary Westfahl and George Slusser (Jefferson, North Carolina: McFarland Publishers, 2009), 96-129.

into their affairs. Other writers have moved in a similar direction; for example, while most people regard Olaf Stapledon's *Star Maker* (1937) as the continuation of his *Last and First Men* (1930), that book actually had a more immediate sequel, the little-known *Last Men in London* (1932), wherein a representative of Stapledon's hyper-advanced Eighteenth Men travels into the past to display an inordinate fascination with the daily life of a typical resident of present-day London. Despite a lengthy introduction justifying "The Future's Concern with the Past,"[101] this interest does not appear logical at all; but it does allow Stapledon to say very little about his future superhumans and their life on Neptune while saying a great deal about what his fellow humans are doing right now.

To say the least, based on our knowledge of human history, it does not seem defensible to project that superbeings will be driven to study and meddle in the affairs of lesser beings as their primary activity. True, there are today numerous people who are dedicated to breeding or nurturing animals like dogs, cats, and horses, and almost every living organism on the planet has attracted at least a few scientists who are fascinated by, and may feel a special bond with, the creatures they are studying. But no human culture as a whole has predominantly focused its energies on the improvement of animals, and it is hard to imagine that a superhuman race would envision its primary purpose as the improvement of humans or other, less advanced species. It is more reasonable to posit, as Clarke does at the conclusion of *Against the Fall of Night* and *Childhood's End*, that members of a superrace would have little if any interest in the doings of their predecessors and would unhesitatingly and permanently withdraw from their company; but while a writer could readily portray this attitude when a story concludes with the creation or discovery of advanced beings, it is a problematic premise when

---

101. Olaf Stapledon, "Introduction: The Future's Concern with the Past," *Last Men in London*, 1932, in *Last and First Men and Last Men in London*, by Olaf Stapledon (Middlesex, England: Penguin Books, 1973, 335-337.

one is beginning a story about such beings.

Fifth, if writers carry on with their efforts to depict a super-human species, they may fall victim to the sentiment of the old saying, "familiarity breeds contempt," and to make these beings seem more and more like ordinary human beings. Thus, in the original film and novel *2001: A Space Odyssey*, the monoliths, and the aliens who constructed them, were implicitly but clearly presented as omniscient, omnipotent, and absolutely incapable of error; they had a plan for the development and improvement of the human species, and they carried it out flawlessly. In Clarke's sequels to *2001*, however, there gradually emerged a sense that the monolith builders were distant, and not always capable, manipulators of humanity, and their machines were seen as deteriorating and potentially inclined to make disastrous mistakes; and those aliens' counterparts in the *Time Odyssey* trilogy, as noted, were downright evil and even less competent. As another example, one might consider the character of Q (John de Lancie), initially presented in the first episode of *Star Trek: The Next Generation* (1987-1994), "Encounter at Farpoint" (1987), as a member of an amazing advanced superrace with knowledge and abilities far beyond those of mere humans; yet as he continued to reappear in future episodes of that series, *Star Trek: Deep Space Nine* (1993-1999) and *Star Trek: Voyager* (1995-2001), he increasingly became a comic character, easily outwitted or outmaneuvered by the humans he loved to interact with and prone to any number of human weaknesses.

Sixth, as another aspect of this tendency to regard superbe-ings as similar to typical humans, writers may resort to human-ity's ancient tendency in confronting an unknown intruder—to immediately classify it as either "friend" or "foe" and respond accordingly—and start to characterize these enigmatic crea-tures in such conventional terms—despite the logical supposi-tion that that an advanced race would inevitably have complex motives not well described by these simple categories. One need not reiterate that evil aliens have long been a mainstay of popular science fiction, but even writers who are intelligent enough to reject such stereotypes may find themselves drifting toward similar portrayals, as was the case in Clarke and Baxter's *Time Odyssey* trilogy. And, if writers are uncomfortable with portrayals of these superbeings as enemies, they can always transform them into friends. That is the scenario of the Clarke and Pohl's *The Last Theorem*: advanced aliens called the Grand Galactics first begin an effort to eradicate the flawed human race, but when one of them visits Earth and sees signs of progress, the Grand Galactics not only reverse their decision and spare humanity from destruction, but also decide, generously and implausibly, to bequeath to humans their guiding role as the guardians of the galaxy.

Even in what is perhaps the greatest science fiction novel to wrestle with the vexing question of the ultimate destiny of intelligent life in the universe, Olaf Stapledon's *Star Maker*, the briefly observed ultimate being is described by the hapless narrator using the language of "friend" or "foe." When the Cosmic Mind that is the combination of all the universe's most developed species finally encounters their universe's creator, the Star Maker, that entity rejects their approach, and the Cosmic Mind resultingly speaks of their creator with what seems like justifiable anger:

> In my agony I cried out against my ruthless maker. I cried out that, after all, the creature was nobler than the creator; for the creature loved and craved love, even from the star that was the Star Maker; but the creator, the Star Maker, neither loved nor had need of love.[102]

But the Cosmic Mind immediately regrets this outburst and works his way to the realization that the Star Maker is, from his limited perspective, somehow both a villain and a hero:

---

102. Olaf Stapledon, *Star Maker*, 1937, in *Last and First Men and Star Maker: Two Science-Fiction Novels by Olaf Stapledon*, by Olaf Stapledon (New York: Dover Books, 1968), 410. Subsequent page references in the text are to this edition.

"Irrationally, yet with conviction, I gave my adoration to the Star Maker as comprising both aspects of his dual nature, both the 'good' and the 'evil,' both the mild and the terrible, both the humanly ideal and the incomprehensibly inhuman" (421). It is indeed striking that, even in this grandest effort to conceive of the inconceivable—a creature infinitely more advanced than humanity—the author finds himself falling back upon crude, anthropocentric concepts of "good" and "evil."

Finally, as writers allow their posited superbeings to be gradually reduced to the status of all-too-human fools, scoundrels, or bosom buddies, their only recourse is, essentially, to start all over again: to indicate that, beyond the once-exalted level of their original creations, there exists an even more advanced race of beings, as high above them as those beings are above humans, and to suggest that this newly unveiled species might actually embody the enigmatic perfection once associated with the first superbeings. This is how Clarke effectively both abandons and relaunches his *2001* saga in the two-sentence conclusion to *3001: The Final Odyssey*, and hints of a similar super-super-race also emerge in the *Time Odyssey* trilogy. As another interesting example, Frederik Pohl's *Gateway* (1977) initially involves an unseen but highly advanced alien race, the Heechee, whose abandoned spaceships are imperfectly exploited by future humans in search of knowledge and wealth. However, as the second novel in the series, *Beyond the Blue Event Horizon* (1980), tells us more about the Heechee, and as the third novel, *Heechee Rendezvous* (1984), actually brings them onstage, we learn that the Heechee, despite their superior technology, are not as superhuman as they once appeared, since they are now hiding near a black hole in order to avoid an even more powerful race, the Assassins, intent upon destroying and refashioning the entire universe. However, after bringing the Heechee down to human-like status and introducing a new race to function as superhuman alternatives to humanity, Pohl's fourth novel in the series, *The Annals of the Heechee* (1987), begins to refashion the Assassins themselves as comforting friends, since their efforts to rid the universe of matter and reconstruct a universe of pure energy are now being viewed as desirable. The stage now is seemingly set for the unveiling of a third race of beings far above the Assassins who might recapture the aura of awe and mystery previously associated first with the Heechee and later with the Assassins, but Pohl instead brought his series to an end—despite the appearance of two later volumes, *The Gateway Trip* (1990) and *The Boy Would Who Live Forever: A Novel of Gateway* (2004), that follow Asimov's example and are both basically "prequels" offering stories that took place before the time of *The Annals of the Heechee*. And this, of course, also makes Pohl's series another example of an epic about humanity's future that concludes not by going forward but by going backward.

Still, it seems clear that, despite the inherent difficulties, or the sheer impossibility, of the task, science fiction writers will always feel the urge to continue their endless odyssey of attempting to envision a future human race that is significantly more advanced than ourselves, or alien races of equivalent stature, even if they invariably find themselves unable to bring their sagas to a satisfactory conclusion. We are compelled to ponder our own eventual destiny and to explore those thoughts in stories, even as we recognize the essential futility of the effort. Perhaps, then, there is an element of truth in Kirby's observation about the true underlying message of the *2001* saga, that "the New Seed is no more than the spirit of our own self-belief, our own confidence in the stubborn rationale which has brought us from the caves to condominiums in the suburbs." In other words, the same drive and determination that will enable humanity to succeed and progress in the future is also leading writers to constantly try, and to constantly fall short, in their efforts to imagine the exact forms that that progress will take. Thus, all of the noble, fruitless struggles to extend a narrative that cannot be meaningfully extended, as examined here, may collectively represent, in their own way, a story that is as interesting and inspirational as *2001: A Space Odyssey* itself.

17. UNASSISTED SUICIDE: THE REMARKABLE SAGA OF *ST. ELSEWHERE*

While the long history of television may include innumerable oddities, I submit that there has never been a series quite like the medical drama *St. Elsewhere* (1982-1988). Perhaps I was initially attracted to the series primarily because, at a time when I was struggling to finally earn my Ph.D. in English and American Literature, it was very appealing to keep hearing the phrase "Dr. Westphall" (even if the spelling was not quite right). I could also explain my interest in the series by noting that it did occasionally drift into the territory of fantasy, as in the episode with an apparently magical Santa Claus ("Santa Claus Is Dead" [1985]) and the one in which Dr. Wayne Fiscus (Howie Mandel) has a near-death experience and encounters a deceased colleague in heaven ("After Life" [1986]). More expansively, I could refer to the show's final episode, "The Last One" (1988)—which indicates that the whole sordid saga of the St. Elegius Hospital was merely the strange fantasy of the autistic child of Dr. Donald Westphall (Ed Flanders)—and argue on that basis that the episode had retroactively recast the entire series as a fantasy; and this could also explain why so many other developments in the series, while not overtly fantastic, did not seem entirely realistic.

However, *St. Elsewhere* actually commanded my attention because, as I came to realize, it was the only television series in history that actively *despised* its audience, the only television series in history that *longed* to drive away viewers, earn miserable ratings, and get cancelled. Paradoxically, even though the series was highly successful in this dogged quest to attract fewer and fewer viewers, it was repeatedly and unexpectedly renewed for another season due to demographic research demonstrating that the program was remarkably good at attracting precisely the sorts of viewers that advertisers craved—masochists?

I kid you not. For the writers of this series, the story conferences for future episodes always began with the question, "All right, *now* what can we do to piss viewers off?" If characters seemed to be getting too popular, like the charmingly cantankerous patient, Mrs. Hufnagel (Florence Halop), or the ebullient young Dr. Elliot Axelrod (Stephen Furst), the series killed them off, preferably in an abrupt and disagreeable manner (Mrs. Hufnagel was crushed to death in her hospital bed; Dr. Axelrod died of a sudden heart attack). Defying a long tradition of admirable doctors on television, the series devised ways to make almost all of its doctors unlikable, for one reason or another. The alcoholic, drug-addicted, accused rapist and all-around cad Dr. Peter White (Terence Knox) was an extreme case, but there were also the perpetually bumbling Dr. Victor Ehrlich (Ed Begley, Jr.); the sadistic and verbally abusive Dr. Mark Craig (William Daniels), who also turned out to be actually responsible for Mrs. Hufnagel's death; that decent doctor but inadequate father, Dr. Westphall; the unstable and ultimately suicidal Dr. Wendy Armstrong (Kim Miyori); the fraudulently unqualified Dr. Jack Morrison (David Morse); and so on. The series cheerfully depicted a hospital in which absolutely everything went wrong, and absolutely everything kept getting worse and worse. I mean, what can one say in defense of a series that, for its obligatory heartwarming Christmas episode, featured the death of Santa Claus?

The irksome twist in the final episode, perhaps the series' culminating achievement in annoying its audience, may reflect the fact that its creators had been driven to absolute fury because, despite all of their best efforts, they were still being enticed, by their network's inexplicable willingness to pay them good money, into filming additional episodes. After all, a year before its last season, the producers, positively convinced that they had finally succeeded in achieving ratings so abysmally low that even skewed demographic research could not stave off cancellation, threw a celebratory cancellation party in anticipation of the inevitable news and filmed the projected final episode, fittingly titled "Last Dance at the Wrecker's Ball" (1987). Of course, they resolved to conclude their series in a manner that would please no one, so they depicted the doomed St. Elegius Hospital about to be demolished by a wrecking ball, with Westphall patiently waiting inside to be destroyed along with his whole wretched hospital. But, dash it all, NBC defied all expectations and renewed the series for yet another season, forcing producers to go back to the drawing board and churn out one last year of episodes wherein the hospital is rescued at the last minute, and then of course even further ruined, by being taken over by a greed-driven HMO.

But this time, the producers took no chances: they filmed their second final episode, designed to be even more irritating than the other one, and informed NBC, with grave finality, that they were bringing their series to a close. And thus, having long ago driven away the vast majority of its potential audience, *St. Elsewhere* finally alienated the few, perversely fascinated viewers who remained by, in effect, *cancelling itself.* I ask you, has there ever been another series in the history of television that so desperately strived to kill itself off? And the fact that this occurred with a series about a hospital, ostensibly devoted to preserving human lives, is one more irony that distinguishes this truly remarkable series.

Unsurprisingly, the series has proved to be less than a huge hit in syndication (though episodes still resurface here and there), and no one has ever proposed staging a reunion episode; so, in the two decades following its end, the series has for the most part achieved the oblivion that its creators so tenaciously fought for. However, like all victims of memorable disasters, the loyal and long-suffering viewers of *St. Elsewhere* can never forget the singular experience of their weekly visits to the hospital from hell.

18. MYTH AND ILLITERACY: BILL AND TED'S EXPLICATED ADVENTURES

(WITH LYNNE LUNDQUIST)

Bill and Ted's Excellent Adventure (1988), apparently little more than a mindless and ephemeral teenage comedy, does not immediately seem an appropriate subject for scholarly explication. Yet the film demands some attention simply as a phenomenon: popular beyond anyone's expectations, the film spawned, among other things, a moderately successful sequel, *Bill and Ted's Bogus Journey* (1991); two television series, one animated and one live-action, both entitled *Bill and Ted's Excellent Adventures* (1990-1991, 1992); a comic book; and even a breakfast cereal, Bill and Ted's Excellent Cereal. At the time of writing, there are also plans for a third Bill and Ted movie, penciled in for release in 2013. And we have personal evidence that this movie at least briefly achieved something of a cult status among some younger filmgoers; when our niece Laura, then sixteen years old, came to visit many years ago, she brought in her single suitcase a videocassette of the movie—and her mother Brenda reported that she always traveled with a copy of it. Furthermore, in giving her a tour of the Los Angeles area, we were obliged to include a new and hitherto unheralded attraction: the city and high school of San Dimas, California, home of Bill and Ted. Clearly, this film meant a great deal to my niece and others of her generation: the question is, why?

In responding to this question, we first note the common position that modern science fiction in all media represents a revival of and return to the narratives and themes of ancient myths—as argued, for example, in Wendy Doniger O'Flaherty's "The Survival of Myth in Science Fiction" (1988) and Alexei and Cory Panshin's *The World beyond the Hill* (1989).[103] And, having repeatedly viewed *Bill and Ted's Excellent Adventure* and its sequel, we conclude that both films validate this argument, each representing a carefully structured and thematically coherent mythic quest which goes to the heart of the issues raised by advocates of a mythic interpretation of science fiction; and a look at the message embedded in these film should prove both exhilarating, and exasperating, to those scholars.

To those who believe that ancient myths represent the best and most satisfying guide to the problems of human existence, the period of time before the development of Western civilization—specifically, the time before the invention and practice of writing—must be seen as a true Golden Age. When stories were maintained purely as oral traditions, storytellers were free to alter and shape their tales to match their listeners' expectations and needs. Historical events and personages could be taken out of context and molded into aesthetically pleasing and meaningful myths and legends. And without the craft of writing to divide society into the literate and the illiterate, something of an egalitarian spirit, one could maintain, permeated pre-historical cultures.

The development of writing changed all this; indeed, as Northrop Frye suggests in his *Anatomy of Criticism* (1957),

---

103. Wendy Doniger O'Flaherty, "The Survival of Myth in Science Fiction," *Mindscapes: The Geographies of Imagined Worlds*, edited by George Slusser and Eric S. Rabkin (Carbondale, Illinois: Southern Illinois University Press, 1988), 16-33; Alexei Panshin and Cory Panshin, *The World beyond the Hill: Science Fiction and the Quest for Transcendence* (Los Angeles: Jeremy R. Tarcher, Inc., 1989).

the practice of writing sets in motion a steady cycle of literary decline, as myths are reduced first to romances, then to mimetic fictions, and finally to "the general pattern of thematic irony."[104] The reasons for this progression, and its relationship to the art of writing, are clear. In a civilized and literate society, stories remained as they were first written, frozen in amber as they first occurred or were created, bound by historical context, and hence not amenable to continuing alteration and evolution; thus, historical fact begins to displace mythic vision. Joseph Campbell's *The Hero with a Thousand Faces* (1949) suggests this opposition of myth and history when he says that "Whenever the poetry of myth is interpreted as biography, history, or science, it is killed."[105] Second, with more information available, scholars became skeptical first of the literal truth, and then of the symbolic value, of the old myths, so that attitudes of skepticism and doubt begin to creep into literature, and the evocative power of the myths is diluted. Finally, since the skill of writing provides knowledge—and power—it becomes a new way to divide society into classes of the dominating— the literate—and the dominated—the illiterate. Indeed, the fact that western males moved rather quickly to withhold knowledge of reading and writing from women and racial minorities—a pattern which endured well into the nineteenth century— demonstrates how writing became an instrument whereby the white, male power structure achieved and maintained control of Western society and, eventually, the entire world.

Therefore, to truly reestablish a harmonious, egalitarian, and mythically guided civilization, it seems, one must completely eliminate literacy, and with it all the remaining vestiges of Western civilization, so as to set up a new civilization again

---

104. Northrop Frye, *Anatomy of Criticism: Four Essays*, 1957 (Princeton: Princeton University Press, 1971), 61. Later page references in the text are to this edition.

105. Joseph Campbell, *The Hero with a Thousand Faces*, 1949 (Princeton: Princeton University Press, 1968), 249. Later page references in the text are to this edition.

based on an oral tradition and the ancient, time-honored values of that tradition.

It is to accomplish these goals that two worthy heroes—William S. Preston and Theodore Logan—will embark on their quest through time in *Bill and Ted's Excellent Adventure*. Their heroic stature is suggested by the title "Esquire"—or squire—which they habitually affix to their names, by the way in which they don armor to literally become knights in medieval England, and by the meaning of their names: William, "protector," and Theodore, "gift of the gods." And they are ideally suited to the task: for although they have emerged from western civilization, they have remained completely separated from it. In the first scene, while playing with their musical instruments, Bill suddenly exclaims, "We're late."

"For what?" Ted responds.

"School, dude."[106] Obviously, Ted has been attending school, but he has been, equally obviously, completely oblivious to the experience. Bill and Ted read only rarely, and are hence completely ignorant of the traditional knowledge of Western culture: to them, Napoleon is simply "a short, dead dude," Julius Caesar is a "salad dressing dude," and Marco Polo is "a water sport."

However, Bill and Ted are very much a part of a new, emerging oral tradition and its popular culture. Their responses to events are childlike and without guile: in a later poker game with Billy the Kid, they cannot maintain a "poker face"—symbolizing the façade of logic and reason that Western culture imposes on its citizens. The first thing they do in the film is videotape themselves: for them, to appear on television, not to be written about in books, constitutes true achievement. Their perspective on history is limited to what they have seen at theme parks—they recall what Abraham Lincoln said at Walt Disney World, and their response to nineteenth-century New Mexico is that it is "just like Frontierland"—and to what they have seen

---

106. *Bill and Ted's Excellent Adventure* (Orion Pictures, 1988).

in movies—to Ted, Lincoln is a man chasing a whale, as he confuses Lincoln's image with that of Gregory Peck as Captain Ahab in the film *Moby Dick* (1956).

The primary focus of their cultural life, however, is rock music: they wish to start a band and become musicians, and while Ted knows nothing about Napoleon and Caesar, he has memorized many rock lyrics; thus, when eloquence is called for, Ted does not consult a mental storehouse of quotations from books, but rather, as Bill puts it, prefers to "recite 'em some lyrics." And Bill's full name—Bill S. Preston—arguably recalls the popular keyboard player who once played with the Beatles, Billy Preston.[107]

Finally, Bill and Ted seem fully attuned to the ancient practices of mythology: when Ted guesses in class that Joan of Arc is "Noah's wife," he demonstrates a desire to take an established personage of recorded history and place her in the context of an ancient and widespread myth of a universal flood.

Because the established powers of the writing-based Western world still wish to maintain their hegemony over this emergent and revolutionary oral culture, Bill and Ted face discipline and punishment for their failure to master its textual lore. Specifically, Bill and Ted are about to flunk their history class—history being the field most closely associated with written records, and hence the subject they are least able to deal with—and with that failing grade, they will be kicked out of school. At that point, Ted's father, a harsh and strict policeman—in Los Angeles County—will send Ted to military school, there to experience the most exaggerated version of European authoritarian education.[108]

---

107. And certainly, the casting of key roles in the first film reinforces their links to rock music, with Bruce Springsteen's saxophonist Clarence Clemons as the leader of the future society, and Go-Gos guitarist Jane Wiedlin as Joan of Arc. The pattern is also seen in the film's sequel, which includes a musician from the group Faith No More and legendary blues singer Taj Mahal as the Gatekeeper of Heaven.

108. The sense, then, that Bill and Ted are budding free spirits imprisoned

However, their history teacher—who is, significantly, African-American, and hence a representative of the various peoples that have been oppressed by Western culture—offers them a way out of their dilemma. If Bill and Ted present a superior oral report, he tells them, they will pass the class. Thus, by means of the communication system of oral culture—speaking—Bill and Ted will be allowed to escape the traditional responsibility to attain success through the communication system of written culture—exams and papers, which they have consistently flunked. And when the camera shows a bemused grin on the instructor's face after he explains this option, one senses that this African-American man has a secret sympathy for those who have avoided, and seek to subvert, the white Western establishment.

To prepare for this report, Bill and Ted first obtain from the library a huge stack of books, but in this film, the major role of books is to serve as a sight gag; clearly, Bill and Ted are incapable of reading through these books in several weeks, let alone one night, and the only reading skill they display in the film is the ability to look up a name in an index and find a reference to it, and the related ability to use a phone book. To get needed historical facts, they start asking various people going into the local Circle K store—the characteristic information-gathering process of an oral culture.

To help Bill and Ted succeed in their formidable task, Rufus, a man from the future, appears to offer assistance. His time machine is, significantly, shaped like a phone booth—repre-

---

by the demands of literacy is reinforced by the film's opening song, "I Can't Break Away," and the fact that San Dimas, or Saint Dismas, was the legendary Good Thief who was crucified next to Jesus, converted to Christianity, and became the patron saint of prisoners. Alternately, the significance of San Dimas could be that he was a thief, and Bill and Ted's chief activity in the film is stealing historical figures out of the past. Finally, as a person who converted to Christianity literally at the last moment—while dying on the cross—Dismas could also be seen as a patron saint of procrastinators, and hence as an appropriate icon for Bill and Ted, who wait until the night before it is due to prepare their important oral report.

senting the telephone, one of the modern inventions which have helped to subvert the power of the written word and promote oral communications. And the booth is powered by an antenna—representing television, the other modern invention which undermines literacy and writing.

The adventure they embark upon perfectly accords in most particulars to the mythic pattern that was long ago outlined in Campbell's *The Hero with a Thousand Faces*. Rufus, of course, is the traditional magical helper who comes to issue the call to adventure and start the hero on his quest. The threshold to the unknown is crossed by means of the time-traveling phone booth, and the twisting threads of the circuits of time that they travel along are a powerful visual image of the labyrinth. The various historical eras they visit could be aptly described as "a dream landscape of curiously fluid, ambiguous forms, where [the hero] must survive a succession of trials" (Campbell 97). Their sojourn in the future is the moment of reconciliation with the spiritual father, and an apotheosis of sorts: the ritualistic arm movements and general air of solemnity there strongly suggest a religious rite. The people they take from the past are the equivalents of the magic token or elixir the hero brings back from the realm of the gods. Bill and Ted's return to their own world is perilous and troublesome, as they face renewed discipline—Bill must do his chores, Ted is told to pack his bags and prepare for military school—and as their tokens from the past are placed in prison. However, they ultimately succeed in their original environment, and Bill and Ted discover that they have attained something of the status of gods, as they incredulously tell the returned Rufus that the people of the future seem to "worship" them. Indeed, they now assume the role of World Redeemers, who will allow us to break "free of the prejudices of our own provincially limited ecclesiastical, tribal, or national rendition of the world archetypes" (Campbell 157-158) and thus construct a new and harmonious world order.

However, what is most interesting about their quest is not so much that it follows mythic patterns—as scholars have shown, that is the case for many modern narratives—but that the quest itself is undertaken on behalf of myth, and in opposition to the sworn enemy of myth—namely, history. The plan that Bill and Ted develop is to kidnap various famous people of the past, with the use of Rufus's time machine, and bring them into the present, so as to participate in their oral report. In doing so, they enact in a new and literal manner the traditional process of myth-making: namely, ripping historical figures out of their proper context and reshaping them in the milieu of a timeless present to respond to and reflect contemporary concerns.

Thus, as seen by Bill and Ted, the philosophy of Socrates is reduced to first an apparent advocacy of ignorance, in the one quotation from him supplied by the film—"The only true wisdom consists in knowing that you know nothing"—and in Ted's empathetic response—"That's us, dude." And Socrates's thoughts about the transitory, tenuous nature of human existence are simplified as the opening of the long-running soap opera *Days of Our Lives* (1965-): "Like sands in the hourglass, so are the days of our lives."

Furthermore, though Socrates was sedentary and reflective, and though Billy the Kid was by most accounts a psychopathic killer, both men are refashioned by their encounter with Bill and Ted into friendly heroes who carry out the daring rescue of Bill and Ted from a medieval execution. And though history suggests that both men were homosexuals, they surface here as conventionally heterosexual males who will later try to pick up two pretty young girls at the San Dimas mall.[109]

The eventual destination of Socrates, Billy the Kid, and the six other historical figures—an oral presentation to the student body of San Dimas High School—is a visual icon for the overall

---

109. Indeed, while the coming oral culture seems amenable to almost all types of people and lifestyles, there remain touches of homophobia: in the first film, after Bill happily discovers that Ted has survived his apparent death and they hug each other, they stand back and say, "Fag." The jocular tone in which they speak cannot change the fact that the word is a homophobic slur. There is a similar scene in the second film.

process of mythification, as people from various different times and cultures are gathered together in one unified pageant, a timeless and ahistorical vaudeville show for present-day listeners.

In addition, despite the seeming randomness in their selection of historical figures, there is in fact a deeper logic in the people that Bill and Ted choose to bring into the present. First, and perhaps most important, there is Socrates, who was the last major intellectual figure in Western history who did not write, who abhorred writing, who argued in fact that the very practice of writing would bring an end to true culture. To representatives of the new oral tradition like Bill and Ted, then, Socrates is the last noble illiterate before Western civilization descended into the error of writing. Therefore, to begin a true oral civilization again, Socrates is the appropriate starting point.

Six of the other chosen figures all share one or more of the following traits: they lacked any formal education—Lincoln, Genghis Khan, Billy the Kid, and Joan of Arc; they accomplished great things at a very early age—Billy the Kid and Joan of Arc; or they managed to obtain power and influence even though they were excluded outsiders—Joan of Arc, a successful woman in a very sexist age; Ludwig van Beethoven, the man of partial African descent who gained a prominent position in European society; and Napoleon Bonaparte, the Corsican who rose to rule France. Thus, they embody all of the characteristics of the ideal citizens of the new age of illiteracy: they are young, ignorant, and outside of existing power structures.

In this company, Sigmund Freud—the eighth chosen figure—seems at first out of place, since his major accomplishments did not come in his youth, he was very well educated, and he was very much part of the power structure of turn-of-the-century Viennese society. The fact that he is notably different from the others is indicated by Bill and Ted's comment that they are grabbing him for "extra credit." Nevertheless, Freud is a crucial presence in their quest; for he was the first to reveal that the intellect and knowledge that seemed to dominate modern Western society were in fact simply a facade for deeper, more primitive emotions, drives that could be well represented by ancient myths (as, for example, in what Freud mythopoeically labeled the Oedipus complex). And his one-time disciple Carl Jung went ever farther, arguing that mythic archetypes are actually embedded in the human brain. Thus, for all his own attachment to an intellectual tradition, Freud's work provides an intellectual basis for rejecting all of the detritus of Western written culture and returning to an illiterate, mythic culture.

Of course, in seizing and celebrating these particular figures from the past, Bill and Ted are not completely exonerating them, for some of them clearly did cruel and brutal things that in no way represent the ideals of the emerging egalitarian and holistic culture of illiteracy: Genghis Khan was a brutal barbarian; Billy the Kid was a feared killer; Napoleon became a ruthless dictator and warrior; and while Joan of Arc is getting better press these days, we should recall that William Shakespeare's *Henry VI* plays portrayed her as an evil witch. However, all of their excesses are implicitly excused in this film because they lived in cruel and brutal times—which were themselves a product of power structures based on literacy—and those times drove them to do evil because they were not provided with satisfactory outlets for their desires. However, taken out of their repressive societies, these people blossom into well-adjusted and productive members of society—a transformation symbolized by the fact that Joan of Arc, when she steps into the phone booth, leaves her sword behind (and the camera lingers on that sword, to emphasize the point).

Transported to the pleasant and increasingly illiterate environment of San Dimas, the rehabilitation of these historical figures is effected. In San Dimas, the demonic zealotry of Joan is channeled into aerobic exercises. In San Dimas, the fighting spirit of Genghis Khan finds release in the symbolic combat of sporting equipment. In San Dimas, the legendary temper of Beethoven is soothed by the marvels of modern keyboard instruments. In San Dimas, the obsessed and megalomaniacal Napoleon becomes a playful fellow who loves ice cream sundaes, bowling, and water slides; indeed, he slips into the water park, Waterloo, by passing as a child.[110] And in San Dimas, the sober-minded, often depressed Abraham Lincoln grows into a cheerful and genial father figure to the new age of illiteracy, with his new philosophy encapsulated in his final statement to San Dimas students: "Be excellent to each other, and party on, dudes!"

In fact, the film depicts San Dimas as something of a utopia in contrast to the past of historical times, which is repeatedly shown to be despotic and evil. In the American West, Bill and Ted are involved in a potentially lethal barroom brawl that ends with their heads sticking through the wall—an image recalling the pillory of Puritan times. When Napoleon first sees them, he instructs his men to "Blow them up." And when they arrive in fifteenth-century Europe, the king first orders them to the iron maiden and then to be beheaded. The pure, unsullied spirits of Bill and Ted face this brutality with plain incomprehension: for as they say, they represent a new world order where Iron Maiden is a popular rock band, not an instrument of torture.

Significantly, Bill and Ted encounter no violence or conflict when they visit time periods before the development of writing. Thus, the Athens of Socrates is a beautiful, Edenic scene, and Bill later remarks that the place was "very tranquil" and looked like the cover of Led Zeppelin's album *Houses of the Holy* (1973).

---

110. Not only is this water park a central symbol of Napoleon's spiritual rebirth—his first trip down a tubular water slide is an image of movement through the birth canal, and his final splash recalls a baptism—but there are other uses of water imagery throughout the film, since water is, as Northrop Frye notes, one traditional symbol of the world of innocence (152-153). Other examples: the blissfully ignorant Ted argues that Marco Polo is "a water sport" and sees Joan of Arc as "Noah's wife," indicating his natural affinity with water; Bill, Ted, and the six people they have seized return to the present moment beside Bill's swimming pool; the cleansing of Bill's house includes washing windows, dishes, and the toilet; Beethoven is fond of Bon Jovi's *Slippery When Wet* album (1986); and of course, the idyllic world of the future, Rufus reports, is distinguished by its large number of water slides.

And their accidental visit to 1,000,000 B.C. is the occasion of a rustic picnic in a lovely pastoral setting, with Ted providing everyone with chocolate pudding cups; while cavemen come upon them as they depart, they carry no weapons to threaten them, further suggesting a pre-historical age of innocence.

When Bill and Ted bring these famous people into the present, their first activity is to help Bill and Ted clean Bill's house—a symbolic representation of the necessary cleansing they will perform to rid modern civilization of its remaining vestiges of literacy and oppression. Still, they still must face the opposition of the still-powerful and repressive culture of literacy, embodied in the figure of Ted's policeman father. The six people they leave at the mall, who essentially engage in playful and harmless activities, are nevertheless arrested and imprisoned, so that Bill and Ted must rescue them.

At this point, they discover that they truly have magical powers: to bring a necessary object to them, all they need do is to make plans, at some future date, to go back in time and put the object there beforehand. Thus, they plan to hide Ted's father's keys behind a sign, and those keys appear; they plan to leave a tape-recorder with a timer to create a diversion, and a tape recorder begins to play. Acquisition of magical powers is, of course, another common development in a standard heroic quest.

The subsequent history presentation is important in that it further emphasizes the elimination of historical context in its way that Bill and Ted describe the people they have brought. Socrates is likened to Ozzy Osbourne as another figure often accused of corrupting young people. Joan of Arc accomplished all her activities, Bill stresses, "by the time she was seventeen"— which must be about the age of Bill and Ted. Beethoven's new favorite music is *Slippery When Wet* (1986) by Bon Jovi. All of these people are now part of humanity's eternal and fluid present instead of its frozen and fixed past.

Finally, like all heroes, Bill and Ted must emerge from their successful adventure with suitable mates. In this case, they are eventually paired with two beautiful princesses from fifteenth-century England. The choice is perfect: unable to learn another language, Bill and Ted must find women who speak English; but committed to a life of happy illiteracy, their ideal women should be untainted by any formal education—and these girls come from England right before the Renaissance, or right before the time when the previously unheard-of concept of educating women first began to tentatively emerge. Thus, the women chosen for them are purely and completely illiterate.

And what of the world that will emerge from Bill and Ted's successful quest? We first see that world in Bill and Ted's brief visit to the future in *Bill and Ted's Excellent Adventure*, and Rufus describes it at the beginning and end of the film. After Bill and Ted succeed as musicians in the group Wyld Stallynz—that is, as uncivilized animals—their music will "end war and poverty," "align the planets," and "bring them into universal harmony"; then, humanity will come into "contact with all forms of life, from extraterrestrial intelligences to common household pests." Manifestly, this culture will be based on oral communication, specifically rock music, and its characteristic activities and attitudes are aptly described in the song we hear playing in the future: "dancing in the streets all night," and "everything will be all right." The future will be a society focused on play, since its features first mentioned by Rufus are that "bowling scores are up," "many golf scores are down," and there are "more excellent water slides" on Earth than on any other known planet. It is also an egalitarian and harmonious society, since its chief figure is an African-American man, surrounded on either side by a woman and a man. Indeed, the final song of the film—"Two Heads Are Better Than One"—specifically announces an end to hierarchy—a pattern of social organization based on having "One" leader—and the heralded beginning of a holistic culture based on the diffusion of power—"Two Heads." Finally, it is obviously a society where few people do any reading, since it is the citizens' habit to wear sunglasses at all times.

When considering how the saga of Bill and Ted has

progressed beyond this film, one can properly discount the two spinoff television series, for their episodes provided little more than routine variations on familiar time-travel stories, utterly lacking in mythic resonance. However, the 1991 sequel *Bill and Ted's Bogus Journey* is another matter: for it presents a reenactment of the original story with even greater stress on the themes of the elimination of literacy and the reestablishment of myth. What was often implicit in the first film is here presented explicitly, making this one of those rare sequels that seem created specifically to validate an interpretation of the original work.

At the start of the second film, we see the future system of education at Bill and Ted University, where all instruction is apparently oral: no books are in sight, and instructor Rufus specifically tells students to do their homework with their headphones on, suggesting that they are learning from tapes, not books. The briefly seen historical figures who appear to assist the class are again appropriate: Thomas Alva Edison, the brilliant inventor who was nevertheless uneducated and virtually illiterate; Johann Sebastian Bach, a prolific composer who did little if any writing; a member of the modern rock group Faith No More; and a twenty-third century punk rocker credited with the invention of a new type of amplifier. Their studies, in fact, seem centered on the history of music, the central art form of their culture, and the one which least demands any literacy or traditional education.

Into this idyllic scene intrudes an evil man, intent upon returning to the past and undoing everything that the music of Bill and Ted has accomplished. His name, De Nomolos, reverses the name Solomon, a famous exemplar of wisdom and purported author of the *Song of Solomon*. His program for restoring order is laid out in a book he is holding—and except for the Book of Records that the Gatekeeper of Heaven writes in, it is the only book seen in the film. To demonstrate his complete villainy, he tells the stunned students that they should carefully study that book to learn about his plans; it may be the first time in their lives that they have been asked to read a book. His plan—to construct perfect robot duplicates of Bill and Ted to kill them and thus prevent their rise to prominence—represents western technology at its worst, the creation of sophisticated machines to replace and oppress people.

In their exploits in this film, Bill and Ted enact overtly mythic patterns that were better concealed in the original movie. Bill and Ted experience the ultimate heroic rite of passage, exemplified by Jesus Christ Himself: they literally die, and they literally rise from the dead. When they are trapped on Earth as ghosts, it never occurs to them to convey any written message to the living, but they enter the bodies of two policemen, and disrupt a seance, to deliver oral messages. They descend into hell—which they complain does not look at all like their album covers—and there they experience nightmarish versions of their early lives, a harsh military camp and a demand to kiss an elderly female relative. This vision of Hell as a repeated nightmare demonstrates the stagnation and oppressiveness of modern western civilization.

Next, Bill and Ted triumph over Death, represented by a black-robed figure as in Ingmar Bergman's film *The Seventh Seal* (1957), by besting him in a series of games—such as Battleship, Clue, table hockey, and Twister—that significantly require little if any reading skill. Death, in fact, becomes their servant, and later the bass player in their band, suggesting the complete domestication of that ancient human enemy.

Bill and Ted then gain entrance into Heaven by answering the question "What is the meaning of life?" with the lyrics from the rock group Poison's song, "Every Rose Has Its Thorn" (1988).[111] When they ask God to direct them to someone who can help them, he sends them a crystalline map with no writing on it; and they find the greatest scientists of history, including Albert Einstein and Benjamin Franklin, engaged not in scientific research but a game of charades, trying to guess the name of a movie—a perfect recreation for an oral culture. They

---

111. *Bill and Ted's Bogus Journey* (Orion Pictures, 1991).

recruit two Martian scientists to help them build good robots to defeat De Nomolos's bad robots, and the Martians bear a striking resemblance to the monsters in Maurice Sendak's *Where the Wild Things Are* (1963)—a children's picture book with minimal writing.

After their crude robots destroy the evil duplicates, their return to San Dimas is momentarily problematic, since De Nomolos appears and threatens to kill them again; but again utilizing their magical power to transform the present by planning to do so in the future, they overcome him with a planted sandbag, cage, and fake gun. In their subsequent concert, broadcast live to the entire world, their first song is "God Gave Rock and Roll to You," further associating the characteristic art form of a newly illiterate culture with religious imagery;[112] and in a series of newspaper headlines and magazine covers, we learn in more detail exactly how their music worked to establish world peace and usher in a new golden era.[113]

Despite both films' general silliness, there is some emotional power in their conclusions, particular in the second film, where one gets a vision of how wonderful the world would be if stupid but good-natured people like Bill and Ted were dominant, instead of educated evil people like De Nomolos. Mythic interpreters of science fiction should be especially pleased by these films, for they explicitly affirm the power of myth, both in their structure and in their message: they are mythic quests specifically about the re-establishment of mythic thinking. But Bill and Ted demand as the price of a new mythic existence the abandonment of Western culture, scholarship, and the written

---

112. It is also worth noting that the band chosen to perform this song (a reworking of a 1973 hit from the band Argent) was Kiss—a band previously noted for appearing only in animal makeup, with overtones of primitivism and paganism.

113. The only incongruous note in this conclusion is the appearance of newspaper headlines; surely, given their espousal of illiteracy, Bill and Ted's triumphs should have been chronicled in television news reports. But that device would have interfered with their music in this case.

word.

As must be emphasized, this position is entirely logical: that is, if myths are what modern people need, then they surely need them in their purest form—oral traditions. Ersatz myths embedded in the written narratives of science fiction and other popular fictions are a poor substitute. And people certainly do not need their minds cluttered with random trivia from the past—history—which totally lacks mythic power and structure. Therefore, there is a paradox here: while scholars of myth might logically join in Bill and Ted's crusade for the abolition of literacy and the establishment of a new illiterate, oral and thoroughly mythic culture, they must also face the fact that one necessary consequence of this development would be the elimination of the scholarly community which supports and maintains mythic research.

From a different scholarly perspective, of course, myths embody both ancient wisdom and ancient stupidity, and the persistence of mythic patterns in modern times might be attributed more to force of habit than their enduring value. And those who hold such opinions can properly gape in horror at the program of Bill and Ted, seeing in their quest not the rebirth of an ancient and superior civilization but rather the return of an undesirable and unenlightened civilization.

Perhaps, though, one can find hints of a mediating position in *Bill and Ted's Excellent Adventure* and its sequel. After all, the tuned-in residents of the future have not entirely abandoned Western science—since, as Rufus explains, their time-travelling ability stems from "modern technology." Reading does endure as an art, even if it is only the reading of a directory of phone numbers needed to reach various times in history. And Bill and Ted in fact learn something from their first quest, since in their final presentation they offer some facts about their assembled historical figures and even—for the first time—pronounce their names correctly; and they learn something from their second quest, since their final confrontation with De Nomolos reveals an unusually sophisticated knowledge of the workings of time paradoxes. Since myth at its highest level may enact the reconciliation and combination of opposites—seen most clearly in the androgynous figures cited by Campbell—Bill and Ted may, then, be effecting a merging of ancient wisdom and modern knowledge, of pre-historical and historical civilization. And this would provide another suggestive interpretation of the song "Two Heads Are Better Than One": to create a truly superior culture, both the old truths of myth and the new truths of science are required. The final achievement of Bill and Ted, thus, could be seen as the third stage in William Blake's progression from innocence to experience to "organized innocence"—bringing, as the song says, "Double the pleasure, triple the fun."

All of this may be a tremendous weight to place upon films whose dominant characteristic is their spirit of uninhibited, mindless fun; but then again, seriousness and frivolity are another pair of opposites which can be joined in myth. Thus, there is the extreme solemnity with which Lincoln delivers the first principle of Bill and Ted—"Be excellent to each other"— and the playful exuberance with which he announces the second principle—"And party on, dudes!" Peter Nicholls's entry on the film in *The Encyclopedia of Science Fiction* (1993) perfectly captures its dual nature by noting that "this charming, silly film...within its own relaxed, adolescent terms is done with great conviction."[114] There is, then, no contradiction in finding a sobering message in silly films; and although what we have said is perhaps not exactly how our niece would have articulated her fondness for Bill and Ted, even she must have dimly discerned the underlying and revolutionary import of the movie that she carried in her suitcase.

---

114. Peter Nicholls, "Bill and Ted's Excellent Adventure," *The Encyclopedia of Science Fiction*, edited by John Clute and Peter Nicholls (New York: St. Martin's Press, 1993), 121.

19. THREE QUESTIONS AND ANSWERS ABOUT SCIENCE FICTION FILMS

1. Which Science Fiction Movie Ending Do You Wish You Could Change?

It probably never would have been considered a masterpiece in any event, but one science fiction film ruined by an absolutely wrong ending was Ivan Reitman's *Evolution* (2001). Having depicted tiny alien organisms that landed on Earth and rapidly generated more and more advanced creatures, up to and including primates, the film should have properly concluded with the development of intelligent humanoid aliens, who would calmly introduce themselves, apologize for all the problems caused by their more ferocious predecessors, and announce plans to gather all of the alien beings together and depart to another world that is not already inhabited by a thriving biosphere. Such an ending would not only have been logical, but it also would have provided a worthwhile commentary on the process of evolution, which was after all the film's title: the idea that, whatever value fierce competitiveness might have in the advancement of species, the best strategy for ultimate success is usually cooperation.

Unfortunately, since such an ending would not have provided the spectacular special-effects fireworks and improbable heroism which contemporary Hollywood lore insists is essential in concluding a sure-fire box-office success, the filmmakers instead opted for the inane emergence of an enormous one-celled organism which could somehow be exterminated, as I vaguely recall, by the desperately improvised application of some Head and Shoulders shampoo—foreshadowing, as seems clear in retrospect, that a lot of investors were going to take a bath, and the film was going down the drain.

2. What Makes a Successful Science Fiction or Fantasy Book Adaptation? Why Do Some Fail?

As the reviewer for Locus Online who normally covers films based on science fiction novels and stories, I have had more than enough opportunities to ponder the question of what goes right—or what goes wrong—when Hollywood employs a work of science fiction literature as its source material. In approaching this subject, I am, first of all, increasingly comfortable with the notion that we are effectively dealing with two separate narrative genres which might be termed text-centric science fiction and media-centric science fiction. The contrasting characteristics should be clear enough to most informed observers: text-centric science fiction, one might say, is unemotional, idea-driven, unpredictable, and disturbingly committed to challenging the status quo, whereas media-centric science fiction is passionate, character-driven, predictable, and comfortingly dedicated to preserving the status quo. Needless to say, most text-centric science fiction comes in the form of prose fiction and most media-centric fiction comes in the forms of films and television programs, but obviously there are some exceptions: *Star Trek* novels are of course media-centric, while rare films like *2001: A Space Odyssey* (1968) could be considered text-centric. And, although I have a personal preference here that goes without saying, I choose to avoid arguments to the effect that one form of science fiction is better than the other; rather, they are simply *different* genres, and people should be free to enjoy one or the other without being condemned as, say, elitists or philistines.

Thus, instead of asserting, as one might, that film adaptations of science fiction stories and novels routinely homogenize, dumb down, or trash their source material, one might better say that works of text-centric science fiction are necessarily being translated into works of media-centric science fiction, and leave it at that. And, from that perspective, most film adaptations indeed "work," since filmmakers are generally careful to add to unsuitable source material all of the valiant heroism, violence, emotional hooks, and jazzy special effects that are essential ingredients in media-centric science fiction. (As one of many examples, one might contrast Steven Gould's gentle, thoughtful novel *Jumper* [1992] with its frenetic, melodramatic film adaptation [2008].) I suspect, though, that the real question I am being asked to address is whether such adaptations "work" for devotees of text-centric science fiction, and the obvious answer is this: when the source material contains interesting, unconventional ideas, and when those ideas somehow survive the process of translation to figure in the released film, then the result might be a media-centric science fiction film that can also be appreciated by people who generally prefer text-centric science fiction.

Consider, for example, *Total Recall* (1990), which for the most part spectacularly departs from its source, Philip K. Dick's story "We Can Remember It for You Wholesale" (1966), in order to present a standard conflict of good versus evil, a plot generally consisting of a series of exciting chase scenes, and so many violent deaths as to defy any efforts to count the corpses. And yet, in that scene where a psychologist calmly confronts Arnold Schwarzenegger's Douglas Quaid and announces that all of the film's preceding events were actually his own hallucinations, the film is suddenly raising the sorts of intriguing questions about illusions and reality that are central to Dick's work; and the film's conclusion is also thought-provoking, as Quaid effectively rejects his original true personality in order to embrace the fake personality that was imprinted upon him, another Dickian moment illustrating the elusive nature of our own identities. The result is a film that is fitfully interesting almost in spite of itself. As a contrasting example to show that text-centric features do not always survive translation, consider *Children of Men* (2006), which is an admirable film in many respects; unfortunately, the filmmakers viewed the story of P. D. James's novel *The Children of Men* (1992) primarily as a pretext to consider how responses to the threat of terrorism can lead to totalitarianism, which I suppose is something worth examining but is far duller and more conventional that James's more novel explorations of how people would live in a world without children, a topic that the film, perversely, generally contrives to ignore.

The broader problem is that it can be difficult for intriguing ideas to persist through what are today the innumerable stages of filmmaking, from the first draft of the script to the final, released film. A good object lesson is the film *I Am Legend* (2007). After watching and reviewing this generally deplorable film, I was surprised to learn that the film had originally employed a version of the surprise ending of Richard Matheson's 1954 novel: the apparently mindless and vicious plague-altered mutants were revealed to be intelligent beings who represented the new, dominant form of humanity, meaning that Will Smith's Robert Neville, previously intent upon murdering them all, was the true monster of the story. Unfortunately, preview audiences reportedly hated the ending, impelling producers to shoot a new ending that recalled a previous adaptation of Matheson's novel, *The Omega Man* (1971), which concludes with a dying Neville messianically bequeathing a cure for the plague to his female companion. On the face of it, this appears to represent yet another instance of Hollywood jettisoning a source's provocative, unsettling concept in order to instead provide familiarity and reassurance. And yet, after watching the original ending online, I must say that I agree with those preview audiences: since the filmmakers had spent almost two hours using every trick in the how-to-make-a-blockbuster book to effectively demonize the mutants, their sudden, last-minute attempt to portray the mutants sympathetically was inept and unpersuasive. Even when making a determined effort to remain faithful to source material, it would seem, Hollywood has trouble dealing with interesting ideas.

3. Bad Guys We Love to Hate: The Best Film Villains in Science Fiction, Fantasy and Horror.

I'm sorry, but try as I may, I cannot muster any strong emotional response to any of the extravagant, larger-than-life villains often found in science fiction films who are presumably the intended focus of this discussion. They simply do not seem real to me, and not because of their amazing abilities or implausibly intricate schemes. Rather, it is the fact that typically they fully understand the villainy of their actions and not only accept, but even relish, their own extraordinary evilness. Such individuals are found in everyday life, but they are rare.

The sort of villains that we do regularly encounter, and that I most readily despise, are the people who do evil things because they are too stupid, or too blinded by self-interest or parochial beliefs, to recognize that they are in fact doing evil things. In other words, I hate the villains who incredibly believe that they are really heroes.

Thus, one character who inspires visceral loathing every time I view his film is Tom Stevens (Hugh Marlowe), the boyfriend of Helen Benson (Patricia Neal) in the original version of *The Day the Earth Stood Still* (1951). Having brilliantly deduced that Helen's housemate Mr. Carpenter is actually the alien Klaatu (Michael Rennie) after her son Bobby (Billy Gray) tells him exactly that, and having confirmed his story by getting jewelers to verify that Klaatu's diamonds resemble none found on Earth, Stevens rushes to the phone to tell the Pentagon where Klaatu is hiding, refusing to listen to Helen's pleadings that his actions might prove catastrophic for the entire human race. Since the authorities have been asking citizens to contact them with any information about the alien, Stevens can readily believe that he is doing the right thing, and he is further motivated by a selfish desire to win the world's admiration and respect as the man who brought an end to the alien menace. It is heartening to watch Helen angrily reject this creep, and to recognize that even though Stevens's actions lead directly to Klaatu's death, his subsequent resurrection and safe return to his home world, along with his stark warning to humanity regarding the true nature of his mission, ensure that Stevens has not only lost a future wife, but also will gain nothing from his traitorous deed.

This raises an interesting question: in the warped, wretched remake of *The Day the Earth Stood Still* (2008), which character most closely corresponds to Tom Stevens? It is not the character named "Tom," who has little to do in this version of the story, but rather Klaatu himself (Keanu Reeves). Like Tom Stevens, Klaatu believes he is doing the right thing by endeavoring to kill every single human on the planet without warning in order to preserve Earth's natural environment. Further, since his race obviously embraces a peculiar moral code which values pristine biospheres more than intelligent beings, there is an element of self-interest in his genocidal activities; one can even imagine that, if he returns to his peers and reports his success in saving Earth from its own nasty inhabitants, he might anticipate receiving some sort of reward—exactly like Stevens. Klaatu further proves that he is a rotten so-and-so with a few random murders and acts of petty theft. And our opinion of him cannot change because he ultimately discerns some merit in the human race and decides to turn off his engines of mass destruction; for heaven's sake, if a man starts firing a machine gun into a crowd and then decides after ten seconds that this is a bad thing to do and stops shooting, does that make him a hero?

The final puzzle is why anyone would choose to transform one of science fiction film's noblest heroes into a despicable scoundrel, but delving into that question would demand consideration of different sorts of villains driven by stupidity, self-interest, and parochial beliefs—namely, the executives who oversee contemporary Hollywood films.

20. THE TEN BEST SCIENCE FICTION AND FANTASY FILMS OF THE TWENTY-FIRST CENTURY...AS OF DECEMBER 31, 2010...AND A PREDICTION ABOUT TEN BEST LISTS TO COME

By one theory, a work of art should be judged primarily by how well it accomplishes its own goals. Thus, anyone would concede that Three Stooges shorts do not offer viewers eloquent dialogue, beautifully framed shots, or thoughtful commentary on the human condition, suggesting that they completely lack merit, yet such films never intended to offer any rewards of that kind; instead, they were designed to make people laugh. And, since innumerable people over the decades have continued to watch and laugh at Three Stooges shorts, they must by this argument be embraced as successful works of art, in the context of their own aspirations.

So, let us apply this principle to the task of evaluating the science fiction and fantasy films of the last decade, considering their own goals and how well they achieved them. This is remarkably easy, since a minute of Internet research can provide us with a list of the ten best science fiction and fantasy films of the last decade, in precise rank order:

1. *Avatar* (2009)
2. *The Lord of the Rings: The Return of the King* (2003)
3. *Pirates of the Caribbean: Dead Man's Chest* (2006)
4. *The Dark Knight* (2008)
5. *Harry Potter and the Sorcerer's Stone* (2001)
6. *Pirates of the Caribbean: At World's End* (2007)
7. *Harry Potter and the Order of the Phoenix* (2007)
8. *Harry Potter and the Half-Blood Prince* (2009)
9. *The Lord of the Rings: The Two Towers* (2002)
10. *Shrek 2* (2004)

The list is copied from a Wikipedia table of the highest grossing films of "the first decade of the twenty-first century." For these films, like all major films nowadays, were primarily designed to make money; and since these genre films accomplished that goal better than any of the others, they must be acknowledged as the ten best films of the decade.

Of course, one may object to this conclusion on any number of minor and major grounds.

As a technical flaw, this list is based upon the common misunderstanding that 2000 was the first year of the new millennium, so that 2000-2009 represents the new century's "first decade." But wiser readers of science fiction know that there was never a year zero, so that 2001 was actually the new millennium's first year—which is why Arthur C. Clarke chose that year as his title, and is why a science fiction website is looking back at 2001-2010 as the millennium's first decade. A proper top ten list using that timeframe, based on data from the Internet Movie Database, would drop *The Lord of the Rings: The Two Towers* and *Shrek 2* to make room for two big hits from 2010, *Toy Story 3* and *Alice in Wonderland*, which would be ranked four and five, while the still-in-theatres *Harry Potter and the Deathly Hallows Part 1* (2010), currently number eleven, is on course to displace its immediate predecessor as the new number ten.

A broader objection would be that, in claiming that these films were primarily focused on making money, I am wrongly elevating what was only one of several motives that included other, more aesthetic concerns. That is, while composing his epic poems, Homer was surely influenced by a desire to keep his royal patrons happy and thus ensure that he would continue to enjoy free room and board, and while crafting his plays, William Shakespeare kept a constant eye on the bottom line; but both writers were also seeking, obviously, to produce deep and meaningful works of art. Couldn't this also be true of contemporary filmmakers? But the problem is that today's films, more so than ever, are controlled at every step of production by innumerable masters, and although one artist can resolve to do something which might displease audiences and reduce profits in order to accord with a personal muse, such developments are impossible when scores of people are involved in every decision, as individual desires are smothered by the one priority everybody has in common, which is making money. True, there may still be a few dinosaurs, like Tim Burton or James Cameron, who can choose and dominate their own productions. However, the *auteur* theory in general, so beloved of critics, may work for François Truffaut's *The 400 Blows* (1959) or Jean-Luc Godard's *Breathless* (1960) but seems nonsensical when applied to modern Hollywood blockbusters.

Thus, I recently read a scholarly article which, in keeping with the attitudes of the tribe, dutifully refers to "Alex Proyas's *I, Robot*" (2004). Give me a break. This film did not come into existence because director Proyas woke up one day and exclaimed, "I have a vision for a story about human beings and robots in the near future which I feel personally compelled to bring to the screen." Rather, it was a film project that probably went through several producers and six script rewrites before Proyas was even brought on board, a film that was massively reshaped to accord with the demands of superstar Will Smith, a film that involved hundreds of visual and technical artists who surely did their work with only minimal feedback from Proyas, a film crediting three "second unit directors" who supervised numerous scenes when Proyas was not even present, and a film that undoubtedly did some final reshooting and reediting solely because certain aspects of the film did not test well with sample audiences. This regrettable but commercially successful film, then, did not emerge from an individual creator, but rather from a vast money-making machine.

Others might grant that these films were focused on profitability, but would argue that applying this as a standard of judgment is crass and meaningless; surely, experienced critics should compile such a list based more on their reasoned judgments about the quality of recent films, not the number of dollars they earned. But the actual flaw in my methodology, I believe, is not that it is incorrect, but that it is premature; to truly measure the merits of a work of art, one must examine its earnings over a long period of time, which is not yet possible in the year 2011. Thus, in their day, Jean Renoir's *The Rules of the Game* (1939) and Orson Welles's *Citizen Kane* (1941) were considered spectacular failures, but I am sure that today, those masterful films are racking up more DVD and downloading sales than any other French or American films released around the same time; and eventually, if not now, they will emerge as the most profitable films of their eras. So, while I am not particularly enamored of some of the films on the list, I can hope that the overlooked gems of this decade I would prefer, like *Jerome Bixby's The Man from Earth* (2007) or *Alien Trespass* (2009), might someday be rediscovered and become big sellers on the direct-download-to-brain market when, say, the *Pirates of the Caribbean* films and the *Avatar* trilogy are long forgotten.

There are other grounds for criticizing the premise of this list: monetary figures might be adjusted to account for inflation, and to really determine how much money a film has earned, one should include not only box-office receipts but sales of ancillary merchandise as well. But such modifications would probably not produce any significant alterations in the rankings. What I find most interesting about the process of compiling the list is that there was no need for me to go through every film and carefully separate the science fiction and fantasy films from the others—because *all* of the top films on the Wikipedia list clearly fell into the categories of science fiction or fantasy. Indeed, looking at the complete list of the fifty most profitable films of the decade, one must go down to number twenty-four before locating a film, *The Da Vinci Code* (2006), that could be termed a realistic drama (though John Clute might regard that film, and the novel which inspired it, as examples of that subgenre of fantasy termed "secret histories"). The only other films on the list that could not have been reviewed at a science fiction website are numbers 38 and 39, *The Passion of the Christ* (2004) and *Mamma Mia!* (2008). The conclusion to draw from this, which Hollywood has already drawn, is that if you want to make massive profits from a film today, it must be a science fiction or fantasy film. And this represents a complete reversal of the attitudes prevalent a half-century ago, when science fiction and fantasy films were usually considered minor projects primarily for children, to be made with little money in order to earn a little more money, while producers with an eye for the big bucks specialized in expansive westerns, glossy soap operas, biblical epics, or socially conscious "message" films. But few people admire those Oscar-winning behemoths today, and producers are now focusing their attention on the still-watched science fiction films of that era that have not yet been profit-ably remade. (Coming to theatres soon: The new *When Worlds Collide* [1951] and the new *Forbidden Planet* [1956].)

This triumph of the science fiction and fantasy film, though, is unlikely to endure, since it seems driven primarily by the appeal of increasingly sophisticated special effects which will become less and less impressive as they become more and more commonplace. In the late nineteenth century, theatres attracted large audiences by employing new technologies to offer amazing spectacles: one could visit Le Théâtre du Grand-Guignol in Paris and watch a man have his head cut off by a guillotine; in New York, a production of *Ben-Hur* presented a chariot race with real horses on stage. But when films came along which could provide even better thrills, such dramas were no longer compelling, and the plays from the period that we remember today are the intimate, character-driven dramas of Henrik Ibsen and Anton Chekhov. Similarly, at a time when commercials and video games have better special effects than *Avatar*, that film will endure in the popular imagination only if people regard it as a thought-provoking and profound story, which strikes me as highly unlikely (but for now, let's leave that argument to posterity). The special effects in *2001: A Space Odyssey* (1968) still look pretty good today, but we keep watching that film solely because of its inexhaustible mysteries, not its visual splendor, unlike another film from the time with equally good effects, Gerry and Sylvia Anderson's insipid *Döppelganger* (aka *Journey to the Far Side of the Sun*) (1969).

Thus, though I initially tried to dodge the responsibility, the task of critics remains not to assess which films are profitable today (since that is covered in news reports anyway), but rather to predict which films might still be profitable twenty, fifty, or one hundred years from today—because, like *Rules of the Game*, *Citizen Kane*, and *2001*, people will still find them interesting. And if playing that game, I might actually place a bet on some of the films on the current list—such as *The Lord of the Rings* trilogy, which lamentably focuses too much on Aragorn's war and not enough on Frodo and Sam's quest but otherwise qualifies as an admirable adaptation of a classic fantasy novel, and *The Dark Knight*, the film which provocatively argues that in order to become a superhero or supervillain, you must be clinically insane. Also in the category of blockbusters today that might be blockbusters tomorrow would be *Inception* (2010), a film I am still in the process of figuring out; *Wall•E* (2008), an iconoclastic meditation on humanity's future in space; and *Eternal Sunshine of the Spotless Mind* (2004), which follows no genre conventions but is nevertheless a clever look at the possible impact of imagined new technology on a future society. Then there are the box-office disappointments, and outright flops, that merit a second look, such as *The Invasion* (2007), which I still believe might someday be accepted as the best adaptation of its oft-film story about pod people; *Looney Tunes: Back in Action* (2003), which should become a perennial favorite like the classic cartoons that inspired it; and *The Hitchhiker's Guide to the Galaxy* (2005), which I initially panned as inferior to previous adaptations, though I have come to appreciate it on its own terms as a kinder, gentler version of Douglas Adams' wacky satire. Finally, there are the under-the-radar films previously referenced: *Alien Trespass*, which uniquely captures both the klutzy charm and genuine virtues of the 1950s science fiction film, and *Jerome Bixby's The Man from Earth*, a true test of the proposition that science fiction is a literature of ideas, since the entire film is merely a filmed conversation between several characters, with nary a special effect in sight, but is fascinating nevertheless.

So, if one counts *The Lord of the Rings* as a single movie released in three parts, I have compiled the desired list, perfectly harmonizing with humanity's strange fixation on the number of digits on our hands to select exactly ten films from the first ten years of the decade as potential candidates for cinematic immortality. And if your favorite didn't happen to make the list, it's entirely possible that is because I never saw it, since I am not in the habit of rushing to the theatre every weekend to check out all the latest releases. Some might say that this makes me unqualified to pick out the decade's best films, but the unfortunate truth is: *everybody* is unqualified for the task.

For, as one further consequence of the current profitability of science fiction and fantasy films, people all over the world are making lots and lots of them. If you search the Internet Movie Database for science fiction films released between January 1, 2001 and December 31, 2010, you will get a list of 1404 films; for fantasy films in the same period, 1657. Have you seen all 3061 of them? I actually scrolled through the list of science fiction films, the overwhelming majority of which I had not even heard of, and it's true that most of them sound pretty dreadful; but how can anybody be sure until they have watched them? Therefore, any list of the decade's most memorable films must be provisional, because there may be some wonderful but unknown films from the last decade just waiting for a Columbus to bring them to the world's attention and put them in competition for future positions on ten best lists.

So, if all of us lack the significant data needed for a proper assessment of this decade's films—long-term monetary earnings and a thorough knowledge of all possible candidates—then why does anyone bother to compile these sorts of lists? The answer is related to the main reason why people are producing all of these science fiction and fantasy films: editors pay good money for writers to generate these retrospective analyses, since people are interested in reading them. Thus, I fell into the trap of writing this essay, and you fell into the trap of reading it. As I have argued elsewhere, major motion pictures are the pyramids of contemporary civilization—massive, collectively constructed monuments that people feel compelled to constantly visit, contemplate, and admire; and because of our cultural fascination with films, any excuse for another look will do.

21. NOTES FROM A MIXED MARRIAGE; OR, THE LADY AND THE MONSTER

To immediately clarify my title, I must explain that both my wife Lynne and I have blonde hair and blue eyes, and are of Northern European descent, so our relationship matches no conventional definition of a "mixed marriage." But if I add that I have been devoted to science fiction for my entire life, while my wife has never had any interest at all in science fiction, then some people will understand exactly what I am talking about.

The divide between us is, first of all, physically evident to anyone who visits our house. All but one of its rooms is furnished and decorated in a stylish, conventional manner recalling the designer homes observed on the Home and Garden Channel, which was long one of my wife's favorite channels. In the rooms on display, one must search very hard to find precisely three understated clues that someone with an interest in science fiction lives in this house: on the bookshelf behind the television in the family room, amidst framed photographs and other mementos, rests the plaque commemorating my Pilgrim Award for lifetime contributions to science fiction and fantasy scholarship; on the wall next to the bathroom, there is a framed certificate of my Hugo Award nomination; and in our living room—after a brief argument—we have placed a small bookshelf to one side that displays all of my published books about science fiction, along with other books and magazines that include something I have written. (The problem now is that this bookshelf no longer has enough room for all of the Westfahl items, so another battle looms about replacing it with a larger and more prominent bookshelf.)

Then, after a guided tour of this impeccably fashionable home, one can open the door at the end of the hallway—which my wife usually closes when company comes—and enter a different world. Here, the walls are covered with bookshelves extending to the ceiling filled with books and magazines, most of them science fiction and fantasy, and the rare empty spaces on the walls, shelves, and computer desk are occupied by various items of memorabilia involving spaceships, super-heroes, and monsters, such as framed pictures of the stars of *Star Trek* and the Justice League of America and a poster and dangling bat from my Carleton College production of *Dracula*. This is My Room, officially referred to as either the "office" or the "library," where I do my writing and singularly control the décor, and the one place in the house which resembles the dwelling of a typical science fiction fan.

Our social lives—if one can say that I have a social life at all—are also very different. My wife loves visiting with her numerous friends and attending their social gatherings, and on rare occasions I will accompany her in going to a friend's party (though I will likely spend more time with the host's cat than with the host) or I will sit with her in our family room talking with guests about various subjects, none of them science fiction. Then, on equally rare occasions, my wife will join me at the one sort of social event I enjoy—a science fiction convention— where at times she will eagerly converse with the few friends I may encounter (indeed, she usually talks to them more than I do). At other times, she amuses herself by softly commenting on the ridiculous fannish costumes or the hideous artwork on display—sadly, with limited space available in the office, there will never be any paintings of winged cats pursuing tiny dragons in our house.

Still, our most common and revelatory conflicts involve

choices in entertainment, since our preferences of course rarely coincide: I gravitate toward science fiction, fantasy, and horror, while my wife loves comedies about a man and woman who meet and seem like complete opposites until, after a series of improbable encounters, they fall in love with each other; it is the archetypal plot of all chick flicks, and a story line that my wife may feel has special relevance to her own experience. Sometimes, though, instead of dragging me to such films, she will agree to watch something that I want to see; for example, I recall one Saturday night, when in keeping with our typically exciting and glamorous lifestyle, we were sitting at home in front of the television. Scrolling through the various options available, I noticed the film *Revenge of the Creature* (1955) and cautiously opined that I would like to turn to that channel, since I had not seen the film in over twenty years. Uncharacteristically, my wife accepted that decision.

As this admittedly less-than-classic film unfolded, my wife, displaying a sincere desire to comprehend why anyone on Earth would want to watch such a movie, kept asking the sorts of logical questions that would occur to any rational viewer. Can't everyone see that this purportedly terrifying "monster" is really just a man wearing a rubber suit? Couldn't they have found some decent actors for these parts? Why would a scaly fish-man be sexually attracted to a normal-looking human woman? And why are people afraid of this aquatic creature, when all they have to do to remain safe is to stay away from the water?

In response, I might have said, there are some things that a man shouldn't have to explain; but the answers are not hard to provide. The shoddy special effects and inadequate acting so typical of 1950s science fiction films are actually key elements in their appeal, since they convey an important message: that these are stories about characters that rich, powerful, successful people simply don't care about and can't identify with. Thus, these cheap, hastily-made films precisely reflect the margin-alized status of the social outcasts they focus on and hope to attract. The *outré* physical appearance of the monster is merely a metaphor for the ways that the outsiders and misfits often attracted to science fiction feel psychologically different from others, and the monster's biologically improbable lusts embody the nerd's fervent longings to date the beautiful high school cheerleaders that he knows in advance will always reject him. And because being abhorred by society can drive people to both love themselves, and hate themselves, with unusual fervor, the behavior of the monster's potential victims, as well as the monster's behavior, is designed to mirror the feelings of the targeted filmgoers: characters deliberately place themselves in close proximity to the monster, and then scream in horror when the monster appears, because they, like the monster itself, both love the monster and hate the monster.

More recently, some discord arose when we went to see the Cal State Fullerton production of *Bat Boy: The Musical*, a rare form of entertainment with some appeal for both of us: I love science fiction, and my wife loves musicals, so why not go see a science fiction musical? But afterwards, I surprised my wife with an angry reaction when she said that the show reminded her of the Walt Disney film and musical *Beauty and the Beast*— because to me, that attractive but irksome romance represents the illusory, comforting, Hollywood version of the monster story, built upon the false assumptions that if society's monsters can be domesticated a little bit, and if society's citizens can learn to be a little bit more understanding of monsters, then the monsters can become genuine members of society, both loving and loved, thoroughly and harmoniously integrated into the social order. But the people whose aberrant personalities make them real-life monsters know that it's all a lie; they know that no matter how hard they try, and no matter how hard others try, they can never be like normal people, and they can never be comfortable in normal society. This is the hard truth long ago recognized by Mary Shelley's Frankenstein monster, who ultimately resolves to leave the civilized world to live and die in the wilderness, and expressed more succinctly by his most memorable cinematic embodiment, Boris Karloff, when he looks at his intended companion in *The Bride of Frankenstein* (1935) and announces that "We belong dead," there being no place for them in this world of normal people. And *Bat Boy: The Musical*, after dangerously flirting with the false promise of *Beauty and the Beast* in its upbeat first act, finally faces up to facts and has its titular hero similarly request, and receive, death. In sum, the concluding song may tell audiences to "Love Your Bat Boy," but inasmuch as the cast members are singing this while they carry his corpse around, the real message is that such relationships will never work out. To compare all of this to *Beauty and the Beast*, simply because of parallel scenes involving pursuing mobs, is to miss the point of the entire musical. I ended the discussion by telling my wife, "You have to be born Bat Boy to know how it feels," and sadly, I wasn't entirely kidding.

To be sure, I know that today, many science fiction fans can happily coexist with people who do not share their interests because they have been drawn into the fold by the new forms of science fiction, created by and for people with good social skills and conventional viewpoints and distinguished by lavish budgets, state-of-the-art special effects, capable actors, and road-tested happy endings. They are the people who enjoy the various *Star Trek* television series, typically centered upon the saga of how strange misfits like Spock, Data, and Seven of Nine are gradually accepted by crewmates and learn how to become fully human, and other similarly ameliorative distortions of the harsh realities conveyed in films like *The Creature from the Black Lagoon* (1954) and its sequels. And did I imply that my wife dislikes all science fiction films? It isn't true, because along with a few comedies, there is at least one science fiction film that she absolutely adores: *E.T.: The Extra-Terrestrial* (1982), that ultimate, abominable exercise in reconsidering the weird outsider as a charming friend which I have regularly excoriated as the worst science fiction film ever made. If you also regard *E.T.* as your favorite science fiction film, then, you are the sort of person who would have no difficulty getting along with people like my wife. You are, from my perspective, one of them. But I grew up with a different sort of science fiction, created by and for people like me who saw themselves as society's rejects, and that is the core issue that now separates me from my wife.

At this point, some may detect a subtle, or not-so-subtle, contradiction in this developing argument. I have said that films affirming the impossibility of relationships between strange outsiders and normal people are truthful, whereas films indicating that such relationships can be established are annoyingly delusional. Yet as I write this, I am, as a self-identified strange outsider, approaching the twenty-seventh anniversary of my marriage to a woman who would happily identify herself as a normal person. How can I say such things can't happen when I would appear to represent a living, breathing counterexample? Well, what my wife and I have achieved during those twenty-seven years is something quite different from what happened in *Beauty and the Beast*, as is illustrated by a third kind of science fiction film in which the monster survives and establishes a carefully calibrated bond with a human woman founded upon mutual respect, an understanding of their differences, and a considerable amount of distance.

The best example here would be the original *The Day the Earth Stood Still* (1951) and its central couple, the alien Klaatu (Michael Rennie) and secretary Helen Benson (Patricia Neal). Clearly, they are attracted to each other; clearly, they form a strong emotional connection based on their mutual fondness for her son Bobby and their commitment to peaceful coexistence; and clearly, they become romantically interested in each other while fully recognizing that they are also fundamentally disparate sorts of beings. Yet Hollywood cannot allow Klaatu and Helen to passionately kiss, get married, and buy a home in the suburbs (the way my wife wanted the film to end), because romantic couples in films, despite their superficial differences, must ultimately be presented as true soulmates, properly destined for a lifetime of harmonious union. And obviously, people like Klaatu and Helen can never be soulmates of this kind. Thus, to symbolize the perpetual and unavoidable division between them, the story had to end with Klaatu returning to outer space, still spiritually united with Helen (who significantly rejects her other suitor and is left with no other companion) but physically separated from her. Precisely the same scenario was repeated more recently in that brilliant reconstruction of the 1950s science fiction film, *Alien Trespass* (2009), wherein another alien, Urp (Eric McCormack), falls in love with a responsive human woman, Tammy (Jenni Baird), but is finally compelled to return home while she remains alone on Earth, still longing for the company of her unusual acquaintance while she leaves town, alone, to seek her destiny.

And that is what largely explains the endurance of our marriage (something which has surely surprised most of our friends): a certain degree of separation. Even during our honeymoon, my wife realized that I needed some time to be by myself, and over the years, we have come to spend many of our evenings apart, as I sit at the computer while my wife talks to friends on the telephone or watches true-crime or medical dramas on television. It may seem an unusual sort of marriage, and my many detractors may seize upon this description of my behavior as proof that I am indeed a contemptible creep. (Fortunately, I have been schooled by bad science fiction films to care little about the opinions of the sorts of people who pick up torches and pitchforks in response to monsters.) Yet this probably represents the only way to make a mixed marriage work. After all, if one endeavors to imagine an alternate ending to *The Day the Earth Stood Still* wherein Klaatu settles down in Washington, D.C. with Helen as Earth's new ambassador from beyond, it should be clear that the relationship would necessarily involve many nights when Helen and Bobby would sit at home by themselves while Klaatu was hard at work in his flying saucer with Gort and the other machines. No doubt Klaatu would often feel guilty, as I do, about his need to be by himself and he would often wonder, as I do, why his wife puts up with him.

Still, my marriage cannot be entirely attributed to the saint-like patience of a remarkable woman burdened with an eccentric husband—because, while we joke about being complete opposites in all respects, ranging from basic personality traits to the way we squeeze toothpaste tubes (she squeezes in the middle, I squeeze at the end), we actually do have some significant things in common: an absolute commitment to the well-being and educational success of our children, a fondness for cats, frugal spending habits, and similar (Democratic) political beliefs and (not very) religious beliefs. We regularly communicate and work together toward our shared goals even while recognizing that we also to a large extent must lead separate lives. Had we instead foolishly strived for a lifetime of complete "togetherness" (that dubious ideal of married life first promoted in the 1950s, and surely a factor in the immediate increase in the rate of divorce), and spent our every waking moment in constant contact, the marriage undoubtedly would have collapsed long ago.

As already intimated, I recognize that reflections of this kind may be becoming incomprehensible to readers in an era when science fiction has been thoroughly integrated into the world of mainstream entertainment, and the aberrant science fiction films of the 1950s that appealed to society's misfits are generally forgotten because they do not lend themselves to conventionally refashioned storylines that comfortingly deal with monsters in the preferred manner by either thoroughly humanizing them (*E.T.*, *My Favorite Martian* (1963-1966), etc.) or thoroughly demonizing them (*Alien* [1979], *Predator* [1987], etc.). Thus, you may think that every science fiction film from the 1950s has already been remade, but consider how assiduously Hollywood producers have avoided remaking those films that feature disquietingly ambiguous aliens or monsters who are both heroes and villains, such as *The Man from Planet X* (1951), *Stranger from Venus* (1954), the aforementioned *The Creature from the Black Lagoon*, *This Island Earth* (1955), and *The Colossus of New York* (1958). They are instead attracted to the films with aliens that embody absolute evil: *The Thing (from Another World)* (1951), *The War of the Worlds* (1953), *Invaders from Mars* (1953), *Invasion of the Body Snatchers* (1956), and so on. And when they finally decided to tackle *The Day the Earth Stood Still*, the accountants who crafted that repugnant, "updated" version (2008) could obviously discern no profits to be made by featuring a distant but sympathetic alien like Rennie's Klaatu or Urp, and instead essentially made its Klaatu (Keanu Reeves) a heartless villain, happy to begin slaughtering Earth's billions of people because we have been insufficiently nice to our trees. When the phrase "science fiction fans" refers only to people who like films like this, there will be no reason to fear that such individuals will have any problems in relating to everyday society and bonding with its members. Already, I believe, today's young people who feel alienated from the world are turning away from the bland, palatable science fiction of their generation and seeking consolation in other forms of entertainment. For example, my daughter Allison, who inherited her mother's social skills, has found and married a man very much like her father (creating her own mixed marriage), but while her husband Steven was once a big fan of Isaac Asimov, he is now more interested in anime and online gaming than science fiction.

However, a better illustration of the changing tastes of today's generation of nerds may be my son Jeremy, who has inherited more than a touch of his father's odd personality. (My wife likes to joke that she married an alien, and later gave birth to an alien.) While he will occasionally appreciate a science fiction film (significantly, only those oldies-but-goodies that still appeal to outcasts like the original *The Day the Earth Stood Still* or *2001: A Space Odyssey* [1968], not any contemporary blockbusters), his favorite diversion is playing video games, interactive narratives often involving a lonely, unattractive individual, like Mario the Plumber, who must struggle through a world filled with hostile forces which kill him again and again until he might finally enjoy, at best, a brief kiss from a beautiful princess before returning to the fray. I hope that this young Klaatu will, like me, someday find his own Helen Benson, who will understand and appreciate his wonderful strangeness and provide him with sufficient space to be who he is. Such unlikely mixed marriages, as I can attest from my own experience, can work out just fine.

A BIBLIOGRAPHY OF GARY WESTFAHL AND LYNNE LUNDQUIST WRITINGS ON FILM (INCLUDING ITEMS REVISED FOR THIS VOLUME)

Lundquist, Lynne. "Myth and Illiteracy: Bill and Ted's Explicated Adventures." *Extrapolation*, 37 (Fall 1996), 212–223.

------. "Victims of a Globalized, Radicalized, Technologized World, Or, Why the Beatles Needed *Help!*" *Science Fiction and the Prediction of the Future: Essays on Foresight and Fallacy*. Edited by Gary Westfahl, Wong Kin Yuen, and Amy Kit-sze Chan. Jefferson, North Carolina: McFarland Publishers, 2011, 120–127.

------, and Gary Westfahl. "Coming of Age in Fantasyland: The Self-Parenting Child in Walt Disney Animated Films." *Nursery Realms: Children in the Worlds of Science Fiction, Fantasy, and Horror*. Edited by Gary Westfahl and George Slusser. Athens, Georgia: University of Georgia Press, 1999, 161–170.

Westfahl, Gary. "A.I.: Artificial Incompetence, or Robots Just Don't Understand: A Review of *I, Robot*." Locus Online website, posted on July 17, 2004. At http://www.locusmag.

com/2004/Reviews/07_Westfahl_IRobot.html .

------. "'All Energy Is Borrowed': A Review of *Avatar*." Locus Online website, posted on December 20, 2009. At http://www.locusmag.com/Reviews/2009/12/all-energy-is-borrowed-review-of-avatar.html .

------. "All the Truths That Are His Life: A Review of *Dreams with Sharp Teeth*." Locus Online website, posted on June 6, 2008. At http://locusmag.com/2008/Westfahl_DreamsWithSharpTeeth.html .

------. "Aye, Robot: A Review of *Wall•E*." Locus Online website, posted on June 29, 2008. At http://locusmag.com/2008/Westfahl_Wall-E.html .

------. "'Backward, Turn Backward, O Time in Your Flight': A Review of *The Curious Case of Benjamin Button*." Locus Online website, posted on December 27, 2008. At http://locusmag.com/2008/Reviews_Westfahl_BenjaminButton.html .

------. "Big Dumb Opticals: Film Considered as the Motion Pyramid." *Interzone*, No. 150 (December 1999), 52–53. Available at the World of Westfahl website at http://www.sfsite.com/gary/ww-columns03.htm . To be revised and republished in *Talking to Aliens—and Ourselves: Science Fiction Columns from Interzone*. By Gary Westfahl. Foreword by David Pringle. Holicong, Pennsylvania: Wildside Press/Borgo Press, forthcoming.

------. "Captain Klaatu and the Planeteers, or, The Day the Face Stood Still: A Review of *The Day the Earth Stood Still*." Locus Online website, posted on December 14, 2008. At http://locusmag.com/2008/Review_EarthStoodStill.html .

------. "Celebrating a Century of Science Fiction Columns with *A Trip to the Moon*." *Interzone*, No. 176 (February 2002), 47–48. To be revised and republished in *Talking to Aliens—and Ourselves: Science Fiction Columns from Interzone*. By Gary Westfahl. Foreword by David Pringle. Holicong, Pennsylvania: Wildside Press/Borgo Press, forthcoming.

------. "A Christmas Cavil, or, It's a Plunderful Life." *Interzone*,

No. 151 (January 2000), 48–49. To be revised and republished in *Talking to Aliens—and Ourselves: Science Fiction Columns from Interzone*. By Gary Westfahl. Foreword by David Pringle. Holicong, Pennsylvania: Wildside Press/ Borgo Press, forthcoming.

------. "Citizen Flynn: A Review of *Tron: Legacy*." Locus Online website, posted on December 20, 2010. At http://www. locusmag.com/Reviews/2010/12/citizen-flynn-a-review-of-tron-legacy/ .

------. "A Civilized Frontier." Review-essay on *Star Trek: The Human Frontier* by Michèle Barrett and Duncan Barrett. *Science Fiction Studies*, 29 (July 2002), 272–276.

------. "Close Encounters for the Third, and Worst, Time: A Review of Steven Soderbergh's *Solaris*." Locus Online website, posted on November 29, 2002. At http://locusmag. com/2002/Reviews/Westfahl11_Solaris.html.

------. "Commercials." *The Encyclopedia of Fantasy*. Edited by John Clute and John Grant. Contributing Editors Mike Ashley, Roz Kaveney, David Langford, and Ron Tiner. Consultant Editors David G. Hartwell and Gary Westfahl. New York: St. Martin's Press, and London: Orbit Press, 1997, 220.

------. "The Dark Side of the Moon: Robert A. Heinlein's *Project Moonbase*." *Extrapolation*, 36 (Summer, 1995), 126–135.

------. "'Desire Is Irrelevant': A Review of *Terminator 3: Rise of the Machines*." Locus Online website, posted on July 4, 2003. At http://www.locusmag.com/2003/Reviews/Westfahl07_ T3.html.

------. "Doing Something Right: A Review of *Serenity*." Locus Online website, posted on October 3, 2005. At http:locusmag. com/2005/Features/10_Westfahl_Serenity.html .

------. "Dull Outcome, No Kids: A Review of *Children of Men*." Locus Online website, posted on December 28, 2006. At http://www.locusmag.com/Features/2006/12/dull-outcome-no-kids-review-of.html .

------. "Dying Is Hard, Comedy Is Easy: A Review of *Stranger*

Than Fiction." Locus Online website, posted on November 13, 2006. At http://locusmag.com/2006/Features/Westfahl_StrangerThanFiction.html .

------. "Earth Needs Martians: A Review of *Mars Needs Moms.*" Locus Online website, posted on March 13, 2011. At http://www.locusmag.com/Reviews/2011/03/earth-needs-martians-a-review-of-mars-needs-moms/ .

------. "The Endless Odyssey: The *2001* Saga and Its Inability to Predict Humanity's Future." *Science Fiction and the Prediction of the Future: Essays on Foresight and Fallacy.* Edited by Gary Westfahl, Wong Kin Yuen, and Amy Chan Kit-sze. Jefferson, North Carolina: McFarland Publishers, 2011, 135-170.

------. "The End of Civilization and Its Discontents: A Review of *The Road.*" Locus Online website, posted on November 29, 2009. At http://www.locusmag.com/Reviews/2009/11/end-of-civilization-and-its-discontents.html .

------. "'Escape to Your Library!' A Review of *Jumper.*" Locus Online website, posted on February 18, 2008. At http://locusmag.com/2008/Westfahl_Jumper.html .

------. "Extracts from *The Biographical Encyclopedia of Science Fiction Film.*" *Foundation: The Review of Science Fiction,* No. 64 (Summer 1995), 45–69. Short essays on "Irwin Allen," "Gerry Anderson," "John Carradine," "Harlan Ellison," "Sir Alec Guinness," "Ray Harryhausen," "Inoshiro Honda," "Gale Anne Hurd," "Chris Marker," "Richard Matheson," "Dame Diana Rigg," "Robby the Robot," "Rod Serling," and "Steven Spielberg." Revised and included in "Gary Westfahl's Biographical Encyclopedia of Science Fiction Film" (q.v.).

------. "Even Better Than the Real Thing: Advertising, Music Videos, Postmodernism, and (Eventually) Science Fiction." *Science Fiction, Children's Literature, and Popular Culture: Coming of Age in Fantasyland.* By Gary Westfahl. Westport, Connecticut: Greenwood Press, 2000, 79–92.

------. "Familiar Invaders: A Review of *Super 8.*" Locus Online website, posted on June 12, 2011. At http://www.locusmag. com/Reviews/2011/06/familiar-invaders-a-review-of-super-8/ .

------. *"Field of Dreams."* World of Westfahl website, posted on September 4, 2007. At http://www.sfsite.com/gary/ww-ref-field01.htm .

------. "For All Maggotkind, or, Swatted Dreams: A Review of *Fly Me to the Moon.*" Locus Online website, posted on August 18, 2008. At http://locusmag.com/2008/Review_FlyMeToTheMoon.html .

------. "From the Back of the Head to Beyond the Moon: The Novel and Film *This Island Earth.*" *Science Fiction, Children's Literature, and Popular Culture.* By Gary Westfahl. Westport, Connecticut: Greenwood Press, 2000, 49-68.

------. "Gary Westfahl's Biographical Encyclopedia of Science Fiction Film." World of Westfahl website, with revised essays from "Extracts from The Biographical Encyclopedia of Science Fiction Film" and "Two Giants of the Cinema of Space-Time: Further Extracts from *The Biographical Encyclopedia of Science Fiction Film*" (q.v.) and new essays; site expanded and updated regularly. Contents as of April 1, 2012 are: "Forrest J. Ackerman," "Nick Adams," "John Agar," "Philson Ahn," "William Alland," "Irwin Allen," "Woody Allen," "Kirstie Alley," "Gerry Anderson," "Michael Anderson," "Sylvia Anderson," "Jack Arnold," "Barbara Bain," "Gene Barry," "Wesley E. Barry," "Paul Birch," "Whit Bissell," "Bill Bixby," "Jerome Bixby," "Chesley Bonestell," "Peter Boyle," "Ray Bradbury," "Adrien Brody," "Tim Burton," "David Butler," "Edward L. Cahn," "James Cameron," "Lewis John Carlino," "Richard Carlson," "John Carradine," "Leo G. Carroll," "Maurice Cass," "Lon Chaney," "Lon Chaney, Jr.," "John Cho," "Sir Arthur C. Clarke," "Phyllis Coates," "Joan Collins," "Sir Sean Connery," "Roger Corman," "Buster Crabbe," "Peter Cushing," "Meyer Dolinsky," "Faith Domergue," "David

Duchovny," "David Duncan," "Harlan Ellison," "Roland Emmerich," "Maurice Evans," "Federico Fellini," "Richard Fleischer," "Louise Fletcher," "D. C. Fontana," "Anne Francis," "Joanna Frank," "John Frankenheimer," "Brendan Fraser," "Frederic Gadette," "Beverly Garland," "William Gibson," "Jeff Goldblum," "Jerry Goldsmith," "Bernard Gordon," "Bert I. Gordon," "Peter Graves," "Lorne Greene," "Sir Alec Guinness," "Earl Hamner, Jr.," "George Harrison," "Ray Harryhausen," "Byron Haskin," "Howard Hawks," "Ben Hecht," "David Hedison," "Robert A. Heinlein," "Charlton Heston," "Sir Alfred Hitchcock," "Inoshiro Honda," "Ron Howard," "Rock Hudson," "Gale Anne Hurd," "Martha Hyer," "Steve Ihnat," "Michael Jackson," "Russell Johnson," "Tor Johnson," "Nathan Juran," "Boris Karloff," "Buster Keaton," "DeForest Kelley," "Erle C. Kenton," "Val Kilmer," "Akira Kubo," "Stanley Kubrick," "Elsa Lanchester," "Martin Landau," "Robert Lansing," "Glen A. Larson," "Jack Larson," "Christopher Lee," "John Lennon," "John Lithgow," "Robert Longo," "Peter Lorre," "Eugene Lourie," "George Lucas," "Bela Lugosi," "William Lundigan," "Patrick Macnee," "Antonio Margheriti," "Chris Marker," "Hugh Marlowe," "William Marshall," "Arlene Martel," "Ross Martin," "Richard Matheson," "Sir Paul McCartney," "Roddy McDowall," "Leo McKern," "Lee Meriwether," "Ricardo Montalban," "Agnes Moorhead," "Billy Mumy," "Eddie Murphy," "Noel Neill," "Kurt Neumann," "John Newland," "Julie Newmar," "Nichelle Nichols," "Jack Nicholson," "Leonard Nimoy," "Simon Oakland," "Arch Oboler," "Willis O'Brien," "Charles Ogle," "George Pal," "Gregory Peck," "Cassandra Peterson," "Walter Pidgeon," "Jack P. Pierce," "Vincent Price," "Anthony Quinn," "Rex Reason," "Rhodes Reason," "George Reeves," "Keanu Reeves," "Michael Rennie," "Dame Diana Rigg," "Robby the Robot," "Cliff Robertson," "Gene Roddenberry," "Majel Barrett Roddenberry," "Carl Sagan," "Archie Savage," "William Schallert," "Roy Scheider," "Arnold

Schwarzenegger," "Peter Sellers," "Lorenzo Semple, Jr.," "Rod Serling," "William Shatner," "M. Night Shyamalan," "Curt Siodmak," "Jerry Sohl," "Steven Spielberg," "Ringo Starr," "Warren Stevens," "Robert Stevenson," "Patrick Stewart," "Glenn Strange," "Theodore Sturgeon," "George Takei," "Rod Taylor," "Marshall Thompson," "Kenneth Tobey," "Ivan Tors," "Thomas Tryon," "Konstantin Tsiolkovsky," "Sir Peter Ustinov," "Robert Vaughn," "Jules Verne," "Max von Sydow," "Sigourney Weaver," "H. G. Wells," "Adam West," "Gary Westfahl," "James Whale," "Robert Wise," "Edward D. Wood, Jr.," "Frank Wu," "Philip Wylie," "George Worthing Yates," "Irvin S. Yeaworth, Jr.." "Michael York," "Robert Zemeckis," and "George Zucco." At http://www.sfsite.com/gary/ww-encyclopedia.htm .

------. "A Glimpse at the Future: A First Look at *FlashForward.*" Locus Online website, posted on September 26, 2009. At http://www.locusmag.com/Reviews/2009/09/glimpse-of-future-first-look-at.html.

------. "Godzilla's Travels: The Evolution of a Globalized Gargantuan." *World Weavers: Globalization, Science Fiction, and the Cybernetic Revolution.* Edited by Wong Kin Yuen, Gary Westfahl, and Amy Chan Kit-sze. Hong Kong: Hong Kong University Press, 2005, 167–188.

------. "Have Spacesuit, Will Dazzle, but I Don't Care If the Sun Don't Shine: A Review of *Sunshine.*" Locus Online website, posted on July 22, 2007. At http://locusmag.com/2007/Westfahl_Sunshine.html .

------. "Hollywood Strikes a Pose: Seven Tales of Triumph, Treachery, and Travail in Old Tinseltown." *Science Fiction, Children's Literature, and Popular Culture: Coming of Age in Fantasyland.* By Gary Westfahl. Westport, Connecticut: Greenwood Press, 2000, 107–120.

------. "Inconstant Man, or, Have Birthday Suit, Will Time Travel: A Review of *The Time Traveler's Wife.*" Locus Online website, posted on August 17, 2009. At http://www.locusmag.com/Reviews/2009/08/inconstant-man-or-have-

------. "An Intelligent Virus: A Review of *The Invasion.*" Locus Online website, posted on August `8, 2007. At http://locusmag.com/2007/Westfahl_Invasion.html .

------. "Interplanetary Man of Mystery: A Review of *Superman Returns.*" Locus Online website, posted on July 2, 2006. At http://locusmag.com/2006/Features/Westfahl_SupermanReturns.html.

------. "In the Midst of Pandemonium, Profundity?: A Review of *Pandorum.*" Locus Online website, posted on October 2, 2009. At http://www.locusmag.com/Reviews/2009/10/in-midst-of-pandemonium-profundity.html .

------. "It Came from Older Space: A Review of *Alien Trespass.*" Locus Online website, posted on April 5, 2009. At http://locusmag.com/2009/Reviews_AlienTrespass.html .

------. "Janeways and Thaneways: The Better Half, and Worse Half, of Science-Fiction Television." *Interzone*, No. 140 (February 1999), 31–33. To be revised and republished in *Talking to Aliens—and Ourselves: Science Fiction Columns from Interzone.* By Gary Westfahl. Foreword by David Pringle. Holicong, Pennsylvania: Wildside Press/Borgo Press, forthcoming.

------. "A Lack of Vision: A Review of *Blindness.*" Locus Online website, posted on October 6, 2008. At http://locusmag.com/2008/Review_Blindness.html .

------. "Lantern Wilder: A Review of *Green Lantern.*" Locus Online website, posted on June 19, 2011. At http://www.locusmag.com/Reviews/2011/06/lantern-wilder-a-review-of-green-lantern/.

------. "Legends of the Fall: Going Not Particularly Far *Behind the Music.*" *Science Fiction, Children's Literature, and Popular Culture: Coming of Age in Fantasyland.* By Gary Westfahl. Westport, Connecticut: Greenwood Press, 2000, 93–106.

------. "'A Life That's All About Death': A Review of *Hereafter.*" Locus Online website, posted on October 18,

2010. At http://www.locusmag.com/Reviews/2010/10/a-life-that%e2%80%99s-all-about-death-a-review-of-hereafter/ .

------. "*The Lord of the Rings: The Fellowship of the Ring* (2001)." *The Greenwood Encyclopedia of Science Fiction and Fantasy: Themes, Works, and Wonders.* Edited by Gary Westfahl. Advisory Board Richard Bleiler, John Clute, Fiona Kelleghan, David Langford, Andy Sawyer, and Darrell Schweitzer. Foreword by Neil Gaiman. Three volumes. Westport, Connecticut: Greenwood Press, 2005, 1153-1155.

------. "Magnificent Obsessions: A Review of *The Dark Knight*." Locus Online website, posted on July 20, 2008. At http://locusmag.com/2008/Westfahl_TheDarkKnight.html .

------. "Martians Old and New, Still Standing Over Us." *Interzone*, No. 168 (June 2001), 57–58. To be revised and republished in *Talking to Aliens—and Ourselves: Science Fiction Columns from Interzone.* By Gary Westfahl. Foreword by David Pringle. Holicong, Pennsylvania: Wildside Press/ Borgo Press, forthcoming.

------. "Me, Robot: A Review of *A.I.*" Locus Online website, posted on July 1, 2001. At http://locusmag.com/2001/Reviews/Westfahl06.html .

------. "Mister and Monster Smith: A Review of *I Am Legend*." Locus Online website, posted on December 16, 2007. At http://locusmag.com/2007/Westfahl_IAmLegend.html .

------. "Mommie Dreariest: A Review of *Coraline*." Locus Online website, posted on February 8, 2009. At http://locusmag.com/2009/Reviews_Coraline.html .

------. "The Monsters Are Due on Merchant Street: A Review of *War of the Worlds*." Locus Online website, posted on June 29, 2005. At http://www.locusmag.com/2005/Features/06_Westfahl_WarWorlds.html.

------. "A Moon for the (Technologically) Misbegotten: A Review of *Moon*." Locus Online website, posted on June 14, 2009. At http://www.locusmag.com/Reviews/2009/06/moon-for-technologically-misbegotten.html .

------. "Mostly Charmless: A Review of *The Hitchhiker's Guide to the Galaxy.*" Locus Online website, posted on May 1, 2005. At http://www.locusmag.com/2005/Features/05_Westfahl_ Hitchhiker.html.

------. "Nolan's Labyrinth: A Review of *Inception.*" Locus Online website, posted on July 18, 2010. At http://www. locusmag.com/Reviews/2010/07/nolan%E2%80%99s-laby-rinth-a-review-of-inception/ .

------. "Not-So-Close Encounters: *Men into Space* and Their Search for Extraterrestrial Life." The Internet Review of Science Fiction, posted on December 11, 2009. Originally at http://www.irosf.com/q/zine/article/10614 . Now available at World of Westfahl website at http://www.sfsite.com/gary/ ww-irsf08.htm . Revised and republished in *The Spacesuit Film: A History, 1918–1969.* By Gary Westfahl. Foreword by Michael Cassutt. Jefferson, North Carolina: McFarland Publishers, 2012, 69-73.

------. "1958: Science Fiction Film's Sense-of-Wonderful Year." Locus Online website, posted on December 17, 2008. At http://locusmag.com/2008/Reviews_Westfahl_1958.html .

------. "Notes from a Mixed Marriage, or, The Lady and the Monster." Locus Online website, posted on August 23, 2010. At http://www.locusmag.com/Perspectives/2010/08/notes-from-a-mixed-marriage-or-the-lady-and-the-monster/ .

------. "The Odyssey Continues: Relevance of '2001' Resounds in 2001." *Florida Today* (February 11, 2001), 15A.

------. "Opposing War, Exploiting War: The Troubled Pacifism of *Star Trek.*" *Science Fiction, Children's Literature, and Popular Culture: Coming of Age in Fantasyland.* By Gary Westfahl. Westport, Connecticut: Greenwood Press, 2000, 69–78.

------. "The Persistence of Memories: A Review of *Looney Tunes: Back in Action.*" Locus Online website, posted on November 18, 2003. At http://www.locusmag.com/2003/ Reviews/11_Westfahl_Looney.html .

------. "Philip K., Diminished: A Review of *The Adjustment Bureau.*" Locus Online website, posted on March 6, 2011. At http://www.locusmag.com/Reviews/2011/03/philip-k-diminished-a-review-of-the-adjustment-bureau/ .

------. "'The Pit of Man's Fears': Revisiting *The Twilight Zone*." Locus Online website, posted on July 18, 2007. At http://locusmag.com/2007/Westfahl_TwilightZone.html .

------. "Ready for Primate Time: A Review of *Rise of the Planet of the Apes*." Locus Online website, posted on August 7, 2011. At http://www.locusmag.com/Reviews/2011/08/ready-for-primate-time-a-review-of-rise-of-the-planet-of-the-apes/

------. Review of *"Planet of the Apes" as American Myth: Race and Politics in the Films and Television Series* by Eric Greene. *The Science Fiction Research Association Review*, No. 223 (May/June 1996), 31–35.

------. Review of *Science Is Fiction: The Films of Jean Painlevé* edited by Andy Masaki Bellows and Marina McDougall with Brigitte Berg. *Isis: Journal of the History of Science Society*, 92 (March 2001), 238–239.

------. "Robert A. Heinlein's *2001: A Space Odyssey*." *Interzone*, No. 163 (January 2001), 54–55. To be revised and republished in *Talking to Aliens—and Ourselves: Science Fiction Columns from Interzone*. By Gary Westfahl. Foreword by David Pringle. Holicong, Pennsylvania: Wildside Press/Borgo Press, forthcoming.

------. "Rocks for Jocks: A Review of *Journey to the Center of the Earth 3D*." Locus Online website, posted on July 13, 2008. At http://locusmag.com/2008/Westfahl_JourneyCenterEarth.html.

------. "Rock Videos." *The Encyclopedia of Fantasy*. Edited by John Clute and John Grant. Contributing Editors Mike Ashley, Roz Kaveney, David Langford, and Ron Tiner. Consultant Editors David G. Hartwell and Gary Westfahl. New York: St. Martin's Press, and London: Orbit Press, 1997, 817–818.

------. "Ronald McDonald." World of Westfahl website, posted on May 26, 2006. At http://www.sfsite.com/gary/ww-ref-ronald01.htm .

------. "A Saucer of Loveableness: A Review of *Cj7.*" Locus Online website, posted on March 10, 2008. At http://locusmag.com/2008/Westfahl_Cj7.html .

------. "A Scent of Wonder: A Review of *Perfume: The Story of a Murderer.*" Locus Online website, posted on December 30, 2006. At http://www.locusmag.com/Features/2006/12/scent-of-wonder-review-of-perfume.html .

------. "Searching for Tomorrow: A Second Look at *FlashForward.*" Locus Online website, posted on March 14, 2010. At http://www.locusmag.com/Reviews/2010/03/searching-for-tomorrow-second-look-at.html .

------. "Seeing Double: A Review of *The Prestige.*" Locus Online website, posted on October 22, 2006. At http://locusmag.com/2006/Features/Westfahl_ThePrestige.html .

------. "Something Old, Something New, Something Borrowed, Something Blue: A Review of *Minority Report.*" Locus Online website, posted on June 24, 2002. At http://www.locusmag.com/2002/Reviews/Westfahl06_Minority.html.

------. "Space Films Before 1950." World of Westfahl website, posted on May 29, 2011. At http://www.sfsite.com/gary/ww-spacesuit01.htm .

------. *The Spacesuit Film: A History, 1918–1969.* Foreword by Michael Cassutt. Jefferson, North Carolina: McFarland Publishers, 2012.

------. "*Superman* (1978)." *The Greenwood Encyclopedia of Science Fiction and Fantasy: Themes, Works, and Wonders.* Edited by Gary Westfahl. Advisory Board Richard Bleiler, John Clute, Fiona Kelleghan, David Langford, Andy Sawyer, and Darrell Schweitzer. Foreword by Neil Gaiman. Three volumes. Westport, Connecticut: Greenwood Press, 2005, 1285-1287.

------. "Tainted Wells: A Review of *The Time Machine.*" Locus Online website, posted on March 11, 2002. At http://www.locusmag.com/2002/Reviews/Westfahl_TimeMachine.html.

------. "Taking a Different Red Pill: A Review of *A Scanner*

Darkly." Locus Online website, posted on July 9, 2006. At http://locusmag.com/2006/Features/Westfahl_AScanner Darkly.html .

------. "Television." "Addenda and Corrigenda," paperback edition, *The Encyclopedia of Fantasy.* Edited by John Clute and John Grant. Contributing Editors Mike Ashley, Roz Kaveney, David Langford, and Ron Tiner. Consultant Editors David G. Hartwell and Gary Westfahl. New York: St. Martin's Press, and London: Orbit Books, 1999, 1076.

------. "The Ten Best Science Fiction and Fantasy Films of the Twenty-First Century...As of December 31, 2010...And A Prediction about Ten Best Lists to Come." Locus Online website, posted on January 17, 2011. At http://www.locusmag. com/Reviews/2011/01/the-ten-best-science-fiction-and-fantasy-films-of-the-twenty-first-century-as-of-december-31-2010-and-a-prediction-about-ten-best-lists-to-come/ .

------. *"This Island Earth." The Critical Companion to Science Fiction Film Adaptations.* Edited by Peter Wright. John Cook, Catriona Miller, and Sue Short. Liverpool: Liverpool University Press, forthcoming.

------. "Thoroughly Modern Mythology?: A Review of *Clash of the Titans.*" Locus Online website, posted on April 5, 2010. At http://www.locusmag.com/Reviews/2010/04/thoroughly-modern-mythology-review-of.html.

------. "'Thrusters on Full': A Review of *Star Trek.*" Locus Online website, posted on May 10, 2009. At http://www. locusmag.com/Reviews/2009/05/thrusters-on-full-review-of-star-trek.html .

------. "Tomorrow Numbly Dies: A Final Look at *FlashForward.*" Locus Online website, posted on May 30, 2010. At http://www.locusmag.com/Reviews/2010/05/tomorrow-numbly-dies-a-final-look-at-flashforward/ .

------. "A Tribute to *St. Elsewhere*: The Series That I Loved, Even Though It Wanted to Be Hated." World of Westfahl website, posted on April 29, 2007. At http://www.sfsite.com/gary/ww-review04.htm .

------. "The True Frontier: Confronting and Avoiding the Realities of Space in American Science Fiction Films." *Space and Beyond: The Frontier Theme in Science Fiction.* Edited by Gary Westfahl. Westport, Connecticut: Greenwood Press, 2000), 55–65.

------. *"The Twilight Zone* (1959-1964)." *The Greenwood Encyclopedia of Science Fiction and Fantasy: Themes, Works, and Wonders.* Edited by Gary Westfahl. Advisory Board Richard Bleiler, John Clute, Fiona Kelleghan, David Langford, Andy Sawyer, and Darrell Schweitzer. Foreword by Neil Gaiman. Three volumes. Westport, Connecticut: Greenwood Press, 2005, 1318-1320.

------. "Two Giants of the Cinema of Space-Time: Further Extracts from *The Biographical Encyclopedia of Science Fiction Film.*" Worlds Enough and Time: Exploring the Space-Time Continuum of Science Fiction and Fantasy. Program of the 1997 Science Fiction Research Association/J. Lloyd Eaton Conference, Long Beach, California. Edited by Gary Westfahl. Privately printed, 1997, [10–11]. Short essays on "Forrest J. Ackerman" and "H. G. Wells." Revised and included in "Gary Westfahl's Biographical Encyclopedia of Science Fiction Film" (q.v.).

------. "Two Maps of Hell: A Review of *Never Let Me Go.*" Locus Online website, posted on September 19, 2010. At http://www.locusmag.com/Reviews/2010/09/two-maps-of-hell-a-review-of-never-let-me-go/ .

------. *"2010*: The Year We Lower Our Expectations." Strange Horizons website, posted on October 18, 2010. At http://strangehorizons.com/2010/20101018/westfahl-a.shtml .

------. "The Warm Equations: A Review of *Martian Child.*" Locus Online website, posted on November 6, 2007. At http://www.locusmag.com/2007/Westfahl_MartianChild.html .

------. "What Is an Animated Movie?" World of Westfahl website, posted on April 22, 2007. At http://www.sfsite.com/gary/ww-animated01.htm .

------. "Where No Market Has Gone Before: 'The Science-

Fiction Industry' and the *Star Trek* Industry." *Extrapolation*, 37 (Winter 1996), 291–301.

------, Rob Bedford, Mike Brotherton, Adam-Troy Castro, Paul Di Filippo, David Gerrold, Paul Levinson, Kevin Maher, Jay Maynard, Gabriel McKee, Kevin Maher, and Michael L. Wentz. "Mind-Meld: Which Sci-Fi Movie Ending Would You Change?" SF Signal website, posted on February 26, 2008. At http://www.sfsignal.com/archives/006323.html .

------, Summer Brooks, Mike Brotherton, Steve Davidson, Gary Farber, Edward M. Lerner, Kevin Maher, Ben Peek, Chris Preksta, Mike Resnick, S. Andrew Swann, and Nar Williams. "Mind Meld: Bad Guys We Love to Hate: The Best Film Villains in SF/F/H (with Various Videos of Villainy)." SF Signal website, posted on October 14, 2009. At http:// www.sfsignal.com/archives/2009/10/mind-meld-the-best-film-villains-in-sffh/ .

------, Christopher David, Tim Holman, Joseph Mallozzi, Derryl Murphy, James Davis Nicoll, Jennifer Pelland, Nick Sagan, and John Varley. "Mind Meld: What Makes a Successful SciFi/Fantasy Book Adaptation? Why Do Some Fail?" SF Signal website, posted on September 17, 2008. At http:// www.sfsignal.com/archives/007185.html .

BIBLIOGRAPHY OF OTHER WORKS CITED

Aelita: Queen of Mars. Mezhrabpom-Rus, 1924.

"After Life." *St. Elsewhere*. New York: NBC-TV, November 26, 1986.

Aladdin. Disney, 1992.

Aldiss, Brian W. *Billion Year Spree: The True History of Science Fiction*. 1973. New York: Schocken Books, 1974.

Alice in Wonderland. Disney, 1951.

Alice in Wonderland. Disney, 2010.

Alien. Brandywine, 1979.

Alien Contamination. [*Contamination*] Alex, 1980.

Alien Trespass. Rangeland Productions, 2009.

Alligator. Alligator, Inc., 1980.

"The Alternative Factor." *Star Trek*. New York: NBC-TV, March 30, 1967.

The Amazing Colossal Man. Malibu Productions, 1957.

Amis, Kingsley. *New Maps of Hell*. New York: Ballantine Books, 1960.

The Angry Red Planet. Sino, 1959.

Apollo 13. Universal, 1995.

"Arena." *Star Trek*. New York: NBC-TV, January 19, 1967.

The Aristocats. Disney, 1970.

Aristotle. *Poetics*. Translated by S. H. Butcher. Introduction by Frank Fergusson. New York: Hill and Wang, 1961.

Armageddon. Touchstone, 1998.

Asimov, Isaac. *Forward the Foundation*. New York: Doubleday,

1993.

------. *Foundation's Edge*. Garden City, New York: Doubleday, 1982.

------. *Prelude to Foundation*. New York: Doubleday, 1988.

Attack of the 50-Foot Woman. Woolner Brothers, 1958.

Attack of the 50-Ft. Woman. [tv movie] New York: HBO, December 11, 1993.

Attack of the Puppet People. Alta Vista Productions, 1958.

Avatar. Fox, 2009.

Babylon 5. [tv series] Syndicated: 1994-1998.

"Balance of Terror." *Star Trek*. New York: NBC-TV, December 15, 1966.

Bambi. Disney, 1942.

Battle for the Planet of the Apes. Twentieth-Century Fox, 1973.

Baxter, John. *Science Fiction in the Cinema*. New York: Paperback Library, 1970.

The Beast from 20,000 Fathoms. Warner Brothers, 1953.

Beauty and the Beast. Disney, 1991.

Beauty and the Beast. [tv series] New York: CBS-TV, 1987-1990.

Beginning of the End. AB-PT Pictures, 1957.

Beneath the Planet of the Apes. Twentieth-Century Fox, 1969.

Bill and Ted's Bogus Journey. Orion Pictures, 1991.

Bill and Ted's Excellent Adventure. Orion Pictures, 1988.

Bill and Ted's Excellent Adventures. [tv series] New York: CBS-TV, 1990-1991; New York: Fox, 1991-1992.

Bill and Ted's Excellent Adventures. [tv series] New York: Fox, 1992.

The Black Cauldron. Disney, 1985.

The Black Scorpion. Amex Productions, 1957.

Blade Runner. Ladd Company, 1982.

Blish, James. *Spock Must Die!* New York: Bantam Books, 1970.

------. *Star Trek*. New York: Bantam Books, 1967.

------. *Star Trek 2*. New York: Bantam Books, 1968.

------. *Star Trek 3*. New York: Bantam Books, 1969.

------. *Star Trek 4*. New York: Bantam Books, 1971.

------. *Star Trek 5*. New York: Bantam Books, 1972.

------. *Star Trek 6*. New York: Bantam Books, 1972.

------. *Star Trek 7*. New York: Bantam Books, 1972.

------. *Star Trek 8*. New York: Bantam Books, 1972.

------. *Star Trek 9*. New York: Bantam Books, 1973.

------. *Star Trek 10*. New York: Bantam Books, 1974.

------. *Star Trek 11*. New York: Bantam Books, 1975.

------, with J. L. Lawrence. *Star Trek 12*. New York: Bantam Books, 1977.

The Blob. Fairview Productions, 1958.

Boersma, Mark. Letter. "Monolith Mail." *2001: A Space Odyssey*, No. 6 (May, 1977), 19.

Bradbury, Ray. "The Fog Horn." 1951. *The Golden Apples of the Sun*. By Ray Bradbury. 1953. New York: Bantam Books, 1954, 1-8.

The Brain Eaters. American International, 1958.

The Brain from Planet Arous. Marquette Productions, 1957.

"Bread and Circuses." *Star Trek*. New York: NBC-TV, March 15, 1968.

Breathless. Les Productions Georges de Beauregard, 1960.

Bride of Frankenstein. Universal, 1935.

Brin, David. *Startide Rising*. New York: Bantam, 1983.

Broadcast News. Amercent Films, 1987.

Brosnan, John. *Future Tense: The Cinema of Science Fiction*. New York: St. Martin's, 1978.

------. "*Project Moonbase*." *The Encyclopedia of Science Fiction*. Edited by John Clute and Peter Nicholls. New York: St. Martin's Press, 1993, 964.

Brown, Fredric. "Arena." 1944. *The Science Fiction Hall of Fame, Volume I*. Edited by Robert Silverberg. 1970. New York: Avon Books, 1971, 281-309.

Brownfield, Paul. "Fly Him to the Moon." [interview with Tom Hanks] *The Los Angeles Times*, Sunday Calendar Section, April 5, 1998, 92.

Buck Rogers. [serial] Universal, 1939.

Buck Rogers in the 25th Century. [short] Harlan Tarbell, 1934.

"By Any Other Name." *Star Trek*. New York: NBC-TV, February 23, 1968.

Campbell, John W., Jr. *Invaders from the Infinite*. 1932. New York: Ace Books, 1961.

------. "Piracy Preferred." 1930. *The Black Star Passes*. By John W. Campbell, Jr. New York: Dorchester Press, 2010, 7-63.

Campbell, Joseph. *The Hero with a Thousand Faces*. 1949. Princeton: Princeton University Press, 1968.

Captain Video and His Video Rangers. [tv series] New York: Dumont, 1949-1955.

Carr, Terry. "The Dance of the Changer and the Three." 1968. *World's Best Science Fiction 1969*. Edited by Donald A. Wollheim and Terry Carr. New York: Ace Books, 1969, 259-274.

Cat-Women of the Moon. [*Rocket to the Moon*] Z-M, 1953.

Children of Men. Universal, 2006.

Cinderella. Disney, 1950.

Citizen Kane. Mercury Productions, 1941.

Clarke, Arthur C. *Against the Fall of Night*. 1953. New York: Pyramid Books, 1960.

------. *Childhood's End*. 1953. New York: Ballantine Books, 1967.

------. *The City and the Stars*. 1956. New York: Signet Books, 1957.

------. *The Fountains of Paradise*. 1979. New York: Ballantine, 1980.

------. *Imperial Earth*. New York: Ballantine, 1976.

------. *The Lost Worlds of 2001*. New York: Signet Books, 1972.

------. "A Meeting with Medusa." 1971. *The Wind from the Sun: Stories of the Space Age*. By Arthur C. Clarke. 1972. New York: Signet Books, 1973, 127-168.

------. "The Other Side of the Sky." 1957. *The Other Side of the Sky*. By Arthur C. Clarke. 1958. New York: Signet, 1959, 26-44.

------. *Rendezvous with Rama*. 1973. New York: Ballantine, 1974.

------. *3001: The Final Odyssey.* 1997. New York: Del Rey/ Ballantine Books, 1999.

------. *2001: A Space Odyssey.* New York: Signet Books, 1968. Based on a screenplay by Stanley Kubrick and Arthur C. Clarke.

------. *2010: Odyssey Two.* New York: Del Rey/Ballantine Books, 1982.

------. *2061: Odyssey Three.* New York: Del Rey/Ballantine Books, 1982.

------, and Stephen Baxter. *Firstborn: A Time Odyssey: 3.* New York: Del Rey/Ballantine Books, 2008.

------, and Stephen Baxter. *Sunstorm: A Time Odyssey: 2.* New York: Del Rey/Ballantine Books, 2007.

------, and Stephen Baxter. *Time's Eye: Book One of A Time Odyssey.* 2004. New York: Del Rey/Ballantine Books, 2005.

------, and Frederik Pohl. *The Last Theorem.* New York: Del Rey/Ballantine Books, 2008.

Close Encounters of the Third Kind. Columbia, 1977.

The Colossus of New York. Columbia, 1958.

Conquest of Space. Paramount, 1955.

Conquest of the Planet of the Apes. Twentieth-Century Fox, 1972.

Conrad, Joseph. *The Nigger of the "Narcissus": A Tale of the Sea.* 1897. New York: Doubleday, 1914.

"The Corbomite Maneuver." *Star Trek.* New York: NBC-TV, November 10, 1966.

The Cosmic Man. Futura Productions, 1959.

The Crawling Eye. [*The Trollenberg Terror*] Tempean Films, 1958.

The Creature from the Black Lagoon. Universal International, 1954.

Curse of the Faceless Man. Robert E. Kent Productions, 1958.

The Dark Knight. Warner Brothers, 2008.

Dark Star. Jack H. Harris Enterprises, 1974.

The Da Vinci Code. Columbia, 2006.

The Day the Earth Stood Still. Fox, 1951.

The Day the Earth Stood Still. Fox, 2008.

Days of Our Lives. [tv series] New York: NBC-TV, 1965-present.

The Deadly Mantis. University International, 1957.

Deep Impact. Paramount, 1998.

Destination Moon. George Pal Productions, 1950.

Dick, Philip K. "We Can Remember It for You Wholesale." 1966. *World's Best Science Fiction 1967.* Edited by Donald A. Wollheim and Terry Carr. New York: Ace Books, 1967, 9-30.

Dickens, Charles. *Oliver Twist.* 1838. New York: Dodd, Mead, 1941.

Le Dirigeable Fantastique. Georges Méliès, 1906.

Dr. Cyclops. Paramount, 1940.

"The Doomsday Machine." *Star Trek.* New York: NBC-TV, October 20, 1967.

Döppelganger. [*Journey to the Far Side of the Sun*] Century 21, 1969.

Doyle, Arthur Conan. *The Lost World.* 1912. New York: Pyramid Books, 1958.

Dumbo. Disney, 1941.

"The Dummy." *The Twilight Zone.* New York: CBS-TV, May 4, 1962.

Durgnat, Raymond. "The Wedding of Poetry and Pulp—Can They Live Happily Ever After and Have Many Beautiful Children?" *Films and Feelings.* By Raymond Durgnat. Cambridge, Massachusetts: M.I.T. Press, 1967), 251-267.

Earth II. [tv movie] New York: ABC-TV, November 28, 1971.

Earth vs. the Flying Saucers. Clover, 1956.

Earth vs. the Spider. American International, 1958.

"Encounter at Farpoint." *Star Trek: The Next Generation.* Syndicated: September 26, 1987.

"The Enemy Within." *Star Trek.* New York: NBC-TV, October 6, 1966.

"Errand of Mercy." *Star Trek.* New York: NBC-TV, March 23, 1967.

Escape from the Planet of the Apes. Twentieth-Century Fox, 1971.

E.T.: The Extra-Terrestrial. Universal, 1982.

Eternal Sunshine of the Spotless Mind. Focus Features, 2004.

Evolution. Columbia, 2001.

Excursion dans la Lune. (*Excursion to the Moon*) Pathé Frères, 1908.

"Eye of the Beholder." *The Twilight Zone.* New York: CBS-TV, November 11, 1960.

Fantasia. Disney, 1940.

Fantasia 2000. Disney, 1999.

"Far Beyond the Stars." *Star Trek: Deep Space Nine.* Syndicated: February 11, 1998.

Fiend without a Face. Producers Associates, 1958.

First Man into Space. Anglo-Amalgamated, 1959.

First Men in the Moon. Columbia, 1964.

Fiske, John. *Understanding Popular Culture.* London and New York: Routledge, 1989.

The Flame Barrier. Gramery Pictures, 1958.

Flash Gordon. [serial] Universal, 1936.

Flash Gordon Conquers the Universe. [serial] Universal, 1940.

Flash Gordon's Trip to Mars. [serial] Universal, 1938.

The Fly. Fox, 1958.

The Fly. Brooksfilms, 1986.

Forbidden Planet. Metro-Goldwyn-Mayer, 1956.

Forbidden World. New World Pictures, 1982.

Foster, Alan Dean. *Star Trek Log One.* New York: Del Rey/ Ballantine, 1974.

------. *Star Trek Log Two.* New York: Del Rey/Ballantine, 1974.

------. *Star Trek Log Three.* New York: Del Rey/Ballantine, 1975.

------. *Star Trek Log Four.* New York: Del Rey/Ballantine, 1975.

------. *Star Trek Log Five.* New York: Del Rey/Ballantine, 1975.

------. *Star Trek Log Six.* New York: Del Rey/Ballantine, 1976.

------. *Star Trek Log Seven.* New York: Del Rey/Ballantine,

1976.

------. *Star Trek Log Eight*. New York: Del Rey/Ballantine, 1976.

------. *Star Trek Log Nine*. New York: Del Rey/Ballantine, 1977.

------. *Star Trek Log Ten*. New York: Del Rey/Ballantine, 1978.

The 400 Blows. Les Films du Carrosse, 1959.

Frankenstein—1970. Aubrey Schenck Productions, 1958.

Franklin, H. Bruce. *Robert A. Heinlein: America as Science Fiction*. New York: Oxford University Press, 1980.

Die Frau im Mond. [*Woman in the Moon*] Fritz Lang-Film, 1929.

From the Earth to the Moon. Waverly, 1958.

From the Earth to the Moon. [tv miniseries] New York: HBO, April 5 -May 10, 1998.

Frye, Northrop. *Anatomy of Criticism: Four Essays*. 1957. Princeton: Princeton University Press, 1971.

Gernsback, Hugo. "The Science-Fiction Industry." *Science-Fiction Plus*, 1 (May, 1953), 2.

Gerrold, David. *The Trouble with Tribbles*. New York: Ballantine Books, 1973.

------. *The World of Star Trek*. New York: Ballantine Books, 1973.

Ghidrah, the Three-Headed Monster. [*San Daikaijû: Chikyû Saidai no Kessen*] Toho Studios, 1964.

The Giant Claw. Clover, 1957.

Gigantis the Fire Monster. [*Gojira no Gyakushû*] Toho Studios, 1955.

Godzilla [*Gojira*] Toho Studios, 1954. Reissued with new footage as *Godzilla, King of the Monsters*. Jewell, 1956.

Godzilla. Centropolis, 1998.

Godzilla: Final Wars. [*Gojira: Fainaru uôzu*] Toho Studios, 2004.

Godzilla 1985. [*Gojira*] Toho Studios, 1984.

Godzilla 2000. Toho Studios, 1999.

Godzilla vs. Biollante. [*Gojira vs. Biorante*] Toho Studios, 1989.

Godzilla vs. Destroyah. [*Gojira vs. Desutoroiâ*] Toho Studios, 1995.

Godzilla vs. King Ghidorah. [*Gojira vs. Kingu Gidorâ*] Toho Studios, 1991.

Godzilla vs. Mechagodzilla. [*Gojira tai Mekagojira*] Toho Studios, 1974.

Godzilla vs. Monster Zero. [*Kaijû Daisenso*] Toho Studios, 1965.

Godzilla vs. the Smog Monster. [*Gojira tai Hedorâ*] Toho Studios, 1971.

Godzilla vs. the Thing. [*Mosura tai Gojira*] Toho Studios, 1964.

Goldstein, Stan, and Fred Goldstein. *Star Trek Spaceflight Chronology.* Illustrated by Rick Sternbach. New York: Pocket, 1980.

Gorgo. King Brothers Productions, 1961.

Gould, Steven. *Jumper.* 1992. New York: Tor Books, 1993.

The Great Mouse Detective. Disney, 1986.

The Green Slime. MGM/Toei, 1968.

Greene, Eric. *"Planet of the Apes" as American Myth: Race and Politics in the Films and Television Series.* Jefferson, North Carolina: McFarland Publishers, 1996.

Gross, Edward. *The Fab Films of the Beatles.* Las Vegas, NV: Pioneer Books, 1990.

------, and Mark A. Altman. *Captains' Logs: The Unauthorized Complete Trek Voyages.* Boston and New York: Little, Brown, and Company, 1995.

Gunn, James, editor. *The New Encyclopedia of Science Fiction.* New York: Viking, 1988.

A Hard Day's Night. United Artists, 1964.

Hardy, Phil. *The Encyclopedia of Science Fiction Movies.* 1984. Minneapolis, Minnesota: Woodbury Press, 1986.

Harry Potter and the Deathly Hallows: Part 1. Warner Brothers, 2010.

Harry Potter and the Half-Blood Prince. Warner Brothers, 2009.

Harry Potter and the Order of the Phoenix. Warner Brothers,

2007.

Harry Potter and the Sorcerer's Stone. Warner Brothers, 2001.

Hays, Sam. Letter. "Monolith Mail." *2001: A Space Odyssey*, No. 6 (May, 1977), 19.

Heinlein, Robert A. "'All You Zombies –.'" 1959. *6 by H.* [*The Unpleasant Profession of Jonathan Hoag*] 1959. By Robert A. Heinlein. New York: Pyramid Books, 1961, 126-137.

------. "Delilah and the Space Rigger." 1949. *The Green Hills of Earth.* By Robert A. Heinlein. 1951. New York: Signet Books, 1952, 13-23.

------. *The Door into Summer.* 1957. New York: Del Rey/ Ballantine, 1986.

------. *Expanded Universe: The New Worlds of Robert A. Heinlein.* New York: Ace Books, 1980.

------. *Have Space Suit—Will Travel.* 1958. New York: Ace, 1969.

-----. *I Will Fear No Evil.* New York: Putnam, 1970.

------. "The Long Watch." 1949. *The Green Hills of Earth.* By Robert A. Heinlein. 1951. New York: Signet Books, 1952, 40-52.

------. *Rocket Ship Galileo.* 1947. New York: Ace, 1969.

------. "Shooting Destination Moon." 1950. *Requiem: New Collected Works by Robert A. Heinlein and Tributes to the Grand Master.* By Robert A. Heinlein. Edited by Yoji Kondo. New York: Tor Books, 1992, 117-131.

------. *Space Cadet.* 1948. New York: Ace, 1969.

------. *The Star Beast.* New York: Scribner's, 1954.

------. *Starman Jones.* 1953. New York: Dell Publishing, 1967.

------. *Time Enough for Love: The Lives of Lazarus Long.* New York: Putnam, 1973.

------. *To Sail Beyond the Sunset.* New York: Putnam, 1987.

Help! United Artists, 1965.

Hendershot, Cyndy. "The Atomic Scientist, Science Fiction Films, and Paranoia: *The Day the Earth Stood Still*, *This Island Earth*, and *Killers from Space*." *Journal of American Culture*, 20:1 (Spring, 1997), 31-41.

Hercules. Disney, 1997.

Hercules: The Legendary Journeys. [tv series] Syndicated: 1995-1999.

Hilliard, Bob, lyrics. Sammy Fain, music. "In a World of My Own." [song] *Alice in Wonderland.* Disney, 1950.

Himmelskibet. [*A Trip to Mars, A Ship to Heaven*] Nordisk, 1918.

The Hitchhiker's Guide to the Galaxy. Touchstone, 2005.

Holdstock, Robert, consultant editor. *Encyclopedia of Science Fiction.* London: Octopus Books, 1978.

Home Alone. Hughes Entertainment/Fox, 1990.

How to Make a Monster. American International, 1958.

The Hunchback of Notre Dame. Disney, 1996.

I Am Legend. Warner Brothers, 2007.

I Dream of Jeannie. [tv series] New York: NBC-TV, 1965-1970.

I Married a Monster from Outer Space. Paramount, 1958.

Inception. Warner Brothers, 2010.

Independence Day. Centropolis, 1996.

"In Praise of Pip." *The Twilight Zone.* New York: CBS-TV, September 27, 1963.

Inseminoid. [*Horror Planet*] Jupiter Film Productions, 1981.

"The Invaders." *The Twilight Zone.* New York: CBS-TV, January 27, 1961.

Invaders from Mars. National Pictures, 1953.

The Invasion. Warner Brothers, 2007.

Invasion of the Body Snatchers. Walter Wanger, 1956.

I, Robot. Fox, 2004.

It Came from Beneath the Sea. Clover, 1955.

It! The Terror from Beyond Space. Vogue, 1958.

I Was a Teenage Frankenstein. Santa Rosa Productions, 1957.

James, P. D. *The Children of Men.* 1992. New York: A. A. Knopf, 1993.

Jaws. Zanuck/Brown Productions, 1975.

Jerome Bixby's The Man from Earth. Falling Sky Entertainment, 2007.

La Jetée. Argos Films, 1962.

Johnson, Shane. *Mr. Scott's Guide to the Enterprise.* New York:

Pocket Books, 1987.

Jones, Raymond F. "The Alien Machine." *Thrilling Wonder Stories*, 34:2 (June, 1949), 74-88.

------. "The Greater Conflict." *Thrilling Wonder Stories*, 35:3 (February, 1950), 92-113.

------. "The Shroud of Secrecy." *Thrilling Wonder Stories*, 35:2 December, 1949), 64-79.

------. *This Island Earth*. Chicago: Shasta Publishers, 1952.

Journey to the Center of the Earth. Fox, 1959.

Jumper. Twentieth-Century Fox, 2008.

The Jungle Book. Disney, 1967.

Jurassic Park. Universal, 1993.

Just Imagine. Fox, 1930.

King Kong. RKO Radio Pictures, 1933.

King Kong vs. Godzilla. [*Kingu Kongu tai Gojira*] Toho Studios, 1962.

Kirby, Jack, writer and artist. "Beast-Killer." *2001: A Space Odyssey*, No. 1 (December, 1976), 1-3, 6-7, 10-11, 14-17, 22-23, 26-27, 30-31.

------. "The Capture of X-51." *2001: A Space Odyssey*, No. 8 (July, 1977), 1-3, 6-7, 10-11, 14-17, 22-23, 26-27, 30-31.

------. "Hotline to Hades." *2001: A Space Odyssey*, No. 10 (September, 1977), 1-3, 6-7, 10-11, 14-17, 22-23, 26-27, 30-31.

------. "Inter-Galactica: The Ultimate Trip." *2001: A Space Odyssey*, No. 6 (May, 1977), 1-3, 6-7, 10-11, 14-17, 22-23, 26-27, 30-31.

------. "Marak!" *2001: A Space Odyssey*, No. 3 (February, 1977), 1-3, 6-7, 10-11, 14-17, 22-23, 26-27, 30-31.

------. "Mister Machine." *2001: A Space Odyssey*, No. 9 (August, 1977), 1-3, 6-7, 10-11, 14-17, 22-23, 26-27, 30-31.

------. "Monolith Mail." *2001: A Space Odyssey*, No. 1 (December, 1976), 19.

------. "The New Seed." *2001: A Space Odyssey*, No. 7 (June, 1977), 1-3, 6-7, 10-11, 14-17, 22-23, 26-27, 30-31.

------. "Norton of New York 2040 A.D." *2001: A Space Odyssey*, No. 5 (April, 1977), 1-3, 6-7, 10-11, 14-17, 22-23, 26-27,

30-31.

------. *2001: A Space Odyssey.* Marvel Treasury Special. New York: Marvel Comics Group, 1976.

------. "Vira the She-Demon." *2001: A Space Odyssey*, No. 2 (January, 1977), 1-3, 6-7, 10-11, 14-17, 22-23, 26-27, 30-31.

------. "Wheels of Death." *2001: A Space Odyssey*, No. 4 (March, 1977), 1-3, 6-7, 10-11, 14-17, 22-23, 26-27, 30-31.

Kogen, Arnie, writer. Mort Drucker, artist. "The Milking of the Planet That Went Ape." *Mad*, No. 157 (March, 1973), 4-11.

Kosmicheskiy Reys: Fantasticheskaya Novella. (*The Space Voyage; The Space Ship*) Mosfilm, 1935.

Lady and the Tramp. Disney, 1955.

The Land Unknown. Universal International, 1957.

"Last Dance at the Wrecker's Ball." *St. Elsewhere.* New York: NBC-TV, May 27, 1987.

"The Last One." *St. Elsewhere.* New York: NBC-TV, May 25, 1988.

Leave It to Beaver. [tv series] New York: ABC-TV, 1957-1963.

Lees, J. D., and Marc Cerasini. *The Official Godzilla Compendium.* New York: Random House, 1998.

Lem, Stanislaw. *Solaris.* 1961. Translated from the French by Joanna Kilmartin and Steve Cox. London: Faber & Faber, 1971.

Lennon, John, and Paul McCartney. "Help!" [song] *Help!* United Artists, 1965.

------. "Ticket to Ride." [song] *Help!* United Artists, 1965.

Let It Be. Apple Corps, 1970.

"Let That Be Your Last Battlefield." *Star Trek.* New York: NBC-TV, January 10, 1969.

Lewisohn, Mark. *The Complete Beatles Chronicle.* 1992. London: Hamlyn, 2003.

Lichtenberg, Jacqueline, Sondra Marshak, and Joan Winston. *Star Trek Lives!* New York: Bantam Books, 1974.

The Lion King. Disney, 1994.

The Little Mermaid. Disney, 1989.

The Little Shop of Horrors. Santa Clara Productions, 1960.

Looney Tunes: Back in Action. Warner Brothers, 2003.

The Lord of the Rings: The Fellowship of the Ring. New Line Cinema, 2001.

The Lord of the Rings: The Return of the King. New Line Cinema, 2003.

The Lord of the Rings: The Two Towers. New Line Cinema, 2002.

The Lost Missile. William Berke Productions, 1958.

The Lost World. Irwin Allen, 1960.

Make Mine Music. Disney, 1948.

Mamma Mia! Universal, 2008.

The Man from Planet X. Mid-Century, 1951.

"The Man Trap." *Star Trek.* New York: NBC-TV, September 8, 1966.

Marshak, Sondra, and Myrna Culbreath, editors. *Star Trek: The New Voyages.* New York: Bantam Books, 1976.

------, editors. *Star Trek: The New Voyages 2.* New York: Bantam Books, 1977.

Mary Poppins. Disney, 1964.

Master of the World. American International, 1961.

Matheson, Richard. *I Am Legend.* New York: Fawcett, 1954.

Un Matrimonio Interplanetario. Latium, 1910.

Maynard, Jeff. *Star Trek Maps.* New York: Bantam Books, 1980.

Melody Time. Disney, 1946.

Melville, Herman. *Moby-Dick, or, The Whale.* 1851. New York: Penguin Books, 2001.

Men into Space. [tv series] New York: CBS-TV, 1959-1960.

"Metamorphosis." *Star Trek.* New York: NBC-TV, November 10, 1967.

Metropolis. Universum Film, 1927.

Miller, Arthur. *Death of a Salesman.* 1949. New York: Dramatists Play Service, 1952.

Mindwarp: An Infinity of Terror. [*Galaxy of Terror*] New World Pictures, 1981.

"Moaning Lisa." *The Simpsons.* New York: Fox, February 11,

1990.

Moby Dick. Moulin Productions, 1956.

Monster from Green Hell. Gross-Krasne Productions, 1958.

Monster on the Campus. Universal International, 1958.

Moon Pilot. Disney, 1962.

Moonraker. United Artists, 1979.

Mothra. [*Mosura*] Toho Studios, 1961.

Mulan. Disney, 1998.

My Favorite Martian. [tv series] New York: CBS-TV, 1963-1966.

Mysterious Island. Columbia, 1961.

Naha, Ed. *The Science Fictionary: An A-Z Guide to the World of SF Authors, Films, & TV Shows.* New York: Seaview Books, 1980.

"The Naked Now." *Star Trek: The Next Generation.* Syndicated: October 3, 1987.

Nash, Bruce, and Greg Nash. *The Star Trek Make-a-Game Book.* New York: Wanderer Books, 1979.

Nicholls, Peter. *"Bill and Ted's Excellent Adventure." The Encyclopedia of Science Fiction.* Edited by John Clute and Peter Nicholls. New York: St. Martin's Press, 1993, 121.

"The Night of the Meek." *The Twilight Zone.* New York: CBS-TV, December 23, 1960.

"Obsession." *Star Trek.* New York: NBC-TV, December 15, 1967.

"Of Late I Think of Cliffordville." *The Twilight Zone.* New York: CBS-TV, April 11, 1963.

O'Flaherty, Wendy Doniger. "The Survival of Myth in Science Fiction." *Mindscapes: The Geographies of Imagined Worlds.* Edited by George Slusser and Eric S. Rabkin. Carbondale, Illinois: Southern Illinois University Press, 1988, 16-33.

Olander, Joseph D., and Martin H. Greenberg, editors. *Robert A. Heinlein.* New York: Taplinger Publishing Company, 1978.

Oliver and Company. Disney, 1988.

"The Omega Glory." *Star Trek.* New York: NBC-TV, March 1, 1968.

The Omega Man. Warner Brothers, 1971.

One Hundred and One Dalmatians. Disney, 1961.

One Million B.C. Hal Roach Studios, 1940.

Orwell, George. *Animal Farm: A Fairy Story*. 1945. New York: Signet Books, 1964.

The Outer Limits. [tv series] New York: ABC-TV, 1963-1965.

Panshin, Alexei. *Heinlein in Dimension*. Chicago: Advent Publishers, 1968.

------, and Cory Panshin. *The World beyond the Hill: Science Fiction and the Quest for Transcendence*. Los Angeles: Jeremy R. Tarcher, Inc., 1989.

"The Paradise Syndrome." *Star Trek*. New York: NBC-TV, October 4, 1968.

Parasite. Embassy Pictures, 1982.

The Passion of the Christ. Icon Productions, 2004.

Peter Pan. Disney, 1953.

Pete's Dragon. Disney, 1977.

Philadelphia. TriStar Pictures, 1993.

Pinocchio. Disney, 1940.

Pirates of the Caribbean: At World's End. Disney, 2007.

Pirates of the Caribbean: The Curse of the Black Pearl. Disney, 2003.

Pirates of the Caribbean: Dead Man's Chest. Disney, 2006.

Planet of the Apes. Twentieth-Century Fox, 1968.

Planet of the Apes. Twentieth-Century Fox, 2001.

Pocahantas. Disney, 1995.

Pohl, Frederik. *The Annals of the Heechee*. 1987. New York: Del Rey/Ballantine, 1988.

------. *Beyond the Blue Event Horizon*. New York: Del Rey/ Ballantine, 1980.

------. *The Boy Who Would Live Forever*. New York: Tor Books, 2004.

------. *Gateway*. 1977. New York: Del Rey/Ballantine, 1978.

------. *The Gateway Trip: Tales and Vignettes of the Heechee*. New York: Del Rey/Ballantine, 1990.

------. *Heechee Rendezvous*. 1984. New York: Del Rey/Ballantine,

1985.

Pollyanna. Disney, 1960.

Pournelle, Jerry. "Introduction: The Insurmountable Opportunity." *The Endless Frontier, Volume II.* Edited by Jerry Pournelle with John F. Carr. New York: Ace Books, 1982, 1-17.

Powell, Sam. Letter. "Monolith Mail." *2001: A Space Odyssey,* No. 5 (April, 1977), 19.

Predator. Amercent Films, 1987.

The Prince of Egypt. Dreamworks, 1998.

The Princess and the Frog. Disney, 2009.

Project Moonbase. Galaxy Pictures, 1953.

Queen of Outer Space. Allied Artists, 1958.

The ? Motorist. Robert W. Paul, 1906.

The Reluctant Astronaut. Universal, 1967.

Reptilicus. American International, 1961.

The Rescuers. Disney, 1977.

The Rescuers Down Under. Disney, 1990.

Return of the Fly. Associated Producers, 1959.

Return to Earth. [tv movie] New York: ABC-TV, May 14, 1976.

"Return to Tomorrow." *Star Trek.* New York: NBC-TV, February 9, 1968.

Revenge of the Creature. Universal International, 1955.

Reynolds, Mack. *Mission to Horatius.* Racine, Wisconsin: Whitman Books, 1968.

Riders to the Stars. A-Men, 1954.

The Right Stuff. Ladd, 1983.

Rise of the Planet of the Apes. Twentieth-Century Fox, 2011.

Rocketship X-M. [*Expedition Moon*] Luppert, 1950.

Rocky Jones, Space Ranger. [tv series] Syndicated, 1954.

Rodan. [*Sora no Daikaijû Radon*] Toho Studios, 1956.

The Rules of the Game. Nouvelles Éditions de Films, 1939.

"Santa Claus Is Dead." *St. Elsewhere.* New York: NBC-TV, December 18, 1985.

Sedgwick, Cristina. "The Fork in the Road: Can Science Fiction Survive in Postmodern, Megacorporate America?" *Science-*

Fiction Studies, 18 (March, 1991), 11-52.

Sendak, Maurice. *Where the Wild Things Are*. New York: Harper & Row, 1963.

Serviss, Garrett P. *Edison's Conquest of Mars*. 1898. Los Angeles: Carcosa House, 1947.

The Seventh Seal. [*Det Sjunde Inseglet*] Svensk Filmindustri, 1957.

"Shore Leave." *Star Trek*. New York: NBC-TV, December 29, 1966.

Shrek 2. Dreamworks, 2004.

The Simpsons. [tv series] New York: 1989-present.

The Six Million Dollar Man. [tv series] New York: ABC-TV, 1974-1978.

"Skin of Evil." *Star Trek: The Next Generation*. Syndicated: April 23, 1988.

Sleeping Beauty. Disney, 1959.

Slusser, George. *The Classic Years of Robert A. Heinlein*. San Bernardino, California: Borgo Press, 1977.

------. "Dimorphs and Doubles: J. D. Bernal's `Two Cultures' and the Transhuman Promise." *Science Fiction and the Two Cultures: Essays on Bridging the Gap between the Sciences and the Humanities*. Edited by Gary Westfahl and Slusser. Jefferson, North Carolina: McFarland Publishers, 2009, 96-129.

------. *Robert A. Heinlein: Stranger in His Own Land*. San Bernardino, California: Borgo Press, 1976.

Snow White and the Seven Dwarfs. Disney, 1937.

Sobchack, Vivian. *Screening Space: The American Science Fiction Film*. New York: Ungar, 1987.

Solaris. Mosfilms, 1971.

Song of the South. Disney, 1946.

Space Master X-7. Regal, 1958.

Space Patrol. [tv series] New York: ABC-TV, 1950-1955.

"Specimen Unknown." *The Outer Limits*. New York: ABC-TV, February 24, 1964.

Stanley, John. *Revenge of the Creature Features Movie Guide*.

Third Revised Edition. Pacifica, California: Creatures at Large Press, 1988.

Stapledon, Olaf. *Last and First Men*. *Last and First Men and Star Maker: Two Science-Fiction Novels by Olaf Stapledon*. By Olaf Stapledon. New York: Dover Books, 1968), 9-246.

------. *Last Men in London*. 1932. *Last and First Men and Last Men in London*. By Olaf Stapledon. Middlesex, England: Penguin Books, 1973, 333-605.

------. *Star Maker*. 1937. *Last and First Men and Star Maker: Two Science-Fiction Novels by Olaf Stapledon*. By Olaf Stapledon. New York: Dover Books, 1968), 249-438.

Star Trek. Paramount, 2009.

Star Trek. [tv series] New York: NBC-TV, 1966-1969.

Star Trek. [tv series] New York: NBC-TV, 1973-1975.

Star Trek: Deep Space Nine. [tv series] Syndicated: 1993-1999.

Star Trek: Enterprise. [tv series] New York: UPN, 2001-2005.

Star Trek: First Contact. Paramount, 1996.

Star Trek: Generations. Paramount, 1994.

Star Trek: The Motion Picture. Paramount, 1979.

Star Trek: Nemesis. Paramount, 2002.

Star Trek: The Next Generation. [tv series] Syndicated: 1987-1994.

Star Trek: Voyager. [tv series] New York: UPN, 1995-2001.

Star Trek II: The Wrath of Khan. Paramount, 1982.

Star Wars. Fox, 1977.

Sternbach, Rick. *Star Trek: The Next Generation: U.S.S. Enterprise NCC-1701-D Blueprints*. New York: Pocket Books, 1996.

Stewart, George R. *Earth Abides*. New York: Random House, 1949.

"A Stop at Willoughby." *The Twilight Zone*. New York: CBS-TV, May 6, 1960.

Stranger from Venus. Rich and Rich, 1954.

Superman. Warner Brothers, 1978.

Superman II. Warner Brothers, 1980.

The Sword in the Stone. Disney, 1963.

Tangled. Disney, 2010.

Tarantula. Universal International, 1955.

Tarzan. Disney, 1999.

Teenage Cave Man. Malibu Productions, 1958.

The Terminator. Hemdale Film, 1984.

Terror from the Year 5000. La Jolla Productions, 1958.

Terror of Mechagodzilla. [*Mekagojira no Gyakushu*] Toho Studios, 1975.

Them! Warner Brothers, 1954.

The Thing (from Another World). Winchester, 1951.

The Thing That Couldn't Die. Universal International, 1958.

Things to Come. London, 1936.

The Thirty-Foot Bride of Candy Rock. Columbia, 1959

This Island Earth. Universal, 1955.

"The Tholian Web." *Star Trek.* New York: NBC-TV, November 15, 1968.

"Time Enough at Last." *The Twilight Zone.* New York: CBS-TV, November 20, 1959.

The Time Machine. Metro-Goldwyn-Mayer, 1960.

Titanic. Fox, 1997.

Tom Corbett, Space Cadet. [tv series] New York: CBS-TV, 1950; New York: ABC-TV, 1951-1952; New York: NBC-TV, 1951, 1954-1955; New York: Dumont, 1953-1954.

"To Save the Future, They Must Rescue the Past." Advertisement for the collector plate *Star Trek IV: The Voyage Home. Parade*, April 10, 1994, 21.

Total Recall. Carolco International, 1990.

Toy Story 3. Pixar/Disney, 2010.

Trimble, Bjo. *The Star Trek Concordance.* New York: Ballantine Books, 1976.

"Turnabout Intruder." *Star Trek.* New York: NBC-TV, June 3, 1969.

12 to the Moon. Luna, 1960.

The Twilight Zone. [tv series] New York: CBS-TV, 1959-1964.

Twilight Zone: The Movie. Warner Brothers, 1983.

2001: A Space Odyssey. Metro-Goldwyn-Mayer, 1968.

2010: The Year We Make Contact. Metro-Goldwyn-Mayer, 1984.

Underwood, Mike. Letter. "Monolith Mail." *2001: A Space Odyssey,* No. 6 (May, 1977), 19.

Unknown Island. Albert Jay Cohen Productions, 1948.

van Vogt, A. E. "Black Destroyer." 1939. *First Flight.* Edited by Damon Knight. 1963. New York: Lancer Books, 1966, 36-66.

Varan the Unbelievable. Toho Studios, 1962.

Verne, Jules. *Twenty Thousand Leagues under the Sea.* 1869. Translated by Anthony Bonner. New York: Bantam Books, 1976.

Voyage sur Jupiter. (*Voyage to Jupiter*) Pathé Frères, 1909.

Le Voyage dans la Lune. (*A Trip to the Moon*) Georges Méliès, 1902.

Le Voyage à Travers l'Impossible. (*The Impossible Voyage*) Georges Méliès, 1904.

Wall•E. Pixar/Disney, 2008.

War of the Colossal Beast. Carmel Productions, 1958.

War of the Satellites. Allied Artists, 1958.

The War of the Worlds. Paramount, 1953.

Wells, H. G. *The War of the Worlds.* 1898. New York: Berkley, 1964.

Westfahl, Gary. "Greyer Lensmen, Or Looking Backward in Anger." *Interzone,* No. 129 (March, 1998), 40–43.

------. *The Other Side of the Sky: An Annotated Bibliography of Space Stations in Science Fiction, 1869-1993.* Holicong, Pennsylvania: Wildside Press/Borgo Press, 2009.

------. "What Science Fiction Leaves Out of the Future, #2: The Day After Tomorrow." The Internet Review of Science Fiction website, posted on March 5, 2009. Originally at http://www.irosf.com/q/zine/article/10528 .

------, George Slusser, and Eric S. Rabkin, editors. *Science Fiction and Market Realities.* Athens: University of Georgia Press, 1996.

When Worlds Collide. Paramount, 1951.

Whitfield, Stephen, and Gene Roddenberry. *The Making of Star Trek*. New York: Ballantine Books, 1968. Actually written by Whitfield, with occasional inserted comments from Roddenberry.

Wilcox, Clyde, and Kevin Wilcox. "New Gateways to Adventure: The Creation and Marketing of Science Fiction Computer Games." *Science Fiction and Market Realities*. Edited by Gary Westfahl, George Slusser, and Eric S. Rabkin. Athens: University of Georgia Press, 1996, 194-206.

Willman, David. "Suspect Stood to Gain from Anthrax Panic." *The Los Angeles Times*, August 2, 2008, A1; also available at http://articles.latimes.com/2008/aug/02/nation/na-anthrax2.

Wingrove, David. *"Project Moonbase." Science Fiction Film Source Book*. Edited by David Wingrove. London: Longman, 1985, 185.

Wright, Bruce Lanier. *Yesterday's Tomorrows: The Golden Age of Science Fiction Movie Posters, 1950-1964*. Dallas, Texas: Taylor Publishing Company, 1993.

Yellow Submarine. Apple Corps, 1968.

Zebrowski, George. *Macrolife*. New York: Harper & Row, 1979.

ABOUT THE AUTHOR

GARY WESTFAHL, now an Adjunct Professor at the University of La Verne, is the author, editor, or co-editor of 23 books about science fiction and fantasy, including the Hugo-nominated *Science Fiction Quotations: From the Inner Mind to the Outer Limits* (2005), *Islands in the Sky: The Space Station Theme in Science Fiction Literature* (1996, 2009), *The Other Side of the Sky: An Annotated Bibliography of Space Stations in Science Fiction, 1869-1993* (2009), and *The Spacesuit Film: A History, 1918-1969* (2012). He has also written hundreds of articles and reviews for various journals, magazines, websites, and reference works, and has appeared in two nationally televised documentaries. In 2003 he received the Science Fiction Research Association's Pilgrim Award for his lifetime contributions to science fiction and fantasy scholarship.